Building a Classical Record Library

By Bill Parker

REVISED EDITION

Published by
Minnesota Public Radio, Inc.
45 East Eighth Street
Saint Paul, Minnesota 55101

Minnesota Public Radio is a producer and broadcaster of fine arts programming. Included in the MPR network of non-profit, non-commercial radio stations are:

KSJN 91.1 FM Minneapolis / St. Paul
KSJN 1330 AM Minneapolis / St. Paul
KSJR 90.1 FM Collegeville / St. Cloud
KCCM 91.1 FM Moorhead / Fargo
KLSE 91.7 FM Rochester / Decorah / Winona / LaCrosse
WSCD 92.9 FM Duluth / Superior
KRSW 91.7 FM Worthington / Marshall / Sioux Falls
KCRB 88.5 FM Bemidji
WGGL 91.1 FM Houghton, MI
KGAC 90.5 FM St. Peter / Mankato

Cover design by Mark L. Simonson.
Book design by Kathe Wilcoxon.

Manufactured in the United States.

ISBN 0-942110-05-6

For a free catalog featuring other classical music books and recordings write Department P
    Minnesota Public Radio
    45 East Eighth Street
    Saint Paul, Minnesota 55101

LISTEN TO AND SUPPORT YOUR LOCAL PUBLIC RADIO STATION!

In memory of My Mother

who died just as this book went to press. The Edna B. Parker Music Scholarship Fund has been established in her honor.

Table of Contents

1 Acknowledgments

3 Introduction

6 How to Use the Listings

7 Things to Think About
  Before You Buy

15 The Middle Ages & Renaissance

19 The Baroque Era
21 Albinoni, Tomaso
22 Bach, Johann Sebastian
30 Handel, George Frideric
34 Pachelbel, Johann
35 Vivaldi, Antonio

39 The Classical Era
40 Beethoven, Ludwig van
54 Haydn, Franz Joseph
57 Mozart, Wolfgang Amadeus

69 The Early Romantics
70 Berlioz, Hector
72 Chopin, Frédéric
74 Glinka, Mikhail
75 Mendelssohn, Felix
78 Paganini, Niccoló
78 Rossini, Gioacchino
79 Schubert, Franz
83 Schumann, Robert
86 Weber, Carl Maria von

89 The Mainstream Romantics
90 Bizet, Georges
90 Borodin, Alexander
92 Brahms, Johannes
100 Bruch, Max
101 Bruckner, Anton
103 Chabrier, Emmanuel
104 Chausson, Ernest
104 Dvořák, Antonin
108 Franck, César
111 Grieg, Edvard
112 Lalo, Edouard
112 Liszt, Franz
114 Massenet, Jules
115 Mussorgsky, Modest
117 Offenbach, Jacques
118 Ponchielli, Amilcare
119 Rimsky-Korsakov, Nikolai
120 Saint-Saëns, Camille
124 Smetana, Bedrich
125 Strauss II, Johann
126 Tchaikovsky, Piotr Ilyich
135 Wagner, Richard

139 The Late Romantics
140 Debussy, Claude
143 Delius, Frederick
143 Dukas, Paul
144 Elgar, Edward
145 Fauré, Gabriel
146 d'Indy, Vincent
146 Mahler, Gustav
150 Rachmaninoff, Sergei
152 Strauss, Richard

157 **The Modern Romantics**
158 Britten, Benjamin
159 Enesco, Georges
159 Falla, Manuel de
160 Holst, Gustav
161 Khachaturian, Aram
162 Ravel, Maurice
167 Respighi, Ottorino
168 Rodrigo, Joaquin
169 Satie, Erik
169 Sibelius, Jan
173 Vaughan Williams, Ralph

175 **The Mainstream Moderns**
176 Bartók, Béla
178 Berg, Alban
178 Hindemith, Paul
179 Honegger, Arthur
179 Janáček, Leos
180 Kodály, Zoltán
180 Milhaud, Darius
181 Nielsen, Carl
181 Orff, Carl
182 Poulenc, Francis
153 Prokofiev, Serge
187 Schönberg, Arnold
187 Shostakovich, Dmitri
189 Stravinsky, Igor
193 Villa-Lobos, Heitor

195 **The Americans**
196 Barber, Samuel
196 Bernstein, Leonard
197 Bloch, Ernest
197 Copland, Aaron
200 Gershwin, George
200 Grofé, Ferde
201 Ives, Charles

203 **Opera**
204 Beethoven, Ludwig van
209 Bellini, Vincenzo
206 Berg, Alban
206 Bizet, Georges
207 Donizetti, Gaetano
207 Gershwin, George
208 Gounod, Charles
208 Leoncavallo, Ruggero
208 Mascagni, Pietro
209 Massenet, Jules
209 Mozart, Wolfgang Amadeus
212 Mussorgsky, Modest
212 Puccini, Giacomo
214 Rossini, Gioacchino
214 Strauss II, Johann
215 Strauss, Richard
216 Verdi, Giuseppe
219 Wagner, Richard

223 **Title Index**

Acknowledgments

Special gratitude for assisting in researching the reviews for this expanded edition is due to Rex Levang, Anthony Machgan, and Dan Donsker.

Once again, several colleagues at Minnesota Public Radio have contributed valuable suggestions and advice: Don Manildi (piano music); Michael Barone and Randy Bourne (Medieval, Renaissance, Baroque, and organ music); and John Michel (all areas). Bruce Morrow of the *Minnesota Daily* contributed much useful information; and I am grateful to Don Vroon of WNED-FM in Buffalo, New York, who kindly provided copies of his *The Record Buyer* articles for comparison.

As in the past, Donna Avery (MPR Director of Publications) and her staff, including Mark Simonson and Kathe Wilcoxon (graphic design), Janis Olson, Carrie Brutscher and Susen Fitzpatrick(typesetting) and Lynea Schultz (indexing), have lent support and hard work to the production of this volume.

Introduction

In the introduction to the first edition of this book (fall, 1981) I wrote that: *Building a Classical Record Library* is conceived as a road map through a well-charted but complex territory. Thousands upon thousands of classical recordings have been issued over the past hundred years. No one person has heard them all; no one person has collected them all. To give a definitive answer to what is worth hearing and owning out of all of this is beyond the scope and competence of any "guide."

In the ensuing three years the situation has grown even more complex, far more so than I could have foreseen. Many hundreds of additional recordings have hit the market. Digital recording techniques and compact discs have become the hot items. Cassettes have greatly improved in quality and increased their share of sales. Record stores are flooded with repackaged "budget tapes." New books and magazines have appeared, increasing the number of reviews to help (or confuse) the prospective buyer.

This new edition is an attempt to sort out as much as possible of this welter of new information and yet stay within the stated bounds of concision. I have added cassette and compact disc catalog numbers and information as necessary, as well as 8 composers and 100 compositions; but I have condensed the format to an essay style with catalog numbers appended. Naturally, all the listings have been revised, reflecting many deletions and additions to the *Schwann Record & Tape Guide.*

The basic method of the book, however, has not changed. It is still a synthesis of published critical opinion, not my personal predilections. Thousands of reviews have been surveyed, digested, and formulated into brief commentaries that are meant to mirror as accurately as possible the general trend of thinking of the most prominent professional writers on classical music recordings.

Despite the 100 added works of music, this edition is still devoted to the "basic repertory" concept, merely expanded, and directed principally to the beginning collector who has not the time to read and compare the mountains of printed reviews, or the money to form a library by the trial and error method.

I continue to avoid going into detail about recordings that have received a significantly negative press. Other publications are available to tell you what is wrong with various records. This one prefers a positive approach; every recording discussed in this book has merited inclusion by achieving a preponderance of good reviews from eminent authorities. Every recording listed is one that is believed to have a better-than-average chance of satisfying a majority of buyers.

No fewer than 15 sources have been consulted for this edition. The most exhaustively researched were *High Fidelity, Stereo Review, Musical America, Ovation,* and *Fanfare* magazines, with selected reviews from *Gramophone, American Record Guide, Opera News,* and *The Magic Flute* (from Canada). A new magazine, *Opus,* has not even published its first issue as this book is written, but I availed myself of their list of "100 Inspired Recordings" included in their charter subscription promotional material. Reference books used include two editions of the *Penguin Guide* (Edward Greenfield, Robert Layton, and Ivan March), *Opera On Record* (Alan Blyth), *The Great Symphonies* (Clive Unger-Hamilton), *The Simon & Schuster Listener's Guide* (Alan Rich), and *Consumers Union Reviews: Classical Recordings* (published by Bobbs-Merrill).

I used five criteria in selecting recordings for inclusion: sonic quality, price, esthetics of interpretation, stature of performing artists, and availability. Obviously one hopes to get a recording that is a good performance, well recorded and manufactured. Many fine recordings are available at low cost and frequently I have preferred to list the "budget" recordings rather than full-price discs or tapes when all other considerations seemed nearly equal. In an effort to present "central" versions suitable especially for the beginning collector — avoiding highly controversial readings however they may appeal to a minority of aficionados and cognoscenti — I have tended to lean towards those recordings that feature eminent and widely recognized artists and ensembles. And I continue to feel that I should stress recordings that have wide distribution and are most likely to be available through a large number of retail outlets; nothing is more frustrating to the user of a guide like this than to drive across town for a record only to be told that the desired label is not carried in stock and must be special-ordered from Switzerland; however fine it may be, it does not represent a convenient choice for the enthusiastic novice, but rather a challenge for the advanced collector and specialist.

This book aims to be as objective as possible. My subjective judgment intrudes only to the extent of weighing masses of often contradictory published opinion. This becomes more difficult in proportion to the disagreement of critics, as exemplified by the wildly divergent reactions to Carlos Kleiber's recent version of Wagner's *Tristan und Isolde* on Deutsche Grammophon. The

Opus editors listed it among their "100 Inspired Recordings" of all time. The writers in *Ovation, Stereo Review,* and *High Fidelity* all found it interesting in many respects but seriously flawed in others. *Gramophone* found it "wholly convincing," and one *Fanfare* critic advised his readers to "drop everything" and run out to buy a copy. But another *Fanfare* reviewer, Henry Fogel — who may have listened to more opera recordings than any living person — lamented that "in the 20 years of listening to music . . . I don't believe I have been more perplexed and disheartened than I have by this release."

This one recording, then, has been both condemned as one of the worst performances ever recorded, and praised as one of the select 100 most inspired issues of recording history, with a whole spectrum of waffling opinion in between. If no one had said anything very good about it I would have simply left it out; but in this case I felt compelled to include it as a possibility, with reservations carefully noted, but definitely as an *alternate* to the Furtwängler version on Seraphim which has achieved a virtually *unanimous* respect as one of the most beloved classics of the catalog.

Recordings appearing in the 1981 edition but not in this one fall into two categories: those no longer in print, and those which are judged to have been superseded by newer versions (or sometimes by *older* versions newly re-released). Frankly, I have been saddened to discover how few, relatively, of the new recordings are really better than the old ones; and how many really great older recordings have been deleted to make way for mediocre performances issued merely to display new technologies. Many manufacturers are rushing to put out anything in digital or on compact disc without much regard to its musical value. I have tried in every case to recommend the sonically most advanced recording, the cheapest recording, and the best performance. Rarely, all three criteria meet in one disc or tape. But at least I have refused to list any "high-tech" *or* "budget" recording unless it has at least a decent reputation for artistic values.

I have approached making decisions on every recording in this book with a heavy sense of responsibility toward the artists, the recording companies, and you, the reader and imminent purchaser. I have tried to choose as fairly as I could. I hope that the result will be a satisfying core collection of great music in great performances, acquired with a minimum of worry, cost, and duplication.

How to Use the Listings

Excellent sound quality of the disc or tape is, for better or worse, a common prerequisite of the recommendations. Many of the greatest conductors and orchestras recorded so long ago that, even though their performances often remain in print as historic testaments, I feel the person building a *basic* library will not want to *start* with them. Some monophonic recordings are nevertheless recommended and are indicated in the listings by the designation **(M)**.

Some "budget" editions may be rated a bit lower than their expensive counterparts (though many are fully their equals) but still be well worth their costs. Budget records (including those commonly called "mid-price" in the record business) are indicated by the designation **(B)**.

In the case of multiple sets, the number of records per box is given in parentheses immediately before the catalog number.

The listings under each composer and title proceed in alphabetical order by the principal artist and do not imply any hierarchy of judgment. Each recording is considered approximately equal in net value to every other listed, with points of variance noted in the editorial comments.

Within the explanatory comments, when the title of a composition is given in SMALL CAPS it indicates that piece is treated in detail elsewhere in the book. Works which are not reviewed or discussed elsewhere appear in regular roman type or italics.

After each catalog number appears an abbreviation in parentheses indicating whether the format is conventional long-playing disc (LP), digital disc (D-LP) cassette tape (CS), or compact disc (CD). In many cases CD numbers are significantly dissimilar from LP and cassette numbers, but often cassette numbers are virtually identical with LP numbers, except perhaps for a letter prefix. I give complete numbers only when I feel it is necessary or helpful for proper identification when buying or ordering; if the numbers are identical for practical purposes, I do not repeat them. If one or more of the formats is not listed for a particular recording, it normally means that it is not available.

If you are not familiar with classical music terminology, be informed that most classical titles are followed by the designation "Op." followed by a number. "Op." is an abbreviation for the Latin "opus," or "work," and is used as an identifier to indicate the chronological sequence of a composer's compositions. Some of the more prolific composers, such as Mozart, Bach, and Schubert, have initials (e.g., K,S,D) instead of "op." These are the initials of the scholars (Köchel, Schmieder, Deutsch) who spent years of their lives doing the cataloging that the busy musicians ignored.

Most titles also bear a letter indicating the key signature of the piece. I have adopted the *Schwann Record & Tape Guide* system of using a capital letter for major keys and a lower case letter for minor keys. Thus, "Concerto in D" means "D major," and "Symphony in g" means "g minor."

At the end of each chapter is a list of works suggested, as the old phrase goes, "for further listening." Specific recordings are not mentioned, since that would take me beyond the scope of this book. But these "next-most-basic" pieces are the ones you are most likely to seek out if you are won over by the ones in the major listings, and by that time you will probably have gained enough confidence in your own judgment to obviate the need for detailed recommendations.

There is rather more to buying a record than having a list of recommended performances to help you. There is the question of whether you should buy a tape instead of a record. And what labels have the best reputation? Where can you purchase records? How should you take care of them once you buy them?

Over the years, in addition to being a classical music radio announcer and producer, and an avid record collector, I have managed four retail record stores in Toledo, Boston, Syracuse, and now in Saint Paul. I have also worked in the wholesale classical record business in sales and promotion. The next chapter is based on my experiences as both buyer and seller.

Things to Think About Before You Buy

Format

It is still true, as I wrote in the old edition, that more vinyl phonograph records exist than tapes. But tapes are catching up, and it is no longer strictly true that LP's are generally of higher quality. Many companies are putting out chromium dioxide prerecorded cassettes that are fully comparable to, and sometimes better than, their corresponding platters. The cartridge, or "8-track" tape, however, has become virtually extinct.

Three years ago, most of the vinyl records in existence were stereophonic analog recordings using the same basic technology which had prevailed since the late 1950s. Some were quadraphonic discs which required four speakers to exhibit their special sonic qualities, but which were totally compatible with the conventional two speakers of stereo. Once touted as the great advance in record-ing technology, "quad" records and their special reproducing equipment never caught on. Though they still exist, their quad characteristics are so irrelevant that in this edition I have not even bothered to add the designation (Q) when they are listed; they are treated the same as any other stereo-analog recording.

Since 1981 the digital recording technique, in which music is fed into a computer, converted into numbers, and decoded back out onto the disc, has for practical purposes replaced the analog method entirely. Almost the only analog discs remaining are older ones still in print, and often knocked down into the "budget" cate-gory. Many of these old analogs, happily, are wonderful perfor-mances and it is a great boon to have them available at reduced cost; a great many of them are listed in this edition. Basically, digi-tal recordings sound brighter and clearer than analog ones by vir-tue of eliminating some of the steps in the manufacturing process which cause what audio technicians call "generation loss." Still, some listeners claim that digital records are not an unalloyed im-provement; that, for instance, strings recorded digitally often sound shrill or glassy. Others maintain this is an auditory illusion, just as early stereo record buyers often insisted that 78s sounded better because it was the sound spectrum they were *used* to.

At least digital records and tapes do not require the purchase of new playback equipment, although of course the better your turntable, speakers and amplifier, the more likely you are to appre-ciate the special qualities of advanced sonics. But then came the compact disc, five inches in diameter, a thin piece of acrylic plastic coated with reflective aluminum, recorded on one side only, scanned by a laser beam instead of played with a stylus, and requir-ing an entirely new (and initially very expensive) playback ma-chine. Suddenly the industry was proclaiming not only the analog *method,* but even the 12-inch vinyl disc, to be obsolescent.

There are several advantages to the compact disc. Since the playing surface suffers no friction, ticks and pops no longer exist. Being "played" by a beam of light, the little disc can never wear out. Despite the small size, more than an hour's worth of music can be stored in the single side, eliminating the old annoyance of "flip-ping" the record in the middle of a symphony. The size also means of course that a lot more music can be stored in a smaller space, and with lighter weight. And the compact disc is, at least theoretically, a far more suitable format for demonstrating digital technology.

On the negative side, there have been complaints of "mutes" on CDs — brief moments when the music disappears altogether. Some CDs are being manufactured with audio compression, which overturns the very advantage the format was invented for. Many original analog recordings are being put onto compact disc, which instead of enhancing them merely magnifies their inherent faults. You cannot "drop the needle" on a CD to hear your favorite passage in the middle of a work; with some equipment you can only select the beginning of movements or major sections by punching a number on the machine corresponding to the section, unless you manually fast-forward (which can take a very long time) or you have the "indexing" feature, which is often absent from either the disc or the player or both. Although the CD can hold nearly 80 minutes of music, many companies shortchange the buyer with as much as 20 minutes less recorded material — and with current prices around $15-$20 per disc, this is no laughing matter. There are even complaints about the packaging, with many people finding it inconvenient and difficult to pry open the plastic cases in which most CDs are sheathed.

Nevertheless, barring the introduction of an even better technology, the compact disc seems to have the potential to send the conventional disc into an irreversible decline. Every one of the problems just enumerated can be corrected, including the high price. It is no doubt merely a matter of time (short, we hope) until all of the bugs are worked out and the CD is accepted as unquestionably superior in every respect. Already, as we go to press, the cost of CD players has in some cases dropped by more than 50%.

But though we may confidently expect the total demise of 12-inch vinyl records, and even of conventional audiotape (already challenged by a floppy-disc digital audio system), it is too early to predict the final triumph of CD. The Japanese are already working on a technology which would produce a "record" the size of a credit card which would presumably be played on a machine that could fit in your hip pocket or purse. This could be overwhelmingly popular with retailers, if not the buying public, since it would no longer be necessary to pay ever-increasing rents for floor space and stores — orders could be filled by mail from the seller's living room. And then, if the march of technology continues at its present exponential pace, I will not be entirely surprised if by the time of my next revision a central computer somewhere will simply transmit any desired musical performance directly into each human brain via electrodes at the push of a button (excuse me, pad) on the front of your combination microwave oven and universal-access terminal.

Labels

When you go in a record shop, you will discuss "labels" with the clerk, not "brands." There are hundreds of these, both "domestic" (made in USA) and "imported." Traditionally, European pressings have been considered generally superior to American ones; this distinction, however, has been constantly becoming less clear, as both American pressing plants improve and some American companies farm out their pressings to European plants. With the rapid advance of technology and the public's enthusiasm for it, it has become imperative for the record companies to produce a high-quality product or fall by the wayside. Many companies are now not only making superior *new* discs and tapes, but are reaching back into their catalogs and remastering *old* recordings for better reproduction on the new equipment. Analog recordings, for instance, can be remastered digitally from the original tapes to sound far better than they used to, since two steps are eliminated, thus eliminating a significant amount of "generation loss."

Concomitant with this development, many record companies are reissuing hundreds of their older catalog exclusively on budget tape, often in the 90-minute format. Sometimes these are remastered, sometimes not, and the programs may or may not correspond to the original issues (sometimes material is patched together from several different albums); but the common denominator is *low price*. Such anthologies have become popular with the advent of the Walkman, presumably inspiring joggers to greater endurance with the aid of "Greatest Hits of the Baroque" and the like. They have also become favored for automobile cassette players: I have a friend who thinks of distances in musical terms — ask him how far it is from Minneapolis to Sioux Falls and he'll reply "about four Beethoven symphonies."

These special 90-minute budget tape lines are *not* detailed in this book. To cover them fairly would literally require another book of at least the same size, and this material is being issued and deleted and rereleased with such dizzying speed that anything I said might be out of date in a few weeks or months. Therefore I have limited myself to the *original source recordings* (disc and corresponding cassette) from which these anthologies are culled.

I can give you only general guidelines: look for the music, artists, and labels you have confidence in; inquire of a reliable record store salesperson as to the audio quality and price; and don't be too fussy, since these tapes are often meant to be heard over inexpensive headphones or to the accompaniment of freeway traffic.

Among the 90-minute budget tapes are Angel's Miles of Music, Classical 90s from CBS, a special Victrola series from RCA, Deutsche Grammophon's Basics, Doubletime, and Walkman Classics, London's Superconcert series, and Classics for Joy from Pro Arte-Quintessence. These currently list at about $6.98. At the $3.98 price level there are a number of lines with the standard 40-60 minute format, including DG's Musikfest, London's Viva, and Classettes from Philips. Cheapest of all is the Allegro series from Moss Music Group.

Keep in mind that these are not the only budget tape lines. These are just the ones that exist on *cassette only* (except Musikfest and Viva) and are designed for quick sale with a mass market in mind. Many other labels, such as Seraphim (from Angel), Stereo Treasury (London), Odyssey and Great Performance (CBS), Gold Seal and the regular Victrola (RCA), Privilege (DG), Vox (Moss), and Quintessence (Pro Arte) are comparably inexpensive but have exactly corresponding LP's and represent the original issues from which the Walkman-type cassettes derive. These are the cassettes which (with their LP's and/or CD's) *are* treated in detail in this book.

In the old edition I listed some labels with comments on their relative quality. I have thought better of doing that this time, not only because the variances in engineering and materials are now generally less pronounced, but also because I do not wish to give the impression that I recommend buying by label. It is true that some labels, like Philips or DG, have justly acquired superior reputations for recording and pressing quality, while others may be less highly regarded. I see no great advantage, however, in spending premium prices for mediocre performances on high-tech labels, when humbler (but still *good*) labels may offer great performances at a cheaper price. Philips and DG do have many great performances, but blindly buying anything because of the "brand name" is not a guarantee of a satisfactory record collection.

At the same time, you should not buy by price alone. A high price in records may or may not guarantee quality. The price of a record is sometimes merely a reflection of how much it cost to produce, not how good it is. Though many full-price recordings are worth their cost, often a budget record or tape will be fully the equal of, or even superior to, its expensive counterparts. A similar comment may be made about artists: yes, Rubinstein and Toscanini and Perlman and Pavarotti are great performers as a rule, but even they have their off days, or suffer from poor sonics or the foibles of their colleagues on a particular record, and some lesser-known musician may surpass them in a given piece of music.

Prices

This is a dangerous subject to discuss, since prices are not likely to remain stable through the life of this book. Some will go up, some down. As a general rule there are three main tiers of prices. In ascending order they are budget, mid-price, and full price. Budgets are currently mostly in the $3.98-$5.98 range, mid-price is mostly at $6.98, although the no-man's-land up to $8.98 might be so defined as well. Certainly full-price can be considered $9.98-$11.98, and there are many high-tech recordings even more expensive, including many imports, and most obviously CD's which may run upwards of $20 each. For the purposes of this book I have chosen not to differentiate between budgets and mid-price recordings. Product in either category, as well as full-price boxed sets that may offer a special price reduction, are designated with the letter **(B)** simply to indicate that there is some kind of inherent price advantage over comparable merchandise. Think of the **(B)** as indicating a "bargain" rather than a "budget" recording.

In considering the purchase of low-price recordings you should keep in mind that budgets fall into three main categories: (1) records that have been in the catalog for a while and have paid their way. The manufacturer may feel the discs are too good to delete, but will not sell at the original price. Most of these are quite comparable in sound quality with more recent releases, though some (and these are usually clearly labelled) are "historic" performances from the pre-stereo era, and though inferior in sound, they are of great value to the sophisticated collector. (2) New recordings by unknown artists, who the company feels are worthy but unable at this time to compete for the dollars with "name" artists, e.g., pianist Alfred Brendel, now recording for the premium Philips label, first came to public attention on the budget Vox / Turnabout line. (3) Licensed recordings. The issuing company plays a flat fee for the original "masters" of out-of-print or non-importable materials locked in the vaults of another company, and thus bypasses production costs and royalties. The savings are passed on to you. Be aware, then, that in buying the budgets you could be getting anything from a 1903 acoustical recording with scratchy surfaces, to a brand-new version of Schubert's Unfinished conducted by John Doe, with innumerable unquestionable treasures strewn in between (often, in fact, a budget disc may be superior in every way to all the full-price recordings of the same music).

Retail selling prices are considered further in our next category:

Where to Buy

Since all record stores theoretically sell exactly the same albums and tapes, competition in record merchandising boils down to price, selection, and service. The larger the store, and the more it is exclusively devoted to selling recordings (as opposed to musical instruments and stereo equipment), the lower its pricing structure will be (usually), and of course the larger its selection. All records carry a "manufacturer's suggested list price," which is almost never charged in any stores. "Chain" shops may sell discs for 1-2 dollars less than "list" and even lower during "label sales" or "store-wide sales." Just remember that when a "40% off" sale is advertised, it commonly means 40% off *list,* not off the store's regular selling price, which may already be 20-30% off list.

Smaller, higher-priced stores may offer better service, especially to the classical buyer, but even the chain stores try to have somebody available with helpful knowledge. The trick, in large stores, is to *specifically ask* for a classical clerk.

Some records and tapes are available only by mail order, for example through the Musical Heritage Society which offers a large catalog of generally fine items at budget price, but at full-price standards. Some of the larger American labels, and independent marketing organizations, offer "record clubs" by mail. These are especially helpful to collectors who do not live near a good record store — but be aware that often, after you get your amazing introductory offer ("ten records for only $1.00!!"), you may thereafter pay full list price; and if you are sent the wrong item, or have a defective, you must mail it back at your own expense. There is also the waiting factor to consider.

Records, like books, often go "out of print." Some stores in larger cities have "cutout" bins at reduced prices, or devote part of their floor space to used records. A few dealers specialize in hard-to-get recordings, often at high prices.

Care and Cleaning

Many a collector has invested hundreds of dollars only to find, after a few months or years, that his records are "worn out." This need not be. Records will, as their makers claim, "last indefinitely with proper care." This means you must make a modest investment in professional accessories as recommended by reputable dealers. Generally, cloths and sprays are a waste of money. The former, like feather dusters, only skim the surface; they do not get down in the grooves and root out microscopic particles whose presence becomes known through your amplifiier. Sprays, while temporarily masking static, actually leave residues in the grooves which gradually build up a layer of gook that makes things worse than ever. The best home record cleaning device is a specially designed brush whose bristles scour the grooves without damaging them, aided by a properly formulated liquid that leaves no traces. Such a cleaner costs more than cloths and sprays, but is indispensable. It can be found at reputable dealers.

Records should be handled only with the palms touching the outer edges of the disc. Never touch the grooves with your fingers — this smears body oils on the surface, which is as bad as, or worse than, the residue from sprays. Protect records from harmful dust by replacing them after use in their "inner sleeves." Ideally, records should be stored upright, away from direct sunlight, and in an area of low humidity.

Incidentally, similar cautions apply to CDs, which can be damaged or destroyed too, despite some overenthusiastic advertising to the contrary. Although the CD "playing surface" is sealed and protected from direct contact, your finger smears and jelly blobs on the outer shield can interrupt the laser beam and cause your music to temporarily disappear. Keep CDs stainless with a soft, lint-free cloth.

Before proceeding to the recording recommendations, please rest assured that in the last analysis there is no substitute for your own taste and experience. All the critics in the world may agree that a certain performance is the greatest, while you may prefer another. That does not mean you are "wrong." Taste in music is terribly subjective. Perhaps you are just ahead of the times, and future generations of reviewers will come around to your viewpoint. This book is merely an attempt to describe the currents of today's prevailing taste. You are welcome to flow with it if it fits your own feelings, or you may just be curious as to how the "experts" differ from you. The only important thing is to let great music into your life, and to let it bring you the profound and lifelong joy that it has to so many other lucky people.

The Middle Ages & Renaissance

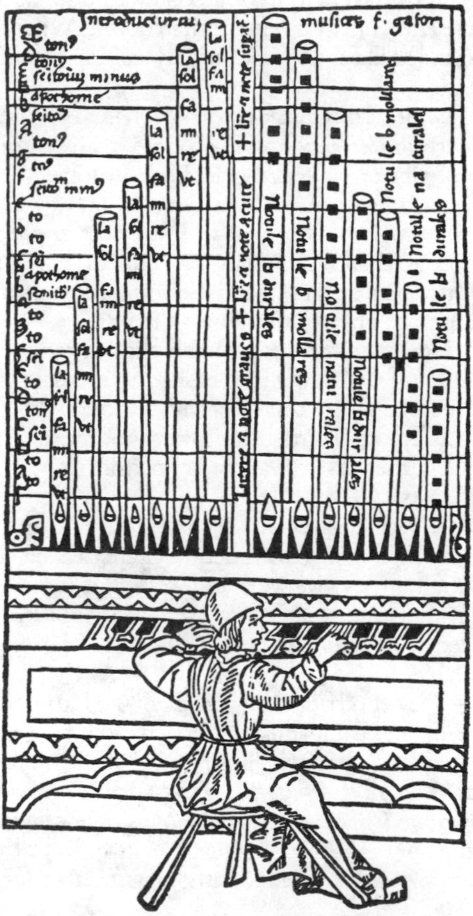

Since very little contemporary concert music has won a wide audience in the past twenty years, the gap has been filled by a renewed interest in very *old* music — the songs and dances and chants whose authors, as often as not, are unknown, but which form the basis for all Western classical music. Gradually we have learned that these works are not only historically important, but also direct in expression and delightful to listen to. In response to this the stereo era has witnessed an ever-expanding stream of issues in the pre-Bach repertoire.

"Early music" however is still a specialized area that falls almost beyond the pale of this book. There is as yet no general agreement as to what may constitute "basic" works written before about A.D. 1600. The great bulk of it is anonymous in origin. Most of it has come down to us through oral tradition, or in a written form whose authenticity is very much in doubt. What this music actually sounded like is a topic of widely varying and often acrimonious dispute.

None of this music is part of what is considered the standard modern concert repertory. If you go to any concert of the Boston Symphony, or the Los Angeles Philharmonic, you may hear Bach, Mozart, Beethoven, Brahms, Franck, Stravinsky, and Takemitsu on the program — but you will not hear any troubadour songs, Gregorian chants, or Renaissance dances (unless they are re-done by Ottorino Respighi). For these you must seek out occasional special recitals, often in museum galleries.

Gregorian chant is probably the one type of early music that comes closest to fitting the "basic" requirements for these listings, but it is like a giant coral reef with a thousand beautiful branches, no one favored particularly over another, and there are wildly different theories as to its correct performance, none of which has proved its case beyond cavil.

Nevertheless, there are some generalized anthology albums which ought to be recommended here to the beginning collector especially. They give wide and well-done samples of the vast and misty thousand years before the Baroque; hearing these, you may be led to dig further among the profusion of recordings now available.

The period from about A.D. 600-1150 was dominated by the type of unaccompanied sacred chant now generally known as "Gregorian," although "Roman" might be more apt. "Plainsong" is another near-synonym. **Vanguard 71217**, titled **A Guide to Gregorian Chant**, is an invaluable single-disc introduction, performed by the **Schola Antiqua**, and including a dictionary of chant terminology. For a larger anthology suitable for extended listening, without scholarly notes, **Columbia** offers a three-record set on **M3X 32329**, convincingly executed by the **Schola Cantorum of Amsterdam Students**; the box carries a permanent "reduced" list price.

What historians call the High Middle Ages, and musicians the Gothic Era, is brilliantly surveyed in a three-record set by **The Early Music Consort of London** on **DG / Archiv 2710 019**. At a much lower price the same forces can be heard in a three-record budget set on **Seraphim SIC-6092**. This is a collection of French secular music from the late Gothic Era (the "ars nova") enticingly billed as **The Art of Courtly Love**. For the cheapest-of-all introductions to the artistry of The Early Music Consort of London and its inimitable late director, David Munrow, try the single disc **Pleasures of the Royal Courts** on **Nonesuch 71326** (LP and CS).

Another inexpensive window on the secular side of Medieval music is provided by **MCA 2504**, a recording of the anonymous **The Play of Daniel**, performed by the **New York Pro Musica** under **Noah Greenberg**. This group was the *first* to make records using "original instruments" (all the rage nowadays) back in 1959. Their influence on subsequent recording history has been incalculable, and though much has changed since their heyday this disc has maintained its status as a classic.

The Renaissance (ca. 1450-1600) is succinctly introduced by another budget three-record box on **Seraphim SIC-6052**, called **The Seraphim Guide to Renaissance Music**. Performing are the **Syntagma Musicum of Amsterdam**.

The entire spectrum of Medieval and Renaissance instrumental music is surveyed in two different two-record sets, both titled **Instruments of the Middle Ages and Renaissance**. Martin Bookspan offers narrative explanation to performances by **Musica Reservata of London** on **Vanguard 71219 / 20**, which includes an 8-page leaflet. More expensive and designed for the more serious enthusiast is **Angel SBZ-3810** (LP and CS) with a 100-page (!) book by David Munrow. The performances, of course, are by his ensemble, The Early Music Consort of London.

If you become an aficionado of early music you will want to keep an eye out for the following names as you explore in greater depth:

Byrd (Keyboard music)

Dowland (Lute music, songs)

Gabrieli (Canzoni for brass)

Josquin des Prez (Masses and motets)

Lasso (Lassus) (Madrigals and motets)

Monteverdi (Madrigals)

Palestrina *(Missa Papae Marcelli)*

Praetorius (*Terpsichore* selections)

Note: Gabrieli is technically a Renaissance composer but gives us our first glimpse of the Baroque. Monteverdi counts as *both* a Renaissance and Baroque composer; his early madrigals mark him as a Renaissance man, but in his later years we must count him as one of the greatest Baroque composers.

The
Baroque Era

Music of the Baroque era (ca. 1600-1750) tends, like twentieth-century music with which it is often held to have abstract affinities, to polarize listeners. Many persons like Baroque music above all other kinds; there is even a sub-species of auditors who listen only to Bach. Other folks can't abide the Baroque. If you belong to the former group, the following list will seem much too brief; if you belong to the latter, you will perhaps not even look at the recommendations. Either choice is yours — but please, avoid the attitude, too often found, that all Baroque music was intended as an innocuous background to reading the newspaper. The least distinguished Baroque music is not far off from that function, but the best of it claims our rapt attention as much as Beethoven or Brahms, and to give it less is to insult the memory of some of the greatest musical geniuses who ever lived.

More than in later music, the Baroque period forces us to pay attention to questions of performance practice. This music went out of fashion almost overnight, at the death of Bach. The first attempts at revival took place nearly a century later, when so much had changed that almost everything about its proper performance was forgotten.

The past twenty years have seen a renaissance of scholarship in this area. Some musicians have espoused the use of the original instruments, or careful reproductions of them. Since these, and the ability to play them, are in short supply, many others have compromised by attempting to reproduce the authentic style of Baroque music as best they can by adapting modern instruments to the Baroque sound, stripping the scores of the accretions of well-meaning Romantic editors, adjusting the ensemble size to the original specifications, and restoring (by means of intelligent conjecture) many of the performance practices so taken for granted by the Baroque composers that they often did not bother to write them out literally.

There are still musicians who think all of this revisionism is nonsense, just as there are those who still believe that the earth is flat, and that the Apollo moon shot took place in a Hollywood studio. I bow here to the prevailing view, and emphasize in the listings those recordings which reflect current thinking — but avoiding as well those which are so absorbed in authenticity that they forget this is also music to enjoy, and to be moved by.

Tomaso Albinoni 1671-1750

Adagio for Strings and Organ (arr. Giazotto)

Albinoni was one of the finest Venetian composers of his day and his music was greatly admired by Bach, who even plagiarized some of it. So we cannot be too critical of the latter-day musicologist Giazotto who took a fragment of Albinoni's music and worked it into the full-length pseudo-Baroque *Adagio* which has become, ironically, "Albinoni's most popular composition."

Since it is a kind of forgery (albeit a magnificent one), it seems silly to recommend recordings that try to force it into the "authentic" mold. Probably the most tasteful approach is that of Marriner and the Academy of St. Martin-in-the-Fields, whose record includes Pachelbel's KANON and other "Baroque hits."

Münchinger's full-price record with the Stuttgart Chamber Orchestra is another favorite album, in a slightly richer style. It has the KANON too, along with Bach's JESU, JOY OF MAN'S DESIRING and other favorites. The older budget disc with the same players has the KANON, and Vivaldi's FOUR SEASONS but not the Bach. The cheapest version is Hickox's; it too includes the KANON and offers Big Orchestra performances, recommended for the hard-of-hearing.

If price is no object, there is the Karajan recording which honestly treats the *Adagio* and the KANON as the elegant fakes they are, and reinforces the image by including the third set of Respighi's ANCIENT AIRS AND DANCES, a deliberate and unrepentant modern glossing of early music. There is also a special CD-only Karajan program with the *Adagio*, the KANON, Mozart's SERENADE NO. 6, Bach's "Air on the G String," Vivaldi's "La Notte" flute concerto, and Gluck's "Dance of the Blessed Spirits."

Hickox, Orchestra. (B)
London Stereo Treasury STS 15441 (LP, CS)

Karajan, Berlin Philharmonic.
DG 2530 247 (LP); 3300 317 (CS)

Karajan, Berlin Philharmonic.
DG 413 309-2 (CD)

Marriner, Academy SMF.
Angel S-37044 (LP, CS)

Münchinger, Stuttgart CO. (B)
London CS 7102 (LP, CS)

Münchinger, Stuttgart CO.
London Jubilee 41007 (LP, CS)

Note: a recent European release features the **Paillard Chamber Orchestra** in newly-recorded versions of the *Adagio*, the KANON, and six others, including JESU, JOY. These are *not* the same as the popular old American RCA versions. No reviews were available for the new versions, and so far only the CD has appeared in this country (**Erato ECD-88020**). If you were one of the old Paillard fans, and are "into" CD's, you might keep an eye out for this one, though it's on a label not carried by all stores.

Johann Sebastian Bach   1685-1750

Brandenburg Concerti (6), S. 1046/51

Along with Vivaldi's FOUR SEASONS, these concerti are probably the most popular of all Baroque instrumental music. A recent Schwann catalog showed 36 complete recordings. Out of the one-fourth of these I have selected as receiving the best reviews, all but one use period instruments or at least simulate Baroque performance practice.

Pinnock's version is among the newest and most favored. Most critics have raved over its clarity, excitement, and faithful scholarship. The sonics, while brilliantly up-to-date, are criticized by *Gramophone* for an alleged "contrived intimacy." Very high marks also for Harnoncourt's more recent (1982) of two recordings on Telefunken, though the division of opinion is wider than for Pinnock.

Fuller's set, described in my previous book as available only by mail, is now in stores. It is still well thought-of, but some think it has slipped a few percentage points; it also takes three discs instead of the normal two, a serious cost consideration. The long-admired Leonhardt box has also been getting edged out of favor, but keep in mind it is the only one giving you a complete printed facsimile of the score (caution: there is another pressing of the same performances, on the same label, *without* the score, with a different catalog number, and cheaper — be sure you know which you're getting).

The recent Linde Consort recording has got much praise for its cohesion and balance, and Marriner is widely liked as well, but nobody rates either higher than second place. Marriner is the only one besides Pinnock available in CD format.

The Collegium Aureum set remains one of the best sellers and is unquestionably the best budget buy on Quintessence. It is also available at a higher price (and better pressing) on an import label. All reviewers like it, and some prefer it to either Harnoncourt or Pinnock or both. This ensemble uses "original instruments" but somehow they always sound quite close to modern ones. For many listeners, especially those who are uneasy with pungent period oboes and spiky strings, the "Golden Guild" offer an ideal compromise.

The one performance of high quality that is definitely not "authentic" is Benjamin Britten's, by far the best of the supposedly "wrong" versions, and attractively priced. If you prefer warm, rich, resonant modern instruments and a plush, blended sound, buy this one. And if your neighbors are period instrument freaks, sneak it home in a plain brown wrapper.

Britten, English CO. (B)
(2) London Jubilee 42005 (LP, CS)

Collegium Aureum.
(2) German Harmonia Mundi 99643 / 4 (LP)

Collegium Aureum. (B)
(2) Quintessence 2075 (LP, CS)

Fuller, Aston Magna Festival.
(2) Smithsonian 3016 (LP)

Harnoncourt, Concentus Musicus.
(2) Telefunken 26.35620 (D-LP, CS)

Leonhardt Consort.
(2) Pro Arte 2PAX-2001 (LP, CS)

Linde Consort.
(2) Angel OBS-3930 (D-LP)

Marriner, Academy SMF.
(2) Philips 6700 045 (LP); 7300 158 / 9 (CS); 400 076 / 7-2 (CD)

Pinnock, English Concert.
*(2) DG Archiv 2742 003 (D-LP); 3383 003 (CS);
410 500/1-2 (CD)*

Concerti (7) for Harpsichord, S. 1052/8

The Leonhardt-Tachezi box is still recommended, but now has serious competition from Pinnock and his English Concert group. Pinnock is not only newer and, to some, even better, but comes in at one less disc with an additional price reduction and is available on CD. *Concerto No. 5 in f, S. 1056* is the most popular of the seven, and both artists offer it separately on a single disc — Leonhardt-Tachezi coupled with Concerti Nos. 2 and 4; Pinnock more generously with Nos. 4, 6, and 7.

Leonhardt, Tachezi, Leonhardt Consort, Concentus Musicus.
(5) Telefunken 56.35049 (LP)

(Nos. 2, 4, 5) Leonhardt, etc.
Telefunken 6.41099 (LP, CS)

Pinnock, English Concert.
(4) DG Archiv 2723 077 (LP); 410 500/1-2 (CD)

(Nos. 4, 5, 6, 7) Pinnock, etc.
DG Archiv 2533 467 (LP); 3310 467 (CS)

Concerti (2) for Violin, S. 1041/2;
Concerto in d for 2 Violins, S. 1043

Most recordings of these three great works have them conveniently together on one disc. Yes, Itzhak Perlman plays them, but Angel splits them between two records, and since there are many excellent (and far more stylish) performances on one disc, there is absolutely no reason to list Perlman or buy him.

Among the "authentic" versions, three stand out; those by the Academy of Ancient Music, the English Concert, and La Petite Bande. The Academy is led by Christopher Hogwood, with soloists Jaap Schröder and Christopher Hirons. Some critics rate this recording at or near the top for style and fluidity, but some think Schröder's instrument is sour and the sound a bit shrill, especially on the CD.

Pinnock conducts the English Concert, with soloists Standage and Willcock, and reviewers are more unanimous in their praise. Even those who slightly preferred one of the others liked this one greatly for its airy fleetness and probing, chamber-style approach.

All major critics also loved violinists Kuijken and van Dael with La Petite Bande, with two of them making it their first choice for vitality and sensitivity.

There are two best choices for performances using modern instruments. The most unusual is that with Gidon Kremer and the St. Martin's Academy. Kremer solos in the first two concerti, then plays *both* parts in the double concerto (by means of overdubbing, of course). Although it's a gimmick, all critics agree it works, and the performance is full of flair and exuberance.

Older and more traditional is the budget version with violinists Menuhin and Ferras, and the Masters Chamber Orchestra. The same critics who loved one or more of the "authentic" versions tended to prefer this one for the modern-instrument approach.

The Harnoncourt and Oistrakh recordings listed in my earlier book seem to have fallen out of favor, the former superseded by better "period" readings, the latter rejected because its age no longer justifies its high price — Menuhin-Ferras are nearly as good and much cheaper.

Kremer, Academy SMF.
Philips 411 108-1 (LP); 411 108-4 (CS); 411 108-2 (CD)

Kuijken, van Dael, La Petite Bande.
Pro Arte PAD-124 (D-LP, CS)

Menuhin, Ferras, Masters CO. (B)
Seraphim S-60258 (LP, CS)

Schröder, Hirons, Hogwood, Academy of Ancient Music.
L'Oiseau Lyre DSDL-702 (D-LP, CS); 400 080-2 (CD)

Standage, Willcock, Pinnock, English Concert.
DG Archiv 410 646-1 (D-LP); 410 646-4 (CS); 410 646-2 (CD)

Italian Concerto in F, S. 971

Although there are several recordings on the piano, this scintillating work absolutely must be heard on the harpsichord, for which it was written.

The best one you are currently likely to *find* is a budget with Igor Kipnis, although it's nobody's ideal choice. The coupling is the beautiful Partita in b, S. 831. The two most favored versions are on hard-to-get labels: Edward Parmentier on Wildboar, with other works by Bach and two by Georg Böhm; and Mireille Lagacé on Calliope with two additional Bach pieces. Both records are imports.

Kipnis. (B)
Angel RL-32126 (LP, CS)

Lagacé.
Calliope 1657 (LP)

Parmentier.
Wildboar 8101 (LP)

Jesu, Joy of Man's Desiring

Originally this was a chorale from Cantata 147. As one of the most beautiful melodies ever conceived it has become better known through many transcriptions: for piano, violin and piano, organ solo, orchestra, even harmonica.

The late E. Power Biggs was America's most beloved organist and his album "The Biggs Bach Book" is a cherished basic library item. It contains many of the favorite chorale melodies, including *Jesu, Joy,* and selections from the "Little Music Book for Anna Magdalena Bach" (the composer's wife).

For orchestral versions there are Münchinger's album discussed under the Albinoni ADAGIO, and Marriner's lovely collection "A Little Night Music," both at full price. Marriner includes Mozart's EINE KLEINE NACHTMUSIK, Haydn's "Toy Symphony," Gluck's "Dance of the Blessed Spirits," Handel's "Largo," and an Entr'acte from Schubert's ROSAMUNDE. The new Paillard CD from Erato is also detailed under Albinoni. In the budget category there is a nice record of short Bach pieces in modern dress by the German Bach Soloists under Helmut Winschermann.

Biggs.
Columbia M-30539 (LP, CS)

Marriner, Academy SMF.
Angel S-37443 (LP, CS)

Münchinger, Stuttgart CO.
London CS 7102 (LP, CS)

Paillard CO.
Erato ECD-88020 (CD)

Winschermann, German Bach Soloists. (B)
Quintessence 7160 (LP, CS)

Magnificat in D, S. 243

This joyful Christmas classic has such complex textures that it absolutely demands the "period" treatment; otherwise it can become an incoherent jumble. The recordings by Harnoncourt and Preston stand out in this field. Both have soloists trained in authentic Baroque singing style. Harnoncourt leads the Vienna Concentus Musicus and his choristers are the Vienna Choir Boys and the Chorus Viennensis. He uses the familiar half-hour score, and has a coupling of Handel's *Utrecht Te Deum.* Preston, with the Academy of Ancient Music and Choir of Christ Church Cathedral, Oxford, presents a somewhat different version. It is in the less familiar (and much longer) edition in the key of E-flat, augmented by Christmas interpolations written for a performance in Leipzig in 1723. The only coupling is a rarely heard Bach motet, about five minutes long. Both recordings have excellent sonics and are full-priced. Preston is longer, but livelier.

Harnoncourt, Concentus Musicus.
Telefunken 6.42921 (D-LP, CS)

Preston, AAM.
L'Oiseau Lyre DSLO-572 PSI (LP)

Mass in b, S. 232

Oddly, there is no really good "authentic" performance of this great work currently available. Joshua Rifkin's "miniaturist" version has attracted much attention but is far too controversial to be recommended as a basic library choice. That honor goes to Corboz, whose full-blown performance has sweep and conviction and carries a low price sticker.

Marriner's much more expensive version is very good, following a compromise approach: women choristers, modern instruments, but small orchestra and a stab at Baroque idioms. It is much brisker than Jochum's digital recording, which is certainly not stylish, but offers radiant dignity and majesty (some call it pomposity).

Corboz, Lausanne Orchestra and Chorus. (B)
(2) RCA FVL 2-5715 (LP)

Jochum, Bavarian Radio Symphony and Chorus.
(3) Angel DSC-3904 (D-LP, CS)

Marriner, Academy SMF.
(3) Philips 6769 002 (LP); 7699 076 (CS) Highlights on **(B)**
Philips Sequenza 6527 099 (LP); 7311 099 (CS)

Organ Music

There are dozens of recordings of Bach organ music. They all have different couplings and there are few unassailably great performances, partly because the organ is notoriously difficult to capture properly on disc or tape. For an introduction to this huge body of music — the greatest ever written for the instrument — I have limited myself to single discs containing at least the Toccata and Fugue in d, S. 565 and / or the Passacaglia and Fugue in c, S. 582.

The living organist who has garnered the widest acclaim for his Bach is Wolfgang Rübsam, who has recorded *all* of these works on a 25-record Philips set! You can get a single disc at budget price with six of the favorites, including the Toccata.

English organist Peter Hurford has also been recording the complete works for Argo, in performances of almost orchestral scope and color. His "sampler" record has both the Toccata and Passacaglia, is recorded digitally, and is available on CD.

E. Power Biggs's Columbia discs are much older, but still very good. MS 6261 is the "most basic" album, with our two key pieces and other favorites, with M 31840 as a good supplement if you would like two Bach organ records. For a more varied program, MS 7269 has the Toccata, four other Bach pieces, and works by six other composers, including a selection from Handel's CUCKOO AND THE NIGHTINGALE and Ives's VARIATIONS ON 'AMERICA.'

Beware of Michael Murray on Telarc (very un-stylish and expensive, despite superior sound) and Marie-Claire Alain on Erato (excellent performances, with both key pieces, but chaotic sonics).

Biggs.
Columbia MS 6261 (LP); 16 11 0160 (CS)

Biggs.
Columbia M 31840 (LP, CS)

Biggs.
Columbia MS 7269 (LP)

Hurford.
Argo 411 824-1 (D-LP); 411 824-4 (CS); 411 824-2 (CD)

Rübsam.
Philips Festivo 6570 118 (LP); 7310 118 (CS)

St. Matthew Passion, S. 244

This mammoth expression of Bach's piety comes in all three flavors: "traditional," called by purists "wrong" (Karajan); "middle-of-the-road," with modern instruments but also with nods toward scholarship and style (Somary and Richter); and "authentic," called by traditionalists "out of tune."

Harnoncourt still represents the only true "original instrument" version. He has only male singers, with boys replacing women as in Bach's day. Somary's "compromise" reading is dramatic, vital, and imaginative, with interesting notes. Richter has the most famous soloists (Mathis, Baker, Schreier, and Fischer-Dieskau), and emphasizes the grandiose aspects of the score while remaining reasonably stylish. Karajan also has good soloists and a slow, solemn, highly polished approach.

Harnoncourt, Concentus Musicus.
(4) Telefunken 46.35047 (LP)

Karajan, Berlin Philharmonic, Vienna Singverein, German Opera Chorus.
(4) DG 2711 012 (LP); 3371 007 (CS)

Richter, Munich Bach Orchestra and Chorus.
(4) DG Archiv 2712 005 (LP); 3376 016 (CS) Highlights on DG Archiv 2531 317 (LP)

Somary, English CO, Ambrosian Singers.
(4) Vanguard 71231/4 (LP)

Suites (4) for Orchestra, S. 1066/9

Sometimes also listed as "Overtures," these Suites are all essential listening, though No. 3 is best known for containing the beloved "Air on the G String."

Fortunately, there are many recordings to choose from and there is hardly a really bad one in the lot. In the bargain category the Collegium Aureum turn in their usual good job, and the newer Pommer recording, with modern instruments but Baroque idioms, is that rare bird, a low-priced digital.

The clear winner with critics in the full-price field is Pinnock, lively, breezy, "correct," and beautifully recorded — though some say the cassette is inferior. Hard on Pinnock's heels are Kuijken and Linde, both also with original instruments. Harnoncourt's newer version is livelier and sonically superior to his old one, still available at reduced price (not listed here).

Reviewers are widely split on Marriner's old and new readings, both of which are still in print. Arguments rage over which is better, but I am listing only the more recent one, since it definitely has better sound and there is no price difference. At least it is considered the best performance using modern instruments.

Harnoncourt, Concentus Musicus.
(2) Telefunken 26.35046 (LP, CS)

Kuijken, La Petite Bande.
(2) Pro Arte 2PAD-205 (D-LP, CS)

Linde Consort.
(2) Angel SB-3943 (D-LP, CS)

Maier, Collegium Aureum. (B)
(2) Quintessence 2702 (LP, CS)

Marriner, Academy SMF.
(2) Philips 6769 012 (LP); 7699 087 (CS)

Pinnock, English Concert.
(2) DG Archiv 2723 072 (LP); 3310 175 (CS)

Pommer, New Bach Collegium Musicum. (B)
(2) Sinfonia 2-700 (D-LP, CS)

George Frideric Handel   1685-1759

Concerti Grossi (12), Op. 6

Considered in Europe the equals of Bach's BRANDENBURG CONCERTI, these works are far less popular in America — for no reason I can fathom.

Pinnock is again favored among the period instrument performances, highly praised by nearly all reviewers and included by *Opus* in their select list of the 100 most inspired recordings of all time. There is a CD of this, along with Iona Brown's widely-liked modern instrument version. Quite similar to Brown is Marriner (they use the same orchestra, after all), but his version has older sound. His impeccable taste may make up for that. The Collegium Aureum set is very good and its gorgeous cover is almost worth the price alone; but it will be available only in stores carrying imports.

Warning: Harnoncourt's recording is one of his worst. Sloppy ensemble and a very idiosyncratic concept of the music.

Brown, Academy SMF.
(3) Philips 6769 083 (D-LP); 7654 083 (CS); 410 048-2 (CD)

Collegium Aureum.
(3) German Harmonia Mundi 99645 / 7 (LP)

Marriner, Academy SMF.
(3) London CSA 2309 (LP)

Pinnock, English Concert.
(3) DG Archiv 2742 002 (D-LP); 3383 002 (CS); 410 897-2 (CD) Nos. 1 and 4 available separately on DG Archiv 410 897-1 (D-LP); 410 897-4 (CS)

Concerto No. 13 for Organ, "The Cuckoo and the Nightingale"

I have chosen this brilliant work to stand as an introduction to Handel's 16 wonderful organ concerti. The most piquant version is that with Harnoncourt and organist Herbert Tachezi. The record is particularly useful for including four other concerti for various instruments, thus whetting the appetite for additional instrumental music of this prolific master.

Stylish and urbane, though perhaps a bit over-reticent, are the performances of this and two other Handel organ concerti by George Malcolm, accompanied by Neville Marriner. The Biggs record discussed under Bach ORGAN MUSIC contains just one movement from *The Cuckoo and the Nightingale,* but it is a wonderful souvenir of his brightly energetic complete set with Sir Adrian Boult, currently out of print.

Biggs.
Columbia MS 7269 (LP)

Malcolm, Marriner, Academy SMF.
Argo ZRG 888 (LP, CS)

Tachezi, Harnoncourt, Concentus Musicus.
Telefunken 6.41270 (LP, CS)

Messiah

Again we have a mixture of period- and modern-instrument versions to choose from, and the critical rankings have pretty well sort-ed themselves out. Recordings of *Messiah* can be amazingly different from one another since Handel himself revised it and performed it with various changes in his own time; it was later edited and revised by Mozart; and conductors right up to our own day have reorchestrated and carved it up pretty much as they have seen fit.

By far the leader among "authentic" versions is that by Hogwood, which has won general enthusiasm for overall vitality and beauty. Even the few carpers have said many good things about it. A majority picked it for their first choice, and it made the *Opus* list of "100 Inspired Recordings." There is a CD, but only of highlights.

The Gardiner performance is even newer, and digitally recorded. It too is well regarded, but most think of it as a fine *alternative* to Hogwood. It is less consistent in its approach to Baroque practices. Dunn's recording is the only good budget version approaching true Baroque style.

Marriner continues to hold the lead among the more recent "compromise" editions. Interestingly, it uses a Hogwood edition of the score, but does *not* use period instruments. About 15 years ago the Davis and Mackerras recordings were considered revelatory in attempting to bring to bear some of the modern scholarship; as musical performances they are very good in their own right and are still in print, but I am not listing them until they are put into the budget category where they belong with honor.

Meanwhile, there does exist a fine budget choice for the old traditional "inflated" approach. Sir Malcolm Sargent's recording is, as Teri Noel Towe wrote in *High Fidelity*, "the clear choice for those to whom authenticity is anathema." And if you simply want to hear the music very much as you hear it in your local Christmas community concert, only done by top professionals, get the Robert Shaw Chorale set.

And what of Harnoncourt, once the *ne plus ultra* of original-instrument *Messiahs*? Almost all reviewers have abandoned him in favor of Hogwood or Gardiner.

Dunn, Handel and Haydn Society. (B)
(3) Sine Qua Non 2015 (LP) Highlights on 2013 (LP)

Gardiner, English Baroque Soloists, Monteverdi Choir.
(3) Philips 6769 107 (D-LP); 7654 107 (CS)

Hogwood, Academy of Ancient Music.
(3) L'Oiseau Lyre D 189 D3 (LP); K 189 K3 (CS) Choruses only on DSLO 613 (LP, CS); 400 086-2 (CD)

Marriner, Academy SMF.
(3) Argo D 18 D3 (LP); K 18 K32 (CS)

Sargent, Royal Liverpool Orchestra, Huddersfield Choral Society.
*(3) Seraphim SIC-6056 (LP, CS) Highlights on S-60220
(LP, CS)* **(B)**

Shaw, Robert Shaw Chorale.
*(3) RCA LSC-6175 (LP) Also repackaged more cheaply as RCA
VCS-7081 (LP) Highlights on LSC-2966 or LSC-3293*

Water Music Suite; Royal Fireworks Music

For the beginning collector I am recommending single discs that
contain highlights from both of these colorful works. By *Water
Music Suite* is usually meant a synthesis of highlights from the
three Suites which make up the complete *Water Music.* The *Royal
Fireworks Music* is only half as long as the complete *Water Music* so
is usually given complete in any case.

Hogwood again leads the way in the "authentic" category,
with most critics finding him both stylish and lively. Available on
CD. Marriner is stylish too, but uses modern instruments. At
budget prices CBS has reissued the famous Boulez performance,
"modern" but sharply etched in rhythm and color.

Boulez, New York Philharmonic (B).
CBS MY 38480 (LP, CS)

Hogwood, Academy of Ancient Music.
L'Oiseau Lyre DSLO 595 (LP, CS); 400 059-2 (CD)

Marriner, Academy SMF.
Argo ZRG 697 (LP, CS)

For those wanting all of this music, the best bargain is the excellent
Collegium Aureum two-record set, with some additional fillers.
Or you can get them on a single disc with just the complete *Water
Music.*

For the complete *Water Music* along with more brilliant
sound but higher price, the preferred choices are Pinnock with
period instruments and Schwarz with modern instruments, both
available on CD. Close second choices (not digital or CD) are
Hogwood (period) and Marriner (modern).

Collegium Aureum (Complete *Water Music, Royal Fireworks,*
two others). **(B)**
(2) Quintessence 2706 (LP, CS)

Collegium Aureum (Complete *Water Music* only). **(B)**
Quintessence 7085 (LP, CS)

Hogwood, Academy of Ancient Music.
L'Oiseau Lyre DSLO 543 (LP, CS)

Marriner, Academy SMF.
Philips 9500 691 (LP); 7300 779 (CS)

Pinnock, English Concert.
DG Archiv 410 525-1 (LP); 410 525-4 (CS); 410 525-2 (CD)

Schwarz, Los Angeles CO.
Delos 3010 (D-LP, CS, CD)

Johann Pachelbel   1653-1706

Kanon in D

I follow the *Schwann Catalog* in spelling this piece the German
way, with a "K." There is no shame in spelling it the English way,
with a "C." Kanon-canon is simply a generic term for a musical
form in which a melody in one part, say the violins, is repeated exactly in another part, perhaps the woodwinds, usually starting a bit
later and overlapping. "Three Blind Mice" is a simple vocal canon.
    Pachelbel was a minor Baroque composer of delightful mini-
atures. Gordon Reynolds of *Gramophone* calls him "a master of
the unmemorable." The most startling thing about him was that
one of his sons became an organist in Charleston, South Carolina.
Much like Albinoni, he would be forgotten today by the general
public if it were not for a modern orchestral arrangement of his little Kanon for three violins and bass.
    The simple, hypnotic charm of the piece seems to have an in-
finite capacity to soothe contemporary harried nerves, especially
the richly accented performance by the Paillard Chamber Orchestra. Their best-selling album with the sickening title "Go for Baroque," containing the Kanon and other short 18th-century
pieces, was out of print for my earlier guidebook but is now back at
budget price. There is also a newer Paillard recording, available on
CD, which is detailed under Albinoni: ADAGIO. The playing is
saccharine, in a style which Stoddard Lincoln in *Stereo Review*
characterized as "(lacking) sufficient character to be truly vulgar."
Nevertheless, though all critics despise it, most non-specialists
adore it, so I am listing it. Far be it from me to challenge the Will of
the People.

Actually, it was not Paillard but Karl Münchinger who first made this hybrid music popular. His classic version is available on either of the two records discussed under the Albinoni ADAGIO, where you will also find more on the Karajan and Hickox albums. The most tasteful version, perhaps, is that by Marriner, which includes the ADAGIO and other short favorites. The Cologne Musica Antiqua and the Academy of Ancient Music have also made recordings of the *Kanon* in its original form, likely to be a disappointment to anyone but the purist.

Hickox, Orchestra. (B)
London Stereo Treasury 15441 (LP, CS)

Karajan, Berlin Philharmonic.
DG 2530 247 (LP); 3300 317 (CS)

Marriner, Academy SMF.
Angel S-37044 (LP, CS)

Münchinger, Stuttgart CO.
London CS 7102 (LP, CS)

Münchinger, Stuttgart CO. (B)
London Jubilee 41007 (LP, CS)

Paillard CO.
Erato ECD-88020 (CD)

Paillard CO. (B)
RCA AGL1-5211 (LP, CS)

Antonio Vivaldi   1678-1741

Four Seasons, Op. 8, Nos. 1-4

Along with *The Rite of Spring*, these are possibly the most over-recorded works of music — the former because conductors are obsessed with proving they can do it, the latter because they sell. Or does the weather have something to do with it?

Standage-Pinnock are the current darlings of the period instrument choices. Their playing manages to strike a balance between refinement and excitement, or as the *Penguin Guide* has it, "between vivid projection and atmospheric feeling." The Archiv pressing is their newer recording and is available on CD. An earlier recording is available either on CRD or Vanguard; critics like this one about as well, but the recordings may be a little harder to find, more expensive, and perhaps not as good quality pressings.

Most widely-liked of the newer modern instrument versions is that with Carmirelli and I Musici, with somewhat less unanimous praise for Oliveira-Schwarz. Both of these also come in the CD format.

Among the "traditional" versions two stand out for musical quality and low price; Münchinger on Jubilee, with a healthy bonus of the Albinoni ADAGIO and Pachelbel KANON; and Fasano's Virtuosi di Roma on Angel Red Line. At full price the best bets are Loveday-Marriner, Kremer-Abbado, and Perlman, in that order.

Of the other "authentic" versions the Harnoncourt is still available only in the two-record set with the other concerti of Op. 8, and has anyway fallen behind Standage-Pinnock in critical favor. But Kuijken-La Petite Bande have been rising in esteem and make at least the best alternate to Standage-Pinnock.

Carmirelli, I Musici.
Philips 6514 372 (D-LP); 7337 275 (CS); 410 001-2 (CD)

Fasano, Virtuosi di Roma. (B)
Angel RL-32053 (LP, CS)

Kremer, Abbado, London Symphony.
DG 2531 287 (LP); 3301 287 (CS)

Kuijken, La Petite Bande.
Pro Arte PAL-1024 (LP, CS)

Loveday, Marriner, Academy SMF.
Argo ZRG-654 (LP, CS)

Münchinger, Stuttgart CO. (B)
London Jubilee 41007 (LP, CS)

Oliveira, Schwarz, Los Angeles CO.
Delos 3007 (D-LP, CD)

Perlman, London Philharmonic.
Angel S-37053 (LP, CS)

Standage, Pinnock, English Concert.
DG Archiv 2534 003 (D-LP); 3311 003 (CS); 400 045-2 (CD)

Gloria in D, RV. 589

Schneidt's spirited recording has come in for extravagant praise as having a fine balance between vigor and historical authenticity, qualities which are sometimes mutually exclusive in Baroque music performances. Preston also uses old instruments and if his joyful reading is behind Schneidt's in critical approval it is only by the smallest margin.

Two other recordings are perhaps less imaginative and up to snuff in their Baroque performance practice, but have other attractions. The lightfooted reading by Corboz has a very low price. Negri's has simply exciting playing and singing, richly recorded, if not the last word in scholarship, but it is listed in the catalogs only in a two-record set with other Vivaldi sacred choral music. There is, however, a single disc version distributed in Europe (Philips 9500 591) which may turn up in some American stores.

Corboz, Lausanne Ensemble. (B)
RCA AGL1-1340 (LP)

Negri, English CO, Alldis Choir.
(2) Philips 6769 032 (LP); 7699 118 (CS)

Preston, Academy of Ancient Music, Christ Church Catholic Cathedral Choir.
L'Oiseau Lyre DSLO 554 (LP, CS)

Schneidt, Vienna Capella Academica.
DG Archiv 2533 362 (LP)

Suggested further listening for budding Baroque fanatics:

Bach
Cantatas Nos. 4, 78, 80, 140, 202
Chromatic Fantasy and Fugue in d for Harpsichord, S. 903
Goldberg Variations for Harpsichord, S. 988
Partita No. 2 in d for Unaccompanied Violin, S. 1004
Well-Tempered Clavier, S. 846/93

Corelli
Concerti grossi (12), Op. 6

Couperin, F.
Pièces de clavecin

Handel
Concerti (16) for organ
The Harmonious Blacksmith (from Harpsichord Suite No. 5)

Rameau
Pièces de clavecin

Scarlatti, D.
Sonatas for harpsichord (selections)

Telemann
Suite in a for Flute and Strings

Vivaldi
Concerti for various instruments and orchestra

The Classical Era

Ludwig van Beethoven   1770-1827

Symphonies (9)

There are, basically, two divergent directions a Beethoven symphony performance may take: one represents the view, common
in the late 19th century and much of the 20th, that Beethoven belongs firmly in the Romantic school; the other sees him as much
closer to the Classical world of Haydn and Mozart. Performances of
the former persuasion may be referred to — not without trepida-
tion — as "old fashioned" or "provincial." Readings of more recent
vintage will sometimes be described as "stylish." Given the subjective nature of these epithets, the reader is advised that in any case a
performance may be great or dreadful depending on considerations that transcend scholarly questions.

Complete Sets

All of these boxed editions contain all nine symphonies, frequently with other short orchestral pieces (usually overtures) as fill. They
are not all fitted together in the same way, however, and the exact
number of discs in each set is indicated by a number in parentheses
immediately before the label and catalog number.

Bernstein, Karajan, and Solti are the names that first spring
to mind nowadays for complete modern recordings, but there are
others that have comparable merits and might even be preferred
for some reason.

Bernstein's expansive readings date from the late 1970s. Nos.
1, 2, 6, and 7 have had the top notices, followed by 3 and 9. Unfortunately No. 5, the most popular symphony, is the worst. Karajan's
set is his third traversal of these works. The playing is particularly
polished, the sound brilliant, the performances straightforward
(some think too impersonal). Solti's Chicago Symphony set requires one disc more than the others, partly because Solti takes
every repeat Beethoven indicated. Noted especially for his sense of
drama, Solti is best liked in Nos. 3, 4, 7, and 9.

Performances by all three are also available singly. Be careful
with Karajan and Solti, since there are also individual albums of
earlier performances by them, Karajan with the same orchestra,
Solti with a different one. These are differentiated in the individual listings below.

Böhm's set with the Vienna Philharmonic and Jochum's with
the Concertgebouw are getting old, but have broad, solid appeal
and are still well worth their reduced price. Haitink is newer and
has beautiful sound. He is more restrained than most; some find
his readings unusually musical, others think them too reserved.
The cheapest (and oldest) sets are by Szell and Toscanini.
Szell is aristocratic, with magnificent performances of Nos. 3 and
5, but highly variable sonics. Toscanini's monophonic sound from
the 1950s is pretty flat, but can still thrill. Not all critics like his
hard-driving style, but these were the first performances to purge
romantic excess from the interpretations and they are truly legendary.

Not all of these sets are true "budgets," but all of them except
Bernstein and Karajan offer some kind of quantity discount price,
currently ranging from about $25 to $75. Bernstein's cassettes are
about $20 cheaper than the LPs.

Bernstein, Vienna Philharmonic.
(8) DG 2740 216 (LP); 3378 090 (CS)

Böhm, Vienna Philharmonic.
(8) DG 2720 116 (LP)

Haitink, London Philharmonic.
(7) Philips 6747 307 (LP); 7699 037 (CS)

Jochum, Concertgebouw. (B)
(7) Philips Festivo 6770 028 (LP)

Karajan, Berlin Philharmonic.
(8) DG 2740 172 (LP); 3378 070 (CS)

Solti, Chicago Symphony.
(9) London CSP 9 (LP, CS)

Szell, Cleveland Orchestra. (B)
(7) Columbia M7X 30281 (LP)

Toscanini, NBC Symphony. (B) (M)
(8) Victrola VIC-8000 (LP)

Symphony No. 1 in C, Op. 21

This symphony is most sensibly coupled with No. 2 to avoid unne-
cessary duplication as you collect. Bernstein is available this way at
mid-price. So is Karajan, but only in his 1962 recording. Karajan's
newer version has the same coupling but costs more. Both are
good.

Bernstein, Vienna Philharmonic. (B)
DG Signature 410 836-1 (LP); 410 836-4 (CS)

Karajan, Berlin Philharmonic. (B)
DG Privilege 2535 301 (LP); 3335 301 (CS)

Karajan, Berlin Philharmonic.
DG 2531 101; 3301 101 (CS)

Symphony No. 2, in D, Op. 36

Same records as listed above under Symphony No. 1

Symphony No. 3 in E-flat, Op. 55, "Eroica"

If you are looking for the most spectacular sound, Dohnányi's disc and CD are both recommended. The reading is subtle and most persuasive. (Marriner has a CD version too, but many critics find the performance too genteel.)

Karajan's 1962 (budget) and 1977 (full price) recordings are both exciting, with some reviewers preferring the older ones. Solti is vivid and powerful. Bernstein, as often, occasions some division of opinion; some think him a bit overdriven, others praise his fresh insights.

Kegel provides an interesting alternative with a rather old-fashioned approach but on a digital recording at budget price. At the other end of the spectrum the Collegium Aureum offer high-stylishness with an original-instrument version that elucidates the music's textures.

Szell and Toscanini hold onto their legendary status on low-priced recordings with sound that is mediocre by today's standards.

Bernstein, Vienna Philharmonic.
DG 2531 310 (LP); 3301 310 (CS)

Collegium Aureum.
Pro Arte PAL-1029 (LP, CS)

Dohnányi, Cleveland Orchestra.
Telarc 10090 (LP, CD)

Karajan, Berlin Philharmonic. (B)
DG Privilege 2535 302 (LP); 3335 302 (CS)

Karajan, Berlin Philharmonic.
DG 2531 103 (LP); 3301 103 (CS)

Kegel, Dresden Philharmonic. (B)
Sinfonia 624 (D-LP, CS)

Solti, Chicago Symphony.
London CS 7041 (LP, CS) Cassette includes bonus of Weber:
OBERON OVERTURE; *the correct catalog number is 5-7057.*

Szell, Cleveland Orchestra. (B)
Odyssey Y 34622 (LP, CS); or CBS MY 37222 (LP, CS)

Toscanini, NBC Symphony. (B) (M)
Victrola VICS-1655 (LP)

Symphony No. 4 in B-flat, Op. 60

With so many good budget recordings of this work it almost seems silly to pay full price, but Solti commands attention with one of his best readings, and most critics have been impressed with the chamber-orchestra version of Tilson Thomas.

At low price there is a fine choice among Jochum, Karajan (1962), Schmidt-Isserstedt, and Szell. Maestro Szell is packaged two ways: with his own Beethoven Fifth on Odyssey, and with Bruno Walter's Schubert SYMPHONY NO. 8 on CBS Great Performance Series. It is the former you want.

Jochum, Berlin Philharmonic. (B)
Quintessence 7139 (LP, CS)

Karajan, Berlin Philharmonic (B)
DG Privilege 2535 303 (LP); 3335 303 (CS)

Schmidt-Isserstedt, Vienna Philharmonic. (B)
London Stereo Treasury STS 15528 (LP)

Solti, Chicago Symphony.
London CS 7050 (LP, CS)

Szell, Cleveland Orchestra.
Odyssey Y 34600 (LP, CS)

Symphony No. 5 in c, Op. 67

With about four dozen recordings of this ultra-popular work circulating, it is little short of miraculous that one can be singled out as the clear favorite of a majority of critics: Carlos Kleiber's overwhelming reading on DG. It is one of the most convincing performances of anything.

For the latest in technology, Ashkenazy holds the lead among versions available in CD format (Giulini and Maazel on CD have stirred up much controversy). Jochum and Karajan are both grand and gripping, each with one budget and one full-price recording. Kegel turns in another fine digital performance at low price.

In the bottom price category, Toscanini (mono), Reiner, and Walter are all coupled with Schubert's SYMPHONY NO. 8. Walter's Beethoven is not among the more sublime ones, but his Schubert is, so at the price it's worth buying. Szell is paired with No. 4 on Odyssey, or on the two-disc Columbia set with Schubert's Eighth and Dvořák's SYMPHONY NO. 9.

Ashkenazy, Philharmonia Orchestra.
London LDR 71040 (D-LP, CS); 400 060-2 (CD)

Jochum, Bavarian Radio Symphony. (B)
Quintessence 7078 (LP, CS)

Jochum, London Symphony.
Angel S-37463 (LP, CS)

Karajan, Berlin Philharmonic. (B)
DG Privilege 2535 304 (LP); 3335 304 (CS)

Karajan, Berlin Philharmonic.
DG 2531 105 (LP); 3301 105 (CS)

Kegel, Dresden Philharmonic. (B)
Sinfonia 601 (D-LP, CS)

Kleiber, Vienna Philharmonic.
DG 2530 516 (LP); 3300 472 (CS)

Reiner, Chicago Symphony. (B)
RCA AGL1-5206 (LP, CS)

Szell, Cleveland Orchestra.
Odyssey Y 34600 (LP, CS); or (2) Columbia MG 30371 (LP)

Toscanini, NBC Symphony. (B) (M)
Victrola VICS-1648 (LP)

Walter, New York Philharmonic. (B)
Odyssey Y 30314 (LP, CS)

Symphony No. 6 in F, Op. 68, "Pastorale"

The standard-setter for years in this most lyrical of Beethoven's symphonies was the recording by Bruno Walter. It is still in print at the lowest possible price. For digital sound and CD format, Ashkenazy, as in the Fifth, takes top honors. In analog stereo at full price there is a beautiful reading by Böhm. And two conductors usually associated with fiery interpretations, Bernstein and Muti, turn in surprisingly appropriate readings of this mostly bucolic music.

Ashkenazy, Philharmonic Orchestra.
London LDR 71078 (D-LP, CS); 410 003-2 (CD)

Bernstein, Vienna Philharmonic.
DG 2531 312 (LP); 3301 312 (CS)

Böhm, Vienna Philharmonic.
DG 2530 142 (LP); 3300 476 (CS)

Muti, Philadelphia Orchestra.
Angel S-37639 (LP, CS)

Walter, Columbia Symphony. (B)
CBS MY 36720 (LP, CS)

Symphony No. 7 in A, Op. 92

Probably first choice for both performance and sound is Bernstein, whose Seventh is thought by many to be the best performance in his entire set. Kleiber is excellent too, but opinion is not as overwhelmingly approving as for his Fifth. He has a new edge, however, with a recently reduced price. Solti is also at his best in this symphony.

The Collegium Aureum provide an unusual reduced-orchestra version in digital sound, approximating the size of Beethoven's own orchestra. Kegel again, as in the Third, brings the opposite view, huge and majestic, digitally recorded, with the price reduced instead of the orchestra.

Among the lower-priced issues, Reiner is breathtaking in remastered early stereo sound. Other good bargain alternatives are Colin Davis and Toscanini (mono). One of the really legendary performances, that of Pablo Casals conducting the Marlboro Festival Orchestra, has recently become available again at budget price; some think it surpasses even Toscanini's wild energy, and it has better sonics.

Bernstein, Vienna Philharmonic.
DG 2531 313 (LP); 3301 313 (CS)

Casals, Marlboro Festival Orchestra. (B)
CBS MY 37233 (LP, CS)

Collegium Aureum.
Pro Arte PAD-123 (D-LP, CS)

C. Davis, London Symphony (B)
Philips Sequenza 6527 141 (LP); 7311 141 (CS)

Kegel, Dresden Philharmonic. (B)
Sinfonia 600 (D-LP, CS)

Kleiber, Vienna Philharmonic. (B)
DG Signature 410 932-1; 410 932-4 (CS)

Reiner, Chicago Symphony. (B)
RCA AGL1-5231 (LP, CS)

Solti, Chicago Symphony.
London CS 6932 (LP); 5-7053 (CS)

Toscanini, NBC Symphony. (B) (M)
Victrola VICS-1658 (LP)

Symphony No. 8 in F, Op. 93

All but one of the following recordings are listed either because they are truly excellent Eighths, or because they are unavoidable couplings with a great Ninth. Odd man out (or in) is Karajan in his early '60s performances coupled with three great Beethoven overtures, at budget price.

Bernstein, Vienna Philharmonic.
(2) DG 2707 124 (LP); 3370 037 (CS)

Böhm, Vienna Philharmonic.
(2) DG 2707 073 (LP)

Giulini, London Symphony.
(2) Angel SB-3795 (LP, CS)

Karajan, Berlin Philharmonic. (B)
DG Privilege 2535 315 (LP); 3335 315 (CS)

Karajan, Berlin Philharmonic.
(2) DG 2707 109 (LP); 3370 109 (CS)

Symphony No. 9 in d, Op. 125, "Choral"

Refer to the list under Symphony No. 8 (excluding the budget Karajan) for some of the finest two-record sets including the Ninth. Others include Ozawa, Solti, and Jochum-Concertgebouw (Jochum-London Symphony is also fine but really ought to be at budget price to compete).

There is an extra attraction to good Ninths on a single disc or tape. Fricsay, Stokowski, Szell, and Toscanini are all classics, but perhaps most enticing, surprisingly, for distinguished interpretation, superior soloists, and excellent remastered sound is the 1966 performance by Schmidt-Isserstedt (singers are Sutherland, Horne, King, and Talvela).

Fricsay, Berlin Philharmonic. (B)
DG Privilege 2535 203 (LP); 3335 203 (CS)

Jochum, Concertgebouw. (B)
(2) Philips Festivo 6570 189 (LP)

Ozawa, New Philharmonia.
(2) Philips 6747 119 (LP); 7505 072 (CS)

Schmidt-Isserstedt, Vienna Philharmonic. (B)
London Jubilee 41004 (LP, CS)

Solti, Chicago Symphony.
(2) London CSP 8 (LP, CS)

Stokowski, London Symphony. (B)
London Stereo Treasury STS 15538 (LP, CS)

Szell, Cleveland Orchestra. (B)
Odyssey Y 34625 (LP, CS)

Toscanini, NBC Symphony. (B) (M)
Victrola VIC-1607 (LP)

(Add the four double sets under Symphony No. 8.)

There is more great Beethoven, of course, beside the symphonies. Here we will recommend some records of his other works, along with basic compositions by Haydn and Mozart. These men were the big three of the Classical period (from perhaps 1750, the year of J.S. Bach's death, to 1827, the death of Beethoven). You may argue that Beethoven belongs in the Romantic era, and certainly he represents a transition into it, but since we are going back in time we will think of the transition in reverse.

Concerti (5) for Piano and Orchestra

You really should have all five of these marvelous concerti, and there are enough fine boxed sets to satisfy. Dominating the head-lines recently has been the Brendel-Levine set, with highly praised performances, first-class sonics (though recorded live in concert), perfect pressings, and a reduced price. It is also the only set available on CD. Hard to beat!

The previous top choice, still very desirable, was Ashkenazy-Solti. There are also two fine budget sets with Arrau-Haitink and Fleisher-Szell; the former is noble and reflective, the latter superbly shaped and propulsive.

Arrau, Haitink, Concertgebouw. (B)
(6) Philips 6768 350 (LP)

Ashkenazy, Solti, Chicago Symphony.
(4) London CSA 2404 (LP, CS)

Brendel, Levine, Chicago Symphony. (B)
(4) Philips 411 189-1 (D-LP); 411 189-4 (CS); 411 189-2 (CD)

Fleisher, Szell, Cleveland Orchestra (B)
(4) Columbia M4X 30052 (LP)

Concerto No. 5 in E-flat for Piano, Op. 73, "Emperor"

If you're not ready to buy a complete set of the Beethoven piano concerti, this is the *one* most people start with. Among those listed above, Arrau and Brendel are not available separately, Ashkenazy and Fleisher are, with Ashkenazy also showing up in a three-record set that includes the most famous concerti of Chopin, Rachmaninoff, Schumann, and Tchaikovsky. Fleisher is on cassette only at present.

At budget price Curzon, Kempff, and Rubinstein-Leinsdorf are also very attractive. Rudolf Serkin-Bernstein are wonderful too on budget disc and tape, but their CD is naturally more expensive. (There is a newer Serkin-Ozawa on all three formats, but it has had decidedly mixed reviews and is very expensive no matter how you buy it.) Bishop-Kovacevich and Davis give an almost Mozartian performances at mid-price which is preferred by some.

Gilels and Pollini are the other preferred choices at regular price.

Ashkenazy, Solti, Chicago Symphony.
London CS 6857 (LP, CS)

Ashkenazy, Solti, Chicago Symphony (with other famous concerti). **(B)**
(3) London CSP 12 (LP)

Bishop-Kovacevich, C. Davis, London Symphony. (B)
Philips Sequenza 6527 177 (LP); 7311 177 (CS)

Curzon, Knappertsbusch, Vienna Philharmonic. (B)
London Jubilee 41020 (LP, CS)

Fleisher, Szell, Cleveland Orchestra. (B)
Odyssey YT 35491 (CS)

Gilels, Szell, Cleveland Orchestra.
Angel S-36031 (LP, CS)

Kempff, Leitner, Berlin Philharmonic. (B)
DG Signature 410 842-1 (LP); 410 842-4 (CS)

Pollini, Böhm, Vienna Philharmonic.
DG 2531 194 (LP); 3301 194 (CS)

Rubinstein, Leinsdorf, Boston Symphony. (B)
RCA AGL1-4220 (LP, CS)

R. Serkin, Bernstein, New York Philharmonic. (B)
CBS MY 37223 (LP, CS); CBS Sony 35 DC-98 (CD-full price)

Concerto in D for Violin, Op. 61

Reviewers have been close to a consensus that the commanding reading by Perlman and Giulini is the best ever in terms of both performance and sound. New as it is, it seems headed towards legendary status. Not so far behind is the broad but intense performance by Mutter and Karajan; Anne-Sophie Mutter was only 17 when she made this record but her technique and insight already matched the masters.

Two recent high-tech versions have debilitating problems: Kremer uses the vulgarly intrusive cadenzas of Alfred Schnittke in his recording with Marriner; and Kondrashin's prosaic conducting does nothing to help Kyung-Wha Chung on a rare off day. The serenely classical Grumiaux performance, long a first choice, is currently only on budget tape. Krebbers is inspired with Haitink but may be hard to find.

Zukerman plays with an undeniably beautiful lush tone, but turns the music into something far more romantic than it is. At full price, this record should be bypassed in favor of any of four budgets: Stern is purer in his delivery, Suk is wonderfully sweet-toned, Szeryng is subtle and patrician, and Gruenberg is warmly eloquent.

Gruenberg, Horenstein, New Philharmonia. (B)
Nonesuch 71381 (LP)

Grumiaux, Galliera, New Philharmonia. (B)
Philips Festivo 7310 051 (CS)

Krebbers, Haitink, Concertgebouw.
Philips 6599 851 PSI (LP)

Mutter, Karajan, Berlin Philharmonic.
DG 2531 250 (LP); 3301 250 (CS)

Perlman, Giulini, Philharmonia Orchestra.
Angel DS-37471 (D-LP, CS); CDC-47002 (CD)

Stern, Bernstein, New York Philharmonic. (B)
CBS MY 37224 (LP, CS)

Suk, Konwitschny, Czech Philharmonic. (B)
Quintessence 7213 (LP, CS)

Szeryng, Schmidt-Isserstedt, London Symphony. (B)
Quintessence 7076 (LP, CS)

Overtures

The most beloved Beethoven overtures are *Egmont, Leonore No. 3,* and *Fidelio.* These are often included as fillers on complete Beethoven symphony sets or on individual discs, and you are likely to get them that way whether you want them or not. No attempt will be made here to indicate all of those couplings.

Instead, I will recommend two recordings devoted exclusively to the overtures. Karajan is the better known with his two-disc set of eleven overtures (DG 2707 046), but for the beginning collection I am listing only the single-disc version which has the five most popular on it, at reduced price. The playing is gorgeous, if you don't mind Beethoven's sometimes deliberately rough textures being smoothed over. Skrowaczewski's three-record budget set with all of the overtures and some intriguing rarities tossed in is less "perfect" but perhaps more engaging.

Karajan, Berlin Philharmonic. (B)
DG Privilege 2535 303 (LP); 3335 303 (CS)

Skrowaczewski, Minnesota Orchestra. (B)
(3) Vox SVBX-5156 (LP, CS)

Quartet No. 14 in c-sharp, Op. 131

Beethoven's 16 string quartets cover the whole spectrum of his creative life. There are various approaches to playing them and most of the best ones are available only in boxed sets. At my last count there were 16 different ensembles in print with various boxes. For the beginner I recommend starting with Beethoven's own favorite quartet in an excellent performance on a single budget disc. If you like it I hope you will go on from there, but analyzing the mountain of complete recordings is, alas, beyond the scope of this little book.

Yale Quartet. (B)
Vanguard Cardinal 10062 (LP)

Sonatas for Piano

Of the 32 sonatas for piano solo, the three most popular are No. 8 in c, Op. 13, "Pathétique," No. 14 in c-sharp, Op. 27, No. 2, "Moonlight," and No. 23 in f, Op. 57, "Appassionata." More often than not all three are fitted onto one record or tape, and the beginning collector can easily get a fine performance this way.

Rudolf Serkin stresses the dramatic in his classic performances, now on a budget label. At full price Kempff follows the score scrupulously but is never glib, and Rubinstein emphasizes the lyrical aspect. The listed Ashkenazy record is the only one that has his fine readings on one disc. If you don't want a side break in the middle of No. 23, get London CS 7226 and CS 7111 which give you all three of the performances plus four additional works.

Ashkenazy.
London CS 7247 (LP, CS)

Kempff.
DG 139 300 (LP); 3300 506 (CS)

Rubinstein.
RCA LSC-3307 (LP); RK-1287 (CS)

R. Serkin. (B)
CBS MY 37219 (LP, CS)

Two other great sonatas are No. 21 in C, Op. 53, "Waldstein," and No. 29 in B-flat, Op. 106, "Hammerklavier." Both of these are available along with the "Appassionata" on a two-record budget set by Kempff, whom many critics consider to have the most accurate view of Beethoven's piano music. There is another budget single disc with Kempff containing No. 21 plus Nos. 15, 24, and 25; with this record you get the "Waldstein" and not the "Hammerklavier," but you avoid duplication of the "Moonlight" and "Pathétique."

Ashkenazy has a "Waldstein" coupled with No. 26, and Arrau's measured but spellbinding "Waldstein" is coupled with No. 17, "Tempest." Ashkanazy's "Hammerklavier," one of the best, is paired with the lovely *Andante favori*. The other classic "Hammerklavier," Rudolf Serkin's, is filled out by some Bagatelles at budget price.

Arrau (21). (B)
Philips Festivo 6570 190 (LP); 7310 190 (CS)

Ashkenazy (21).
London CS 7256 (LP, CS)

Ashkenazy (29).
London CS 7255 (LP, CS)

Kempff (21, 29). (B)
(2) Quintessence 7130 (LP, CS)

Kempff (21). (B)
DG Privilege 2535 291 (LP); 3335 291 (CS)

R. Serkin (29). (B)
CBS MP 38893 (LP, CS)

Sonatas for Violin and Piano No. 5 in F, Op. 24, "Spring," No. 9 in A, Op. 47, "Kreutzer"

Perlman and Ashkenazy bring youthful spontaneity to their stylish readings but you must buy two discs or cassettes to get the two most beloved of the ten sonatas. They are together, however, on a single CD, which still doesn't save you any money. These artists are the clear choice if you decide to get all of these sonatas; their boxed set is (5) London CS 2501 (LP, CS).

For Nos. 5 and 9 on one disc Menuhin and Kempff are still recommended. For a newer, digital recording, Ughi and Sawallisch are grandly persuasive. All of these are preferable to the budget recordings and worth a little extra.

Menuhin, Kempff (5, 9).
DG 2531 300 (LP); 3301 300 (CS)

Perlman, Ashkenazy (5).
London CS 6958 (LP, CS)

Perlman, Ashkenazy (9).
London CS 6845 (LP, CS)

Perlman, Ashkenazy (5, 9).
London 410 554-2 (CD)

Ughi, Sawallisch (5, 9).
RCA CRC1-4956 (D-LP, CS)

Trio No. 6 in B-flat, Op. 97, "Archduke" (Piano, Violin, Cello)

The outstanding modern recording is that by Perlman, Harrell, and Ashkenazy, offering rich expression, integrated ensemble, deep understanding, and a perfectly balanced recording. Trio No. 7 is a bonus.

At budget price the Suk Trio 1967 recording is among the finest in a long line, but has no coupling.

Perlman, Harrell, Ashkenazy.
Angel DS-37818 (D-LP, CS)

Suk, Chuchro, Panenka. (B)
Quintessence 7082 (LP, CS)

Franz Joseph Haydn   1732-1809

Concerto in E-flat for Trumpet

Most critics rate the Schwarz recording first for sound, pressing quality, and performance. It was not listed last time because it was hard to find and had a very high price. Delos now has wider distribution and has lowered its disc and cassette price. It is also the only performance currently available on CD. Johann Nepomuk Hummel's best-known piece, a trumpet concerto in the same key, is on the flip side.

Güttler's brilliant playing is featured with works of Molter and Leopold Mozart (Wolfgang's father) on a mid-price digital disc. Stringer and Marriner offer excellent budget value with bonuses of horn and organ concerti. Cheapest of all is Maurice André's earlier version with concerti of Handel and Michael Haydn (Joseph's brother).

Much publicity has centered on the Winton Marsalis album on CBS. Marsalis is a fine jazz trumpeter, but classical reviewers feel his work here, though technically secure, is stiff and unconvincing.

André, Stadlmair, Munich CO. (B)
DG Musikfest 413 260-1 (LP); 413 260-4

Güttler, Pommer, New Bach Collegium Musicum. (B)
Sinfonia 602 (D-LP, CS)

Schwarz, "Y" Chamber Symphony of New York.
Delos 3001 (D-LP, CS, CD)

Stringer, Marriner, Academy SMF. (B)
London Stereo Treasury STS 15546 (LP, CS)

The Creation

Next to Handel's MESSIAH, this is the best known and loved oratorio. Critics are almost unanimous in giving the palm to Marriner's recording with soloists Mathis, Baldin, and Fischer-Dieskau for overall quality.

Karajan has two recordings. The newer one (available on CD) was recorded live and has some sonics problems, and reviewers generally feel that his older version, listed here, has better singing and orchestral playing (soloists are Janowitz, Ludwig, Fischer-Dieskau, Krenn, and Berry.)

Kuijken's 1982 original-instrument version has won lavish praise for vitality and authenticity but is on a hard-to-get label.

Karajan, Berlin Philharmonic, Vienna Singverein.
(2) DG 2707 044 (LP); 3370 005 (CS)

Kuijken, Collegium Vocale, La Petite Bande.
(2) Accent 8228/29

Marriner, Academy SMF.
(2) Philips 6769 047 (LP); 7699 154 (CS)

Quartet in C, Op. 76, No. 3, "Emperor"

Haydn wrote 82 string quartets, not a one of them without worth. This is merely the best known, thanks in part to its set of variations on the Austrian national anthem.

The Varsovia (Latin for Warsaw) Quartet have a beautiful performance coupled with one of Haydn's best early quartets, Op. 3, No. 5, "Serenade," whose slow movement is often heard as an encore piece all by itself.

One of the finest ensembles in the world, the Quartetto Italiano, is available at budget price with the quartet Op. 33, No. 2, "Joke." The eminent Amadeus Quartet are also available at low price with a coupling of Mozart: QUARTET NO. 17, "HUNT."

Amadeus Quartet. (B)
DG Signature 2543 502 (LP); 3343 502 (CS)

Quartetto Italiano. (B)
Quintessence 7170 (LP, CS)

Varsovia Quartet.
Pro Arte PAD-112 (D-LP, CS)

Symphonies

Haydn's 104 symphonies, like his quartets, are all worth hearing. One of the great recording projects of the 1970s was a complete edition with Antal Dorati and the Philharmonia Hungarica at budget price on 48 records in 10 boxes with excellent notes, now listing at $285. The overall level of quality is amazing and it is certainly a bargain of its kind, but few collectors will need to invest in it at the outset. Fortunately, many of the more popular symphonies are available on single Dorati discs and cassettes.

Several other conductors are famous for their Haydn, too, and in individual instances may outshine Dorati. I will recommend some smaller boxed sets containing several desirable symphonies, and then list good single-disc recordings.

One of the best deals is Jochum's budget box of the greatest symphonies, Nos. 93-104. These are joyful, dramatic, noble readings with a great orchestra and beautiful sound though the style is what one must now call old-fashioned, since it does not take into account recent scholarly discoveries and points of performance practice. The best "authentic" set is that by Derek Solomons on CBS, but with one exception the symphonies included are not among the better-known ones.

Leonard Bernstein, whose Mozart symphonies are better forgotten, had a surprising knack for Haydn. His brightly vivid and vigorous readings of the "Paris" symphonies, Nos. 82-87, are available in a budget box.

George Szell was famous in his day for Haydn symphonies, but the budget set of Nos. 93-98 has inferior sonics; in a comparable per-disc price category, Jochum is a better bet and gives you the great six last symphonies not in Szell's set. Denis Vaughan's two three-record sets encompassing Nos. 82-94 are also fine performances, but with somewhat faded sound and a relatively high price must be left for the advanced collector only.

Bernstein, New York Philharmonic. (B)
(3) Columbia D3S 769 (LP)

Dorati, Philharmonia Hungarica. (B)
(6) London Stereo Treasury STS 15319/24 (LP)

Jochum, London Philharmonic.
(6) DG 2720 091 (LP)

Among other conductors who have made rich contributions to the Haydn symphonic repertoire Neville Marriner and Sir Colin Davis stand out. The following list of single discs, grouped by conductor, represents those which have received the most glowing reviews, and is restricted to the more popular symphonies. To this may be added Szell's single disc/tape of Nos. 93 and 94, widely considered his best Haydn performances, on CBS MY 37761 **(B)**.

Dorati, Philharmonia Hungarica.
45, 42. *London Stereo Treasury STS 15444 (LP)* **(B)**
88, 89. *London Stereo Treasury STS 15442 (LP)* **(B)**
92, 90. *London Stereo Treasury STS 15446 (LP)* **(B)**
93, 94. *London Stereo Treasury STS 15319 (LP)* **(B)**
95, 96. *London Stereo Treasury STS 15320 (LP)* **(B)**
97, 98. *London Stereo Treasury STS 15321 (LP)* **(B)**
99, 100. *London Stereo Treasury STS 15322 (LP)* **(B)**
101, 102. *London Stereo Treasury STS 15323 (LP)* **(B)**
103, 104. *London Stereo Treasury STS 15324 (LP)* **(B)**

Marriner, Academy SMF.
45, 101. *Philips 9500 520 (LP); 7300 676 (CS)*
85, 84. *Philips 6514 117 (LP); 7337 117 (CS)*
92, 104. *Philips 9500 304 (LP)*
94, 96. *Philips 9500 348 (LP); 7300 594 (CS)*

C. Davis, Concertgebouw.
92, 91. *Philips 410 390-1 (D-LP); 410 390-4 (CS)*
93, 94. *Philips 6514 192 (D-LP); 7337 192 (CS)*
95, 96. *Philips 6514 193 (LP); 7337 193 (CS)*

Bernstein, New York Philharmonic.
94, 101. *Columbia M 32101 (LP, CS)*
97, 98. *Columbia M 35844 (LP, CS)*

Wolfgang Amadeus Mozart   1756-1791

Concerto in A for Clarinet, K. 622

Jack Brymer, one of the great classical clarinetists, has two recordings in print, one with the late Sir Thomas Beecham, the other
with Neville Marriner. The Beecham is much older but gracious
and enchanting, with a coupling of Mozart's Bassoon Concerto
and a low price. The Marriner is newer, costs twice as much, but has
the Bassoon Concerto and an additional work, and offers an even
deeper and more heartfelt contribution from the soloist. Marcellus
and Szell at low price are also very attractive, especially with a fine
SINFONIA CONCERTANTE on the reverse.

Brymer, Beecham, Royal Philharmonic. (B)
Seraphim S-60193 (LP) (B)

Brymer, Marriner, Academy SMF.
Philips 6500 378 (LP)

Marcellus, Szell, Cleveland Orchestra. (B)
CBS MY 37810 (LP, CS)

Concerti (4) for Horn, K. 412, 417, 447, 495

The late Dennis Brain has achieved almost mythological status as a French horn player. Usually I would not consider a monophonic recording at full price to be a good first choice for a beginning collection, but this time an exception must be made. Karajan conducts, the sound is quite clear, and the performances are uniquely excellent.

If Brain had never been born we would surely call Alan Civil and Barry Tuckwell the great hornists in the world. They each have two stereo recordings in print, and happily for us the critics rate their budget versions as the best in each case.

There is one fine performance using Mozart's "original instrument," the valveless horn. It is considerably harder to play well, but Hermann Baumann handles it with aplomb accompanied by Harnoncourt. Do not confuse the version listed with an inferior one with Baumann on the same label, featuring the Salzburg Mozarteum Orchestra.

Baumann, Harnoncourt, Concentus Musicus.
Telefunken 6.41272

Brain, Karajan, Philharmonia Orchestra. (M)
Angel 35092 (LP, CS)

Civil, Klemperer, Philharmonia Orchestra. (B)
Angel RL-32028 (LP, CS)

Tuckwell, Maag, London Symphony. (B)
London Jubilee 41015 (LP, CS)

Concerti for Piano

No composer created a greater legacy of concerti of many kinds than Mozart, for the piano 27 in all. The most popular are Nos. 9, 14, 15, 17, and 19 through 27, and these will be emphasized in the following recommendations.

Many fine pianists play Mozart well, but none in recent years has more successfully made it his specialty than Murray Perahia. In the much shorter listings of my earlier book he did not appear because there were only a few records and famous concerti were paired with ones not considered "basic" enough for that edition. Now our horizon has expanded, there are several more recordings, and Perahia's performances have continued to grow in depth and beauty. His is now *the* name that first comes to mind in speaking of these works as a group.

Virtually all of the other pianists listed are more famous for their work on other composers, mostly Beethoven, Chopin and Schubert; but they have each made one or more Mozart recordings too good to be ignored. Malcolm Bilson has made the finest record using the historic fortepiano of Mozart's day.

Special mention must be made of the listed recording of Nos. 20 and 27 by the late Sir Clifford Curzon with Benjamin Britten conducting. Made in 1970 but not released until 1983, it has already mysteriously disappeared from the Schwann Catalog, though London Records says it is still in print. All reviewers gave it unusually superlative notices for extraordinary beauty and insight, and *Opus* put it in their select list of 100 all-time inspired recordings. Your dealer may not carry it if he orders from Schwann's listings, so set him straight.

Perahia, English CO
9, 21. *Columbia M 34562 (LP, CS)*
14, 24. *Columbia M 34219 (LP, CS)*
15, 16. *CBS IM 37824 (D-LP, CS, CD)*
17, 18. *CBS IM 36686 (D-LP, CS, CD)*
20, 11. *Columbia M 35134 (LP, CS)*
22, 8. *Columbia M 35869 (LP, CS)*
25, 5. *CBS IM 37267 (D-LP, CS)*
26. *CBS IM 39224 (D-LP, CS)*
27, 12. *Columbia M 35828 (LP, CS)*

Ashkenazy, Philharmonia Orchestra
17, 21. *London CS 7104 (LP, CS)*
19, 24. *London CS 7174 (LP, CS)*
22. *London CS 7211 (LP, CS)*
23, 27. *London LDR 71007 (D-LP, CS); 400 087-2 (CD)*

Brendel, Marriner, Academy SMF
20, 24. *Philips 6500 533 (LP)*
22. *Philips 9500 145 (LP); 7300 521 (CS)*
25. *Philips Sequenza 6527 085 (LP); 7311 085 (CS) (B)*
27, 18. *Philips 6500 948 (LP); 7300 383 (CS)*

21, 24. Badura-Skoda, Prague CO. (B)
Quintessence 7123 (LP, CS)

9, 11. Bilson, Gardiner, English Baroque Soloists.
DG Archiv 410 905-1 (LP); 410 905-4 (CS)

20, 27. Curzon, Britten, English CO.
London CS 7251 (LP, CS)

19, 22. DeLarrocha, Segal, Vienna Symphony.
London LDR 71066 (D-LP, CS); 410 140-2 (CD)

21, 22. Kempff, Klee, Bavarian Radio Symphony.
DG 2531 372 (LP); 3301 372 (CS)

17, 27. Klien, Skrowaczewski, Minnesota Orchestra. (B)
Candide 31119 (LP); CT-2275 (CS)

21. Klien, Kehr, Mainz CO. (B)
Turnabout 34504 (LP); CT-2207 (CS)

21, 12. Lupu, Segal, English CO.
London CS 6894 (LP); cassette has different coupling of Nos. 20 and 27 on London 410 278-4, at mid-price

14, 23. Moravec, Vlach, Czech Philharmonic. (B)
Quintessence 7107 (LP, CS)

25. Moravec, Vlach, Czech Philharmonic. (B)
Quintessence 7108 (LP, CS)

19, 23. Pollini, Böhm, Vienna Philharmonic.
DG 2530 716 (LP); 3300 716 (CS)

19, 25. R. Serkin, Abbado, London Symphony.
DG 410 989-1 (D-LP); 410 989-4 (CS); 410 989-2 (CD)

20, 12. R. Serkin, Abbado, London Symphony.
DG 2532 053 (D-LP); 3302 053 (CS); 400 068-2 (CD)

Concerto No. 5 in A for Violin, K. 219

Mozart wrote his five violin concerti as a teenager. The last three are much the best, and the fifth the most popular for its final movement in "Turkish" style.

Of recent recordings that by Iona Brown with the St. Martin's Academy is a model of interpretation, and though it is a digital recording it has been issued at budget price. The only drawback is the coupling of No. 1, perhaps the least interesting of the five.

The older budgets by Szeryng and Menuhin are comparably fine performances in older sound, but with the better Concerto No. 3 as the pairing in each case. Stern is at his Mozartian best in the Fifth that forms part of the two-record budget set with Mozart OVERTURES, PIANO CONCERTO NO. 21, EINE KLEINE NACHTMUSIK, and SYMPHONY NO: 41, all with George Szell conducting.

Perlman's recording, the only one currently available on CD, can be recommended for sonics and for Perlman's ravishing playing, though his understanding of Mozart style is somewhat open to question.

Brown, Academy SMF. (B)
London Jubilee 411 707-1 (D-LP); 411 707-4 (CS)

Menuhin, Bath Festival Orchestra. (B)
Angel RL-32000 (LP, CS)

Perlman, Levine, Vienna Philharmonic.
DG 2532 080 (D-LP); 3302 080 (CS); 410 020-2 (CD)

Stern, Szell, Cleveland Orchestra. (B)
(2) Columbia MG 30841 (LP)

Exsultate, Jubilate, K. 165

This brilliant motet for soprano (originally castrato) and orchestra receives excellent recording from Philips and radiant singing from Kiri Te Kanawa. Three additional choral works round out the program, including the enchanting *Ave, verum corpus*, K. 618.

Te Kanawa, C. Davis, London Symphony.
Philips 6500 271 (LP)

Overtures

As with the Beethoven overtures discussed earlier, some of these show up as fillers for Mozart symphony recordings and are not detailed here.

There are two outstanding recordings devoted exclusively to Mozart overtures, each with nine of them, though they are not all the same ones. Sir Colin Davis is the old standard and cheap, though the sound is a bit rough. Marriner is musically just as good, with much better sound but a higher price.

C. Davis, Royal Philharmonic. (B)
Seraphim S-60037 (LP)

Marriner, Academy SMF.
Angel DS-37879 (D-LP, CS); CDC-47014 (CD)

Quartets

Although many of Mozart's string quartets are great chamber-music works, they do not seem to have the immediate appeal of

much of his other music. They have to grow on you. As an introduction for the beginner, I recommend the fine budget recording
by the Amadeus Quartet of the Quartet No. 17 in B-flat, K. 458,
"Hunt" (the German cover will say "Jagd"). This is probably
Mozart's most popular and accessible quartet, and it is coupled
with Haydn's QUARTET IN C, "EMPEROR." A more basic Classical-
era quartet recording could not be imagined.

Amadeus Quartet. (B)
DG Signature 2543 502 (LP); 3343 502 (CS)

Quintet in A for Clarinet and Strings, K. 581

Out of a number of very good recordings, one stands out as just a
degree better than the others in every respect: De Peyer with the
Amadeus Quartet, joined with an equally excellent version of the
beautiful Oboe Quartet (soloist Lothar Koch). Among the low-
priced choices, the relatively unknown artists George Silfies and
the Giovanni Quartet provide a pleasant surprise with a thorough-
ly musicianly account, excellent sound, and a coupling of the fine
Quintet for Piano and Winds, K. 452.

You may have read about the recent flap at the Berlin Philharmonic when conductor Herbert von Karajan appointed Sabine
Meyer as principal clarinetist without first consulting the other
members of the orchestra, as tradition demands. Ms. Meyer's
notoriety might tempt you to buy her recording on DG, but be
warned that some critics have complained about alleged faults
such as rigid phrasing and an excessively smooth approach. The
worst scandal however is the coupling, a piece attributed to Carl
Maria von Weber but actually by a minor composer named Küff-
ner. After receiving complaints, DG changed the back jacket liner
but not the cover. If you find a copy of the original issue you might
want to get it as a collector's conversation item (DG 410 670-1).

De Peyer, Amadeus Quartet.
DG 2530 720 (LP)

Silfies, Giovanni Quartet. (B)
Turnabout 37013 (LP, CS)

Requiem, K. 626

Over the years, critics have frequently lamented the absence of a
truly great recording of Mozart's last masterpiece, the *Requiem*,

left incomplete at his death and "finished" rather unsatisfactorily by his pupil Süssmayr.

For some years the Colin Davis recording on Philips led the field, though the choral work and engineering came in for some drubbing. Then Marriner's version on Argo introduced Professor Franz Beyer's corrections to the score; this and better sonics seemed to offer hope, but again there were complaints about the chorus, and some thought the whole performance to be on the limp side. Harnoncourt, also using the Beyer edition, provided a spectacularly dramatic performance on Telefunken; but detractors felt it was some distance from representing accurately the Classical style.

All of these have recently been put in the shade by a version conducted by Peter Schreier, better known as one of the finest tenors specializing in Mozart. All reviewers surveyed praised the committed performance and the vivid recording (there is a CD); the *Gramophone* critic proclaimed it his "desert island" choice.

Alas, just as I thought the last word had been written on this subject for a while, L'Oiseau Lyre announced the imminent release of a *Requiem* by Christopher Hogwood and the Academy of Ancient Music, using a yet newer edition of the score by C.R.F. Maunder, omitting Süssmayr's Sanctus, Osanna, and Benedictus. Hogwood's current eminence in "authentic" Mozart performance demands respect, and I am listing the recording although I have not heard it and there has been no time for the accumulation of critical opinion. I am assuming that it will be of interest at least for the lifetime of another edition — that of this book!

Hogwood, Academy of Ancient Music.
L'Oiseau Lyre 411 712-1 (D-LP); 411 712-4 (CS); 411 712-2 (CD)

Schreier, Dresden State Orchestra, Leipzig Radio Chorus.
Philips 6514 320 (D-LP); 7337 320 (CS); 411 420-2 (CD)

Serenade in G, K. 525, "Eine kleine Nachtmusik"

Mozart's closest approach to a "pop hit," the "Little Night Music" has even inspired a Broadway musical of the same name. Out of a profusion of recordings I have selected the few most attractive buys.

Levine is digital, has a coupling of the very desirable "POST-HORN" SERENADE, and has been placed by critics among the top three versions. Marriner has already been detailed under Bach: JESU, JOY OF MAN'S DESIRING, and Szell under the discussion of Stern's performance of Mozart: CONCERTO FOR VIOLIN NO. 5.
Three other budgets give good value: Collegium Aureum

with Divertimento No. 7; Colin Davis with SERENADE NO. 6 and some German Dances; and Kertész with SYMPHONY NO. 36.

Collegium Aureum. (B)
Quintessence 7087 (LP, CS)

C. Davis, Philharmonia Orchestra. (B)
Seraphim S-60057 (LP, CS)

Kertész, Vienna Philharmonic. (B)
London Stereo Treasury STS 15506 (LP)

Levine, Vienna Philharmonic.
DG 2532 098 (D-LP); 3302 098 (CS); 410 085-2 (CD)

Marriner, Academy SMF.
Angel S-37743 (LP, CS)

Szell, Cleveland Orchestra. (B)
(2) Columbia MG 30841 (LP)

Other Serenades:

The brief but lovely Serenade No. 6 in D, K. 239, "Serenata Notturna," comes with the Davis EINE KLEINE NACHTMUSIK mentioned above.

The classic recording of No. 7 in D, K. 250, "Haffner," by Boskovsky and the Vienna Mozart Ensemble is to be had at budget price on London Stereo Treasury STS 15414 (LP).

The same group are equally fine in the "Posthorn" Serenade, No. 9 in D, K. 320 on Stereo Treasury STS 15415 (LP). But the excellent Collegium Aureum are equally attractive at the same price on Quintessence 7118 (LP, CS). And Levine's recommended EINE KLEINE NACHTMUSIK has this as a coupling.

Three recordings vie for top attention in the Serenade No. 10 in B-flat for 13 Winds, K. 361: the Berlin Philharmonic Wind Ensemble on DG 2532 089 (D-LP), 3302 089 (CS); DeWaart and the Netherlands Wind Ensemble on Philips 839 734 (LP); and the Collegium Aureum on budget-priced Quintessence 7125 (LP, CS).

Sinfonia Concertante in E-flat for Violin and Viola, K. 364

A fine budget recording with members of the Cleveland Orchestra comes as a coupling on the Marcellus record already recommended under the CONCERTO FOR CLARINET. With two other superior budgets available (though with less "basic" couplings), there is no reason to spend much for your first version of this work.

Druian, Skernick, Szell, Cleveland Orchestra. (B)
CBS MY 37810 (LP, CS)

Loveday, Shingles, Marriner, Academy SMF. (B)
London Stereo Treasury STS 15563 (LP, CS)

Suk, Škampa, Redel, Czech Philharmonic. (B)
Quintessence 7106 (LP, CS)

Sonata No. 11 in A for Piano, K. 331

With its infectious third movement, the "Rondo alla Turca," this is the most popular of Mozart's 17 piano sonatas. The simplest and most painless way to acquire it is as the bonus on Walter Klien's budget recording of the CONCERTO FOR PIANO NO. 21.

Klien. (B)
Turnabout 34504 (LP)

Symphonies

The best known Mozart symphonies are Nos. 29, 35 "Haffner," 36 "Linz," 38 "Prague," 39, 40, and 41 "Jupiter." The symphony once numbered 37 turned out to be by Haydn's brother Michael and no longer appears in catalogs under Mozart.

The four conductors whose names are most widely recognized for Mozart symphonies are Hogwood, Marriner, Colin Davis, and Szell. *Fanfare* called Hogwood's recently completed seven-volume set of the complete symphonies on original instruments "*the* discographic event of the '80s." Hogwood is to these works what Dorati was in the '70s to the Haydn symphonies (q.v.). In terms of authenticity, supported by beautiful recording and scholarly notes, no one can touch Hogwood; but the performances can be faulted for occasional lapses in ensemble, awkward phrasing, and other inconsistencies.

There are a few single discs by Hogwood of the favorite symphonies, as listed below, but if you get interested in the whole series you might start with Vol. 6 containing Nos. 31, 35, and 38-41 on L'Oiseau Lyre D172D (D-LP); K172K (CS).

Marriner's group play their modern instruments with finesse and perfect balance, but some reviewers grumble that the conductor fusses too much with Mozart's dynamic markings.

Davis has a long reputation for all of Mozart's music, and his 1960s symphony recordings with the BBC Symphony were considered among the most idiomatic and tasteful. His newer series with the Dresden State Orchestra also wins generally warm reviews, without any serious reservations that I have noted.

Szell's Mozart takes a frankly Big Orchestra approach but is distinguished by sharp wit, keen drama, and polished playing — if a little short on geniality.

The Szell recordings are eminently worth having, especially at low price, but they are packaged rather confusingly. No. 41 can be had in the two-record collection of various Mozart works with Szell discussed under CONCERTO FOR VIOLIN NO. 5. Here are the other symphony availabilities:

35, 39. *CBS MY 38472 (LP, CS)* **(B)**

35, 39, 40, 41. *(2) Columbia MG 30368 (LP only)* **(B)**

35, 40. *Odyssey YT 35492 (CS only)* **(B)**

39, 41. *Odyssey YT 35493 (CS only)* **(B)**

40, 41. *CBS MY 37220 (LP, CS)* **(B)**

This kind of head-splitting confusion is endemic with CBS Masterworks Division. More than any other record company they love to recycle recordings in several different combinations. Sometimes the same recording is simultaneously available on different catalog numbers at both budget and full price. I have always found the situation unconscionable and advise buyers to exercise caution to avoid duplication or overcharging.

Other recommended performances are available as follows:

29, 39. C. Davis, Dresden State Orchestra.
Philips 6514 205 (D-LP); 7337 205 (CS)

29, 28. Marriner, Academy SMF.
Philips 9500 652 (LP)

35, 36. Hogwood, Academy of Ancient Music.
L'Oiseau Lyre DSLO 602 (LP, CS)

35, 36. Kubelik, Bavarian Radio Symphony.
CBS IM 36729 (D-LP, CS, CD) N.B.: Kubelik's Mozart is anachronistic in style, but warm and "human" in excellent sound.

36, EINE KLEINE NACHTMUSIK. Kertész, Vienna Philharmonic. (B)
London Stereo Treasury STS 15506 (LP)

38, 39. Böhm, Vienna Philharmonic.
DG 2531 206 (LP); 3301 206 (CS)

38, 41. C. Davis, BBC Symphony. (B)
Philips Festivo 6570 087 (LP); 7310 087 (CS)

38, 39. Kubelik, Bavarian Radio Symphony.
CBS IM 36730 (D-LP, CS, CD)

38, 39. Maag, Philharmonia Hungarica. (B)
Turnabout 34339 (LP)

39, 41. C. Davis, Dresden State Orchestra.
Philips 410 046-2 (CD only)

40, 41. Böhm, Vienna Philharmonica.
DG 2530 780 (LP); 3300 780 (CS)

40, 31. Hogwood, Academy of Ancient Music.
L'Oiseau Lyre DSDL 716 (D-LP, CS); 410 197-2 (CD)

41, 28. C. Davis, Dresden State Orchestra.
Philips 6514 206 (D-LP); 7337 206 (CS)

41, Schubert SYMPHONY NO. 8. Jochum, Boston Symphony.
DG 2530 357 (LP)

The best-loved works of the Classical era, beyond those listed above, are fairly represented in this supplementary list:

Bach, C.P.E.
Concerto in A for Cello, W. 172

Beethoven
Concerto No. 3 in c for Piano, Op. 37
Concerto No. 4 in G for Piano, Op. 58
Missa Solemnis in D, Op. 123
Quartet No. 8 in e, Op. 59, No. 2 "Rasumovsky"
Quartet No. 9 in C, Op. 59, No. 3 "Rasumovsky"
Quartet No. 15 in a, Op. 132

Boccherini
Concerto in B-flat for Cello and Orchestra

Haydn
Concerto in D for Harpsichord, Op. 21

Mozart
Concerto No. 1 in G for Flute and Orchestra, K. 313
Concerto No. 2 in D for Flute and Orchestra, K. 314
Quartet No. 19 in C, K. 465 "Dissonant"

The
Early Romantics

The Romantic movement in music hatched in the midst of Mozart's career, left the nest about the time of Beethoven's *Eroica* symphony, soared throughout the nineteenth century, became ungainly early in the twentieth, and is currently an endangered species. It is well known, however, for more examples of it are on display in our concert hall museums than any other musical bird.

Romantic music has won wider acceptance than any other type of concert music, and the largest number of works on any "basic repertory" list come from the Romantic composers — facts which are reflected in our next listings. We begin here with the "early Romantics," whose compositions often show strong links to the Classical period but unquestionably have a "new" rhapsodic, sometimes even sentimental, quality, that sounds quite different from the polished politeness of the preceding era.

Hector Berlioz   1803-1869

La Damnation de Faust, Op. 24

Sir Colin Davis has been the most eminent Berlioz advocate of our time and his recording is a true "classic." But he has run into severe competition from another musical knight, Sir Georg Solti, whose more recent digital and CD version has better sound and has received virtually nothing but rave reviews for dramatic excitement, choral quality, subtlety and sparkle — "sheer sonic bedazzlement," said *Ovation.*

C. Davis, London Symphony, Ambrosian Singers.
(3) Philips 6703 042 (LP)

Solti, Chicago Symphony Orchestra and Chorus.
(3) London LDR 73007 (D-LP, CS) Highlights on 410 181-2 (CD only)

Harold in Italy, for Viola and Orchestra, Op. 16

Every one of these four recordings has been chosen by one or more critics as the best available, so you are not likely to go wrong whatever you nab. Three, thankfully, are budgets. Keep in mind that the magical Primrose-Beecham is monophonic.

Menuhin-Davis, on the oldest stereo recording, treat the

work very much as a concerto. Suk and Fischer-Dieskau (conducting, not singing) are the most probing and thoughtful. Zukerman-Barenboim go for a richly romantic sound and dramatic flair.

Menuhin, C. Davis, Philharmonia Orchestra. (B)
Angel RL-32077 (LP, CS)

Primrose, Beecham, Royal Philharmonic. (M) (B)
Odyssey Y 33286 (LP)

Suk, Fischer-Dieskau, Czech Philharmonic. (B)
Quintessence 7103 (LP, CS)

Zukerman, Barenboim, Orchestre de Paris.
Columbia M 34541 (LP, CS)

Roman Carnival Overture

Respectable if not definitive performances from Barenboim of three French "basics" at budget price. But if you don't mind a whole record of Berlioz overtures, the classic Davis is distinctively exciting.

Barenboim, Orchestre de Paris. (B)
DG Signature 410 833-1 (LP); 410 833-4 (CS)

C. Davis, London Symphony. (B)
Philips Sequenza 6527 179 (LP); 7311 179 (CS)

Symphonie fantastique, Op. 14

At opposite ends of the price/sound spectrum are Beecham and Paita, neither of whom I can recommend to the beginning collector. No matter Beecham's wonderful performance, the recording cannot deliver sound vivid enough to convey all of this highly colored score; and though Paita has his cadre of immoderate admirers, his records on the Lodia label from Switzerland are hard to find and currently list for $17.98 per disc.

More reasonable, with a virtuosic performance and brilliant digital sound, is the Maazel version on Telarc (generally favored over his CBS disc). Davis and Karajan, outstanding in analog, also create confusion with two recordings apiece; those listed below are the better ones, so check catalog numbers carefully before buying.

Freccia is ardently vivid on budget, with a generous bonus of

the Hungarian March recorded with a "cannon drum" 15 feet in
diameter!

C. Davis, Concertgebouw.
Philips 6500 774 (LP); 7300 313 (CS)

Freccia, Royal Philharmonic. (B)
Quintessence 7057 (LP, CS)

Karajan, Berlin Philharmonic.
DG 2530 597 (LP); 3300 498 (CS)

Maazel, Cleveland Orchestra.
Telarc 10076 (D-LP, CD)

Frédéric Chopin   1810-1849

Concerto No. 1 in e for Piano, Op. 11

Artur Rubenstein, with his elegance, grand sweep, and poetic insight, established himself for most our century as the most widely
admired interpreter of Chopin. His throne is now being occu-
pied by Vladimir Ashkenazy. Of course, other fine pianists make
good Chopin records too.

Rubinstein's very special accounts of Concerti Nos. 1 and 2
are available in a two-record budget set with a bonus of the great
Andante Spianato and Grande Polonaise. Do not be hoodwinked
into buying the two separate records on RCA at full price, with no
filler.

Several excellent pianists whose readings of No. 1 are available at full price (e.g., Zimerman, Ax, Perahia, Argerich) are fa-
tally compromised by their engineers, their conductors, or both.
Gilels and Pollini make much better bargains on their budget
discs.

Gilels, Ormandy, Philadelphia Orchestra. (B)
Odyssey Y 32369 (LP, CS)

Pollini, Kletzki, Philharmonia Orchestra. (B)
Seraphim S-60066 (LP, CS)

**Rubinstein, Skrowaczewski, New Symphony of London (in
No. 1), Rubinstein, Wallenstein, Symphony of the Air
(in No. 2). (B)**
RCA VCS-7091 (LP)

Concerto No. 2 in f for Piano, Op. 21

For Rubinstein, see under CONCERTO NO. 1. Not a good budget in the lot for this work, and not a clear leader at full price either. Those listed have all come in for mostly positive comments. Argerich is paired with the Schumann CONCERTO FOR PIANO, Ax and Zimerman with shorter Chopin pieces, and Ashkenazy rather oddly with the Bach Harpsichord Concerto No. 1 in a piano version.

Argerich, Rostropovich, National Philharmonic.
DG 2531 042 (LP); 3301 042 (CS)

Ashkenazy, Zinman, London Symphony.
London CS 6440 (LP, CS), or on *(3) London CSP 12,* (B) *described under Beethoven* CONCERTO NO. 5 *(LP, CS)*

Ax, Ormandy, Philadelphia Orchestra.
RCA ARL1-2868 (LP, CS)

Zimerman, Giulini, Los Angeles Philharmonic.
DG 2531 126 (LP); 3301 126 (CS)

Piano Anthologies

One of the major recording projects of recent years has been Ashkenazy's 15 discs of all Chopin's solo piano music. The performances are almost uniformly wonderful but the layout is abominable: the recordings made in *reverse* chronological order (except for volume 1) and the volume numbers not corresponding to the order of issuance. Thus volume 15, the "last" one, contains the composer's juvenilia. Volume 7 on London CS 7235 (LP, CS) gives perhaps the best selection of mature works, including the SONATA NO. 2. But if you have a CD player, get Ashkenazy's "Favorite Chopin" CD on London 410 180-2, an apt assortment of the most popular pieces (not available on disc or cassette).

Rubinstein has four single disc anthology albums worth getting, though unfortunately RCA keeps them at full price, as follows:

LSC-4000 (LP); RK-1172 (CS)

LSC-4016 (LP); RK-1236 (CS)

LSC-3322 (LP); RK-1302 (CS); R8S-1302 (8-track!)

LSC-3339 (LP); ARK1-0858 (CS)

A sublime pianist insufficiently known in this country is the Czech Ivan Moravec, whose digital recording on Vox 9059 (D-LP, CS) cannot be over-praised. The best anthology for Horowitz fans is on Columbia M 30643 (LP, CS), and a very basic budget disc is Vanguard Cardinal 10059 (LP) (B) with Guiomar Novaes.

Sonata No. 2 in b-flat for Piano, Op. 35

This is the piece containing the infamous "Funeral March." For Ashkenazy, see the preceding section. Rubinstein and Perahia both have fine versions, each coupled with the Sonata No. 3

Ashkenazy.
London CS 7235 (LP, CS)

Perahia.
Columbia M 32780 (LP)

Rubinstein.
RCA LSC-3194 (LP)

Mikhail Glinka   1804-1857

Russlan and Ludmila: Overture

The Ormandy is in a two-record budget set of overtures called "Curtain Raisers," featuring also performances by Bernstein and Szell, and including the "basic" ORPHEUS IN THE UNDERWORLD OVERTURE by Offenbach, Rossini's WILLIAM TELL, and others.

Previn's luscious-sounding anthology adds some of the best performances of Debussy's PRELUDE TO THE AFTERNOON OF A FAUN, Falla's THREE-CORNERED HAT DANCES, and Barber's ADAGIO FOR STRINGS.

Rostropovich and Solti both offer fiery all-Russian programs, each with Mussorgsky's NIGHT ON BALD MOUNTAIN as a coupling. Rostropovich also gives Rimsky-Korsakov's CAPRICCIO ESPAGNOL,

and Solti adds Borodin's PRINCE IGOR OVERTURE AND POLOV-
TSIAN DANCES.

Ormandy, Philadelphia Orchestra, et al. (B)
(2) Columbia MG 35188 (LP)

Previn, London Symphony.
Angel S-37409 (LP, CS)

Rostropovich, Orchestre de Paris.
Angel S-37464 (LP, CS)

Solti, London Symphony.
London CS 6785 (LP, CS)

Felix Mendelssohn   1809-1847

Concerto in e for Violin, Op. 64

There are so many excellent recordings of this concerto, you would
really have to work to pick a bad one. Some of the best, with their
couplings, are: Cho-Liang Lin (with Saint-Saëns: CONCERTO FOR
VIOLIN NO. 3); Heifetz, Kyung-Wha Chung, Milstein, Zuker-
man, and Stern-Ormandy (with Tchaikovsky: CONCERTO FOR
VIOLIN); Mutter, Perlman, Ricci, Suk, and Ughi (with Bruch:
CONCERTO FOR VIOLIN NO. 1); and Stern-Ozawa (with the two
Beethoven *Romances*).

But the best of all *in the Mendelssohn,* by general consensus,
is Kyung-Wha Chung with Dutoit and the Montreal Symphony.
The soloist is alternately delicate and dazzling, the accompaniment splendid, and the recorded sound superior.

Cho-Liang Lin, Thomas, Philharmonia Orchestra.
CBS IM 39007 (D-LP, CS, CD)

Heifetz, Munch, Boston Symphony.
*RCA LSC-3304 (LP); RK-1284 (CS), or at higher price on the re-
mastered RCA ARP1-4567 (LP, CS)*

Kyung Wha-Chung, Dutoit, Montreal Symphony.
London LDR 71058 (D-LP, CS); 410 011-2 (CD)

Milstein, Abbado, Vienna Philharmonic.
DG 2530 359 (LP)

Mutter, Karajan, Berlin Philharmonic.
DG 2532 016 (D-LP); 3302 016 (CS); 400 031-2 (CD)

Perlman, Previn, London Symphony.
Angel S-36963 (LP, CS), or with Brahms: CONCERTO FOR VIOLIN, *Bruch:* CONCERTO NO. 1 FOR VIOLIN, *and Tchaikovsky:* CONCERTO FOR VIOLIN *in a box,* (3) *Angel SCZ-3912 (LP, CS)*

Ricci, Gamba, London Symphony. (B)
London Stereo Treasury STS 15402 (LP)

Stern, Ormandy, Philadelphia Orchestra. (B)
CBS MY 36724 (LP, CS)

Stern, Ozawa, Boston Symphony.
CBS IM 37204 (D-LP, CS, CD)

Suk, Ančerl, Czech Philharmonic. (B)
Quintessence 7098 (LP, CS)

Ughi, Prêtre, London Symphony.
RCA ARC1-4955 (D-LP, CS)

Zukerman, Bernstein, New York Philharmonic.
Columbia MS 7313 (LP)

Hebrides (Fingal's Cave) Overture

The pleasantest, most basic, and best-sounding way to obtain this work is on Dohnányi's digital recording of SYMPHONY NO. 4, with a bonus of the soothing overture *Calm Sea and Prosperous Voyage.*

Dohnányi, Vienna Philharmonic.
London LDR 10003 (D-LP, CS)

A Midsummer Night's Dream, Incidental Music, Op. 21, 61

The complete music is more than the beginning collector is likely to want. The most famous parts are the Overture, Scherzo, Nocturne, and Wedding March: the records listed contain at least these.

Three of four, happily, are budgets. Ansermet's classic 1960 version still sounds good and is paired with basic highlights from Schubert's ROSAMUNDE. Szell is brisk and gleaming and coupled

with the SYMPHONY NO. 4. Kubelik is fine, offers four additional
overtures, and is at the lowest price of all. Davis's reading is powerful, with a brilliantly fleet coupling of SYMPHONY NO. 4.

Ansermet, Suisse Romande. (B)
London Stereo Treasury STS 15580 (LP, CS)

C. Davis, Boston Symphony.
Philips 9500 068 (LP); 7300 480 (CS)

Kubelik, Bavarian Radio Symphony. (B)
DG Musikfest 413 253-1 (LP); 413 253-4 (CS)

Szell, Cleveland Orchestra. (B)
CBS MY 37760 (LP, CS)

Octet in E-flat for Strings, Op. 20

Mendelssohn was all of 16 when he wrote this enchanting chamber-music masterpiece, best known for its breezy Scherzo. With
the classic 1966 I Musici recording currently unavailable, the elegant St. Martin's Academy, with a generous bonus of the Op. 87
Quintet, is the clear first choice.

Academy SMF Chamber Ensemble.
Philips 9500 616 (LP)

Symphonies (5)

Masur's graceful, elegant readings make the most attractive
package at low price.

Masur, Leipzig Gewandhaus Orchestra. (B)
Vanguard Cardinal 10133/6

Symphony No. 4 in A, Op. 90, "Italian"

There are good budgets by Previn, Klemperer, and Szell; Previn is
perhaps the most rhythmically infectious, and adds an overture
and Prokofiev's SYMPHONY NO. 1. Szell is paired with MIDSUMMER
NIGHT'S DREAM, Klemperer with Schumann's SYMPHONY NO. 4.
At full price there is Dohnányi with the HEBRIDES OVERTURE and
one other, and Davis with MIDSUMMER NIGHT'S DREAM.

C. Davis, Boston Symphony.
Philips 9500 068 (LP); 7300 480 (CS)

Dohnányi, Vienna Philharmonic.
London LDR 10003 (D-LP, CS)

Klemperer, Philharmonia Orchestra (B)
Angel RL-32110 (LP, CS)

Previn, London Symphony. (B)
RCA AGL1-2703 (LP, CS)

Szell, Cleveland Orchestra. (B)
CBS MY 37760 (LP, CS)

Niccolò Paganini   1782-1840

Concerto No. 1 in D for Violin, Op. 6

Michael Rabin's remains the classic account, coupled with
Wieniawski's hyper-romantic Concerto No. 2 on a budget recording. Only Perlman comes close, but at full price he must be an
alternate.

Rabin, Goossens, Philharmonia Orchestra. (B)
Seraphim S-60222 (LP, CS)

Gioacchino Rossini   1792-1868

Overtures

All listed recordings contain the *William Tell* Overture. It is included among overtures by other composers on the "Curtain Raisers" album discussed under Glinka: RUSSLAN AND LUDMILA, and
if you want an all-Rossini program there is a companion two-disc
budget album with performances by Bernstein and Szell.

There are also a number of good single-disc budgets. I have
dropped Gamba in favor of Reiner and Serafin, who are even taut-
er and more "Toscaninian." Giulini is the most stylish and musical.

At full price Abbado's RCA album is outstanding in every way (preferable, I think, to Chailly's newer but scrappier version), and Marriner is unique in using newly revised orchestrations that show us a leaner, more classical Rossini. Another record I have dropped is Karajan's. Though polished and suave, it is short on Rossini's most essential ingredient: humor.

Abbado, London Symphony.
RCA ARL1-3634 (LP, CS)

Bernstein, Szell. (B)
(2) Columbia MG 35187 (LP)

Bernstein, Szell, Ormandy. (B)
(2) Columbia MG 35188 (LP)

Giulini, Philharmonia Orchestra. (B)
Seraphim S-60058 (LP, CS)

Marriner, Academy SMF.
Philips 9500 349 (LP); 7300 595 (CS)

Reiner, Chicago Symphony. (B)
RCA AGL1-5210 (LP, CS)

Serafin, Rome Opera Orchestra. (B)
DG Privilege 2535 365 (LP); 3335 365 (CS)

Franz Schubert   1797-1828

Quartet No. 14 in d, D. 810, "Death and the Maiden"

From all the reviews surveyed the impression was strong that the recent Juilliard is the most balanced choice as a very "central" performance, with excellent sound at full price.

Among the budgets, the Guarneri and Vienna Philharmonic Quartet versions are fine old standards, and each includes another short chamber work.

Guarneri Quartet. (B)
RCA AGL1-4928 (LP, CS)

Juilliard Quartet.
CBS M 37201 (LP, CS)

Vienna Philharmonic Quartet. (B)
London Stereo Treasury STS 15410 (LP)

Quintet in A, D. 667, "Trout"

Brendel and the Cleveland Quartet have the best notices among newer recordings, with a performance of great logic and precision. The budget with Rudolf Serkin and friends is an old standard whose sonics have been improved on the recent reissue. Panenka and the Smetana Quartet give a balanced, sparkling reading (one of the best ever) on another budget, but be warned that careless manufacture causes an unbelievable "wow" at the beginning of side one. Once you live through that, all is enchantment.

Brendel, Cleveland Quartet.
Philips 9500 442 (LP); 7300 648 (CS); 400 078-2 (CD)

Panenka, Smetana Quartet. (B)
Quintessence 7101 (LP, CS)

R. Serkin, Laredo, Naegele, Parnas, Levine.
CBS MY 37234 (LP, CS)

Rosamunde: Incidental Music, Op. 26 (D. 797)

As with Mendelssohn's A MIDSUMMER NIGHT'S DREAM, I am recommending recordings with the best-loved selections from the complete music. Mendelssohn is the coupling for Ansermet's radiant reading with a fine SYMPHONY NO. 8.

C. Davis, Boston Symphony.
Philips 410 393-1 (D-LP); 410 393-4 (CS); 410 393-2 (CD)

Ansermet, Suisse Romande. (B)
London Stereo Treasury STS 15580 (LP, CS)

Songs (Lieder)

Soprano Elly Ameling, mezzo-soprano Dame Janet Baker, contralto Christa Ludwig, and baritones Dietrich Fischer-Dieskau and Gérard Souzay are all great art-song interpreters and provide a nice range of voices in which to listen to these sublime miniatures. Each recording listed has a selection from among the most beloved of Schubert's more than 600 *Lieder.*

Ameling, Baldwin.
Philips 6500 704 (LP); 7300 790 (CS)

Ameling, Demus. (B)
Quintessence 7099 (LP, CS)

Baker, Parsons. (B)
Seraphim S-60380 (LP, CS)

Fischer-Dieskau, Moore.
Angel S-36341 (LP)

Ludwig, Parsons.
Angel S-36462 (LP)

Souzay, Baldwin. (B)
Philips Sequenza 6527 103 (LP); 7311 103 (CS)

Symphony No. 5 in B-flat, D. 485

Marriner has the newest sound, though more than one critic has thought it bass-heavy and deficient in detail. There is no consensus on the interpretation either, though it still outpointed all the other full-price versions. Note that the LP and cassette are coupled with Symphony No. 3, the CD with No. 4, just to make it more confusing.

It may just be safer to stick with Klemperer at budget price, with the more "basic" pairing of SYMPHONY NO. 8. Klemperer's approach is controversial too, but the *Fanfare* critic put it nicely when he called it "perverse but compelling."

Klemperer, Philharmonia Orchestra. (B)
Angel RL-32038 (LP, CS)

Marriner, Academy SMF.
Philips 6514 149 (D-LP); 7337 149 (CS); 410 145-2 (CD)

Symphony No. 8 in b, D. 759, "Unfinished"

Previously recommended under their respective couplings were Colin Davis (with ROSAMUNDE); Jochum (with Mozart: SYMPHO-

NY NO.41); Klemperer, Reiner, Toscanini, and Walter (with Beethoven: SYMPHONY NO. 5); and Szell with the Beethoven and
with Dvořák: SYMPHONY NO. 9 in the double set.

Two additional budgets show their conductors at their very
best: Giulini, coupled with Brahms: VARIATIONS ON A THEME BY
HAYDN (much better than his later Chicago Symphony version on
DG); and Kertész, coupled with three Schubert overtures.

C. Davis, Boston Symphony.
Philips 410 393-1 (D-LP); 410 393-4 (CS); 410 393-2 (CD)

Giulini, Philharmonia Orchestra. (B)
Seraphim S-60335 (LP, CS)

Jochum, Boston Symphony.
DG 2530 357 (LP)

Kertész, Vienna Philharmonic. (B)
London Stereo Treasury STS 15476 (LP)

Klemperer, Philharmonia Orchestra. (B)
Angel RL-32038 (LP, CS)

Reiner, Chicago Symphony. (B)
RCA AGL1-5206 (LP, CS)

Szell, Cleveland Orchestra.
(2) Columbia MG 30371 (LP)

Toscanini, NBC Symphony. (M) (B)
Victrola VICS-1648 (LP)

Walter, New York Philharmonic. (B)
Odyssey Y 30314 (LP, CS)

Symphony No. 9 in C, D. 944, "The Great"

The late conductor Josef Krips left his finest legacy in his classic recording — warm, stylish, direct, well recorded, and low-priced.
This is an overall first choice, but for newer sound Karajan's Angel
recording takes precedence over his older DG. Karajan is bolder
than Böhm and Haitink, less controversial than Giulini, and more
exhilarating than Klemperer.

Karajan, Berlin Philharmonic.
Angel SZ-36545 (LP)

Krips, London Symphony. (B)
London Stereo Treasury STS 15140 (LP)

Trio No. 1 in B-flat, Op. 99 (D. 898)

For a single disc the budget Suk Trio is bright, buoyant, and un-beatable. The other choices are at full price on double sets with the great, but perhaps less immediately attractive, Trio No. 2 in E-flat. Szeryng-Fournier-Rubinstein have been a much-praised standard for some years, but to paraphrase Brahms any fool can hear that they are not together all the time. And at full price I cannot prefer them over two newer and radiant performances.

The Odeon Trio give joyful, uplifting performances digitally recorded with two additional Schubert chamber works. The three Frenchmen are more poetically intimate, with beautiful analog sound and far more beautiful packaging. Their cassette, curiously, is half the price of their album; but they do not include fillers as do the Odeon, and their import label will be harder to find.

Odeon Trio.
(2) Pro Arte 2PAD-202 (D-LP)

Pasquier, Pidoux, Pennetier.
(2) French Harmonia Mundi 1047/8 (LP, CS)

Suk, Chuchro, Panenka. (B)
Quintessence 7111 (LP, CS)

Robert Schumann   1810-1856

Carnaval, Op. 9

Three pianists stand out: Rubinstein for his scintillating lyricism, Arrau for his probing thoughtfulness, DeLarrocha for her poetic vision. Beware of the *Penguin Guide*'s extreme enthusiasm for Barenboim; their view is emphatically not shared by other reviewers. All recordings have fillers of other short piano works.

Arrau.
Philips 802 746 PSI (LP)

DeLarrocha.
London CS 7134 (LP, CS)

Rubinstein. (B)
RCA AGL1-4879 (LP)

Concerto in a for Piano, Op. 54

With some personal anguish I am dropping the record by the sublime pianist Dinu Lipatti. Though budget-priced, its sound is so
faded that I concede it belongs to the advanced collector and is not
the first one to buy; especially since there are at least three truly
great performances in much better sound at the same price — the
raptly poetic Moravec, the alternately tender and majestic Rubinstein, and the profoundly nuanced Rudolf Serkin. At full price,
Ashkenazy is the most dramatic, Zimerman the most exuberant.

Ashkenazy, Segal, London Symphony. (B)
(3) London CSP 12 (LP) contents discussed under Beethoven:
CONCERTO FOR PIANO NO. 5*)*

Moravec, Neumann, Czech Philharmonic. (B)
Quintessence 7153 (LP, CS) (with Franck: SYMPHONIC
VARIATIONS*)*

Rubinstein, Giulini, Chicago Symphony. (B)
RCA AGL1-4880 (LP) (with Noveletten*)*

R. Serkin, Ormandy, Philadelphia Orchestra. (B)
CBS MY 37256 (LP, CS) (with the Quintet, Op. 44)

Zimerman, Karajan, Berlin Philharmonic.
DG 2532 043 (D-LP, CS) (with Grieg: CONCERTO FOR PIANO*)*

Symphonies (4)

Proving, perhaps, the ephemeral nature of music criticism, the
Kubelik set described here three years ago as "the newest...and, by
all accounts, the best," subsequently came in for some negative
criticism and has already been deleted! Bernstein is gone, too, but
Karajan remains at full price and Szell at budget, joined by the distinguished Sawallisch set somewhere in between.

Karajan, Berlin Philharmonic.
(3) DG 2709 036 (LP)

Sawallisch, Dresden State Orchestra.
(3) Arabesque 8102 (LP); 9102 (CS)

Szell, Cleveland Orchestra. (B)
(3) Odyssey Y3 30844 (LP, CS)

Symphony No. 1 in B-flat, Op. 38, "Spring"

George Szell was sometimes faulted for a lack of warmth. This is not a problem in his sunny view of the "Spring" Symphony, very "basically" coupled with SYMPHONY NO. 4, at budget price. At the same price Klemperer may be even a better performance, but the only coupling is the *Manfred Overture*.

Klemperer, New Philharmonia. (B)
Angel RL-32063 (LP, CS)

Szell, Cleveland Orchestra. (B)
CBS MY 38468 (LP, CS)

Symphony No. 2 in C, Op. 61

A really satisfactory single disc is currently hard to come by. Ansermet is warmly romantic if not stylistically perfect, at low price.

Ansermet, Suisse Romande. (B)
London Stereo Treasury STS 15285 (with Manfred Overture*)*

Symphony No. 3 in E-flat, Op. 97, "Rhenish"

Giulini and Haitink both have recent digital recordings coupled (again!) with the *Manfred Overture*. Both have received many positive reviews, but there have also been significant negative ones. *Stereo Review,* for example, calls Giulini's version "the most magical" to appear in over forty years, while *High Fidelity* says the performance is "sluggishly labored" with "inexplicably thick" sonics. I will not tell you not to buy these discs, but for your first time it seems to me much better to get the budget Solti — lyrical, rich playing and mellow sound, and a much more generous coupling of the SYMPHONY NO. 4.

Solti, Vienna Philharmonic. (B)
London Stereo Treasury STS 15575 (LP, CS)

Symphony No. 4 in d, Op. 120

All three listings are budgets, and have been previously recommended under their respective couplings. Things could be worse!

Klemperer, Philharmonia Orchestra. (B)
Angel RL-32110 (LP, CS) (with Mendelssohn: SYMPHONY NO. 4)

Solti, Vienna Philharmonic. (B)
London Stereo Treasury STS 15575 (LP, CS)
(with SYMPHONY NO. 3)

Szell, Cleveland Orchestra. (B)
CBS M 38468 (LP, CS) (with SYMPHONY NO. 1)

Carl Maria von Weber   1786-1826

Invitation to the Dance, Op. 65

Barenboim's anthology is unusually well done with rich recording.
The other overtures are Weber's *Oberon*, Mendelssohn's *A Midsummer Night's Dream*, Mozart's *Marriage of Figaro*, Nicolai's
The Merry Wives of Windsor, and — you guessed it — Schumann's
Manfred! (See under Schumann; if you manage to get every piece
in this book without accumulating four or five *Manfreds*, let me
know how you did it.)

Bernstein's record is an all-Weber program with the three
great overtures, *Der Freischütz*, *Oberon*, and *Euryanthe*, but the
sound is harsh compared to DG's. If Angel ever puts its excellent
but ancient Karajan record on budget, I might list it.

Barenboim, Chicago Symphony.
DG 2531 215 PSI (LP); 3301 215 PSI (CS)

Bernstein, New York Philharmonic.
Columbia M 33585 (LP)

Overtures

In the old book I lamented the passing of the budget Kubelik all-
Weber overture record and recommended Karajan instead. Now it
is gone too! It seems nobody wants a whole recording of these delightful pieces. The catalog does show two budget Kubelik records
now, but each has only one Weber overture. The three most popular ones show up on the Bernstein record discussed under INVITA-
TION TO THE DANCE and on Klemperer's budget which also in-

cludes the overture to Humperdinck's *Hansel and Gretel*. The *Oberon* overture is included on Barenboim's disc listed above, and comes also on the Solti record previously recommended with Beethoven: SYMPHONY NO. 3).

Barenboim, Chicago Symphony.
DG 2531 215 PSI (LP); 3301 215 PSI (CS)

Bernstein, New York Philharmonic.
Columbia M 33585 (LP)

Klemperer, Philharmonia Orchestra. (B)
Angel RL-32079 (LP, CS)

Solti, Chicago Symphony.
London CS 7050 (LP); 5-7057 (CS)

Additional delights from the early Romantic era would include:

Mendelssohn
Elijah, Op. 70 (oratorio)

Schubert
Marche Militaire No. 1 in D
Moments Musicaux, Op. 94 (D. 780)
Sonata in B-flat for Piano, Op. posth. (D. 960)
Wanderer Fantasie for Piano, Op. 15 (D. 760)
Die Winterreise, Op. 89 (D. 911)

Schumann
Kinderscenen, Op. 15
Songs (selections)

The Mainstream Romantics

Georges Bizet   1838-1875

L'Arlésienne Suites; Carmen Suites

Recordings listed are limited to those with both works represented. Among full price choices Abbado is preferred over Marriner by reviewers for energy and sonics. On budget, Markevitch evinces his usual incomparable verve in excellent sound, and the extraordinary Stokowski is genial or glittering as required in a recording made just before his death at age 95. Be careful: Stokowski's is still shown in the catalogs at both full and budget prices; naturally, buy the budget (its sonics will amaze you).

Abbado, London Symphony.
DG 2531 329 (LP); 3301 329 (CS)

Markevitch, Lamoureux Orchestra. (B)
Philips Festivo 6570 107 (LP)

Stokowski, National Philharmonic. (B)
CBS MY 37260 (LP, CS)

Symphony No. 1 in C

Marriner wins back his laurels with his classic light and elegant performance reissued at budget price, coupled with Prokofiev: SYMPHONY NO. 1. (Bernstein's famous old record of the same pairing, available at the same price, is now generally rated below Marriner for both style and sonics.)

Marriner, Academy SMF. (B)
London Jubilee 41065 (LP, CS)

Alexander Borodin   1833-1887

Prince Igor: Overture; Polovtsian Dances

Of the recordings listed only those by Shaw and Solti have both these colorful excerpts from Borodin's opera on one disc or tape.

Shaw, coupled with Stravinsky's FIREBIRD SUITE, is especially exciting in the Borodin. The digital sound is highly impactful and a
splendid CD is available. Solti's record is described under Glinka:
RUSSLAN AND LUDMILA OVERTURE.

The main melody of the *Polovtsian Dances* (sometimes
spelled *Polovetsian*) was used for the tune of "Strangers in
Paradise" in the Broadway musical *Kismet*. There are five excellent
budget discs; your selection may depend on the couplings, all of
which are more or less "basic." For the *Prince Igor Overture* alone,
Ansermet's budget record is jam-packed with the SYMPHONY NO.
2 *and* NO. 3. (Ansermet's companion low-price disc with the
Polovtsian Dances and Rimsky-Korsakov's SCHEHERAZADE is *not*
recommended because of shoddy choral work.)

Ansermet, Suisse Romande. (B)
London Stereo Treasury STS 15149 (LP) (with SYMPHONY NO. 2,
Symphony No. 3)

Barenboim, Chicago Symphony. (B)
DG Privilege 2536 379 (LP); 3336 379 (CS) (with Mussorgsky:
NIGHT ON BALD MOUNTAIN, Rimsky-Korsakov: CAPRICCIO
ESPAGNOL *and* RUSSIAN EASTER OVERTURE)

Fremaux, Monte Carlo Opera Orchestra. (B)
*DG Musikfest 413 255-1 (LP); 413 255-4 (CS) (with Fricsay and
Berlin Radio Symphony conducting* Ponchielli: DANCE OF THE
HOURS *and ballet music of Gounod and Verdi)*

Kubelik, Vienna Philharmonic. (B)
Seraphim S-60106 (LP)

Markevitch, London Symphony. (B)
*Philips Festivo 6570 191 (LP); 7310 191 (CS) (with
Rimsky-Korsakov:* RUSSIAN EASTER OVERTURE, *Tchaikovsky:*
OVERTURE 1812)

Szell, Cleveland Orchestra. (B)
(2) Columbia M2X 787 (LP) (with Rimsky-Korsakov: CAPRICCIO
ESPAGNOL, *Tchaikovsky:* CAPRICCIO ITALIEN, *others)*

Quartet No. 2 in D

You'll hear some of these melodies in *Kismet* too. Could Borodin
have believed his lovely string quartet would become a hit on the
Great White Way? The classic Quartetto Italiano version has just
been deleted, leaving the road open for the wonderfully romantic

Concord Quartet version at budget price, coupled with Dvořák:
QUARTET NO. 12.

Concord Quartet. (B)
Turnabout 37009 (LP); CT-7009 (CS)

Symphony No. 2 in b

The Ansermet and Kubelik budget versions are both described
under PRINCE IGOR: OVERTURE; POLOVTSIAN DANCES. Both are
good: Ansermet has much more music; Kubelik's is the greater
performance.

Ansermet, Suisse Romande. (B)
London Stereo Treasury STS 15149 (LP)

Kubelik, Vienna Philharmonic. (B)
Seraphim S-60106 (LP)

Johannes Brahms   1833-1897

Academic Festival Overture, Op. 80

At full price Szell's classic combination of this with the TRAGIC
OVERTURE and VARIATIONS ON A THEME BY HAYDN is well-nigh
indispensable. There is also a Szell budget coupled with SYM-
PHONY NO. 4. Next best version of the three orchestral pieces
together is Solti's, at lower price. Another budget has Klemperer
in the *Academic* and SYMPHONY NO. 3.

Klemperer, Philharmonia Orchestra. (B)
Angel RL-32050 (LP, CS)

Solti, Chicago Symphony. (B)
London Jubilee 41062 (LP, CS)

Szell, Cleveland Orchestra.
Columbia MS 6965 (LP)

Szell, Cleveland Orchestra. (B)
CBS MY 37778 (LP, CS)

Concerto No. 1 in d for Piano, Op. 15

Gilels-Jochum have long been the classic, but the new Ashkenazy-Haitink, available in CD, is widely regarded as equally great. At full price Bishop-Kovacevich and Colin Davis must be dropped as no longer competitive, with inferior sound; and though Pollini-Böhm have many admirers, they have as many detractors. At the budget level Fleisher-Szell, Rubinstein-Reiner, and Serkin-Szell all have noble credentials.

Ashkenazy, Haitink, Concertgebouw.
London LDR 71052 (D-LP, CS); 410 009-2 (CD)

Fleisher, Szell, Cleveland Orchestra. (B)
Odyssey Y 31273 (LP, CS)

Gilels, Jochum, Berlin Philharmonic.
DG 2530 258 (LP)

Rubinstein, Reiner, Chicago Symphony. (B)
RCA AGL1-4890 (LP, CS)

R. Serkin, Szell, Cleveland Orchestra. (B)
CBS MY 37803 (LP, CS)

Concerto No. 2 in B-flat for Piano, Op. 83

The sublime Gilels-Jochum, unlike its counterpart of CONCERTO NO. 1, has disappeared from the catalog. I can only assume that DG is planning a budget reissue of this very famous recording; watch for it. Meanwhile there is the almost equally famous Gilels-Reiner version on another budget label.

Ashkenazy-Haitink have not had as unanimous praise as for their First, but most comment has been positive. Rubinstein's fourth and greatest recording, with Ormandy, is available only at full price, unlike the Rubinstein First with Reiner. Bishop-Kovacevich and Davis are good enough in their Second to be worth full price.

At budget price Fleisher-Szell and Serkin-Szell are again recommendable, and I feel this time I should include the legendary early stereo Richter-Leinsdorf; in 1960 critic Claudia Cassidy called it "the Brahms Second of a lifetime," and in September, 1984, *Musical America*'s Robert E. Benson called it "still one of the most exciting performances of the music ever put on disc...and more pleasing to the ear than most contemporary digital recordings."

Ashkenazy, Haitink, Vienna Philharmonic.
London 410 199-1 (LP); 410 199-4 (CS); 410 199-2 (CD)

Bishop-Kovacevich, C. Davis, London Symphony.
Philips 9500 682 (LP); 7300 777 (CS)

Fleisher, Szell, Cleveland Orchestra. (B)
Odyssey Y 32222 (LP, CS)

Gilels, Reiner, Chicago Symphony. (B)
RCA AGL1-5235 (LP, CS)

Richter, Leinsdorf, Chicago Symphony. (B)
RCA AGL1-1267 (LP, CS)

Rubinstein, Ormandy, Philadelphia Orchestra.
RCA LSC-3253 (LP); RK-1243 (CS)

Serkin, Szell, Cleveland Orchestra. (B)
CBS MY 37258 (LP, CS)

Concerto in D for Violin, Op. 77

Out of two dozen available recordings, Mutter's is the only one on CD, and it is also one of the best with its accomplished playing and wide range of moods. Surprisingly, Perlman is a bit off in this work, but his boxed set listed under Mendelssohn: CONCERTO FOR VIOLIN is still worthwhile for the other great performances in it. Three great versions — Heifetz, Oistrakh, and Szeryng — are all happily reissued on budget labels.

Heifetz, Reiner, Chicago Symphony. (B)
RCA AGL1-4909 (LP)

Mutter, Karajan, Berlin Philharmonic.
DG 2532 032 (D-LP); 3302 032 (CS); 400 064-2 (CD)

Oistrakh, Szell, Cleveland Orchestra. (B)
Angel RL-32096 (LP, CS)

Perlman, Giulini, Chicago Symphony.
(3) Angel SCZ-3912 (LP, CS)

Szeryng, Monteux, London Symphony. (B)
*RCA AGL1-5216 (LP, CS); also available on (B) Victrola
ALK1-4494 (CS only)*

Concerto in A for Violin and Cello, Op. 102

Perlman, with Rostropovich and Haitink, edges out Mutter-Meneses-Karajan in this work, with more than half the major critics naming it first choice among all recordings. A slight minority prefer the older Oistrakh-Rostropovich-Szell for first place. Almost all like Mutter and friends very much, however, and it is a fine alternative at full price. The best budget is Suk-Navarra-Ancerl, always listed among the choicest few. Mutter and Suk both add the TRAGIC OVERTURE as a coupling.

Mutter, Meneses, Karajan, Berlin Philharmonic.
DG 410 603-1 (D-LP); 410 603-4 (CS)

Oistrakh, Rostropovich, Szell, Cleveland Orchestra.
Angel S-36032 (LP, CS, 8-track)

Perlman, Rostropovich, Haitink, Concertgebouw.
Angel SZ-37680 (LP, CS)

Suk, Navarra, Ancerl, Czech Philharmonic. (B)
Quintessence 7203 (LP, CS)

German Requiem, Op. 45

Large choral works, like operas, have become so expensive to record nowadays that new releases are becoming ever rarer; so I was astonished to find a current Schwann Catalog listing 13 complete recordings of this work. But not half as astonished as I was to find, after plowing through stacks of reviews, that most critics still prefer the two listed in my book three years ago — the '60s versions by Karajan and Klemperer, especially the latter with its unique combination of serenity and power.

Karajan (soloists Janowitz and Wächter), Berlin Philharmonic, Vienna Singverein.
(2) DG 2707 018 (LP) (with VARIATIONS ON A THEME BY HAYDN)

Klemperer (soloists Schwarzkopf and Fischer-Dieskau), Philharmonia Orchestra and Chorus.
(2) Angel SB-3624 (LP, CS)

Hungarian Dances (Orchestral Versions)

Again duplicating the situation in my earlier book, the budget Dorati and Reiner recordings are best buys. Dorati has nothing but *Hungarian Dances* on his record; Reiner has a smaller selection but a flip side of the most popular SLAVONIC DANCES of Dvořák.

Dorati, London Symphony. (B)
Mercury 75024 (LP, CS)

Reiner, Vienna Philharmonic. (B)
London Stereo Treasury STS 15009 (LP)

Symphonies (4) (Complete)

Three omissions perhaps call for explanation: (1) I am finally relegating the monophonic Toscanini set to the "historical" category for more advanced collectors. (2) I did not list the Solti set last time, and shall not this, despite some complaints. I have yet to find a major critic who gives this admittedly popular and best-selling box unqualified approval. No. 1 is often criticized for being too tense, No. 2 for lacking charm, No. 3 for being ponderous, and No. 4 for peculiar idiosyncrasies. None is really bad, none really great, and Solti fans may be surprised at the general lack of visceral excitement. It is the "brand name," not the actual contents, that sells this set. (3) The live 1983 Bernstein performances have occasioned too much controversy to be listed as safe "first choices," except for No. 3 which I have conceded in the individual listings. Bernstein's performances are almost always highly personal, with much vitality, but often marked by those qualities which critics like to call "wayward" or "idiosyncratic." These are buzz words that alert you to a recording that may depart in significant degree from the established principles of a "direct" or "straightforward" interpretation. To the extent that Bernstein or other conductors stray from accepted canons they are increasingly less likely to be listed in this book; this does not mean the performance is bad or wrong; but that it is probably not the one you should start with to discover how the piece is normally played. Conductors like Bernstein who are brave enough to take chances should be admired. Perhaps by the next edition of this guide his Brahms symphonies will have convinced the reviewers and will be considered norms by which other versions are measured. Right now, they are not.

Even with these three major omissions, there are five recommendable "first time" complete sets of the Brahms symphonies. Karajan's is the best known, sporting beautiful orchestral playing and engineering, though some feel his readings are sometimes too slick and homogenized. It is the most expensive set.

At just a hair over "mid-price" Haitink is an excellent investment with all four performances getting good to excellent reviews. The sound is very fine and the performances are not available individually. There is a special price also on Levine, an exciting set which some find overly streamlined. These are available separately and I have included No. 2 in the individual listings for those who would rather pick and choose among conductors.

The budget boxes by Szell and Kertész are excellent values, especially with the symphonies fitted onto three discs instead of four.

Haitink, Concertgebouw. (B)
(4) Philips 6747 325 (LP); (3) 7699 011 (CS)

Karajan, Berlin Philharmonic.
(4) DG 2711 022 (LP); 3371 041 (CS)

Kertész, Vienna Philharmonic. (B)
(3) Vox SVBX-5125 (LP); CT-2190 (#1), CT-2191 (#2, 3), CT-2192 (#4) (CS)

Levine, Chicago Symphony. (B)
(4) RCA CRL4-3425 (LP)

Szell, Cleveland Orchestra. (B)
(3) Columbia D3S 758 (LP)

Symphony No. 1 in c, Op. 68

Karajan is the standard at full price. The newer Giulini, available on CD, has many admirers, but some of the tempos are questionable and overall the performance is conceded to be unconventional.

There are at least five excellent low-price editions. Horenstein, Krips, Böhm, and Szell are old favorites in this work. The "sleeper" is Günter Wand, a fine German conductor who has eschewed the limelight while making a specialty of Bruckner and Brahms. His Brahms First is a magnificent recent performance in stunning digital sound at a low price.

Böhm, Berlin Philharmonic. (B)
DG Privilege 2535 102 (LP)

Giulini, Los Angeles Philharmonic.
DG 2332 056 (D-LP); 3302 056 (CS); 410 023-2 (CD)

Horenstein, London Symphony. (B)
Quintessence 7028 (LP, CS)

Karajan, Berlin Philharmonic.
DG 2531 131 (LP); 3301 131 (CS)

Krips, Vienna Philharmonic. (B)
London Stereo Treasury STS 15144 (LP)

Szell, Cleveland Orchestra. (B)
CBS MY 37775 (LP, CS)

Wand, North German Radio Symphony. (B)
Sinfonia 626 (D-LP, CS)

Symphony No. 2 in D, Op. 73

Karajan and Levine are both exceptional at full price in singles
from their respective complete sets, and Szell is the best budget
with a bonus of the TRAGIC OVERTURE.

Karajan, Berlin Philharmonic.
DG 2531 132 (LP); 3301 132 (CS)

Levine, Chicago Symphony.
RCA ARL1-2864 (LP, CS)

Szell, Cleveland Orchestra. (B)
CBS MY 37776 (LP, CS)

Symphony No. 3 in F, Op. 90

Of Bernstein's performances discussed under the complete
Brahms symphonies earlier, No. 3 is generally considered the best,
and he includes the structurally important exposition repeat in the
first movement which Karajan, to his detriment, omits. Bernstein
also includes the VARIATIONS ON A THEME BY HAYDN.
    Among budgets Szell is again superb and the record is made
even more attractive with a coupling of his own unforgettable
HAYDN VARIATIONS. Klemperer, slow but architecturally impressive, is also a good buy with a bonus of the ACADEMIC FESTIVAL
OVERTURE.

Bernstein, Vienna Philharmonic.
DG 410 083-1 (LP); 410 083-4 (CS); 410 083-2 (CD)

Klemperer, Philharmonia Orchestra. (B)
Angel RL-32050 (LP, CS)

Szell, Cleveland Orchestra. (B)
CBS MY 37777 (LP, CS)

Symphony No. 4 in e, Op. 98

Karajan is especially famous for his Fourth, a powerful reading
with gorgeous orchestral sonority. The four budgets listed are all

deservedly very famous recordings and I would not hesitate to buy the first one that came to hand.

Giulini, Chicago Symphony. (B)
Angel RL-32036 (LP, CS)

Karajan, Berlin Philharmonic.
DG 2531 134 (LP); 3301 134 (CS)

Kertész, Vienna Philharmonic. (B)
London Jubilee 41055 (LP, CS)

Reiner, Royal Philharmonic. (B)
Quintessence 7182 (LP, CS)

Szell, Cleveland Orchestra. (B)
CBS MY 37778 (LP, CS)

Tragic Overture, Op. 81

The Szell budget described under SYMPHONY NO. 2, and the Szell full-price issue and Solti budget recommended under ACADEMIC FESTIVAL OVERTURE contain this work, and it is also included in Karajan's complete symphony box. Suk-Navarra and Mutter et al. have it on their recordings of the CONCERTO FOR VIOLIN AND CELLO.

Karajan, Berlin Philharmonic.
(4) DG 2711 022 (LP); 3371 041 (CS)

Mutter, Meneses, Karajan, Berlin Philharmonic.
DG 410 603-1 (D-LP); 410 603-4 (CS)

Solti, Chicago Symphony. (B)
London Jubilee 41062 (LP, CS)

Suk, Navarra, Ančerl, Czech Philharmonic. (B)
Quintessence 7203 (LP, CS)

Szell, Cleveland Orchestra.
Columbia MS 6965 (LP)

Szell, Cleveland Orchestra. (B)
CBS MY 37776 (LP, CS)

Variations on a Theme by Haydn, Op. 56a

All but one of the best recordings have been recommended under previous listings: the full price Szell and budget Solti under

ACADEMIC FESTIVAL OVERTURE and TRAGIC OVERTURE: a budget
Szell and full price Bernstein under SYMPHONY NO. 3; and it
comes as a filler on the Karajan GERMAN REQUIEM. Additionally it
is coupled with Dvořák: SYMPHONY NO. 8 in a recording by Bruno
Walter that is available on CD.

Bernstein, Vienna Philharmonic.
DG 410 083-1 (D-LP); 410 083-4 (CS); 410 083-2 (CD)

Karajan, Berlin Philharmonic, et al.
(2) DG 2707 018 (LP)

Solti, Chicago Symphony. (B)
London Jubilee 41062 (LP, CS)

Szell, Cleveland Orchestra.
Columbia MS 6954 (LP)

Szell, Cleveland Orchestra. (B)
CBS MY 37777 (LP, CS)

Walter, Columbia Symphony. (B)
CBS MP 38889 (LP, CS); CBS Sony DC 113 (CD)

A note on the Brahms Edition:

In 1983 DG issued a ten-volume set of 62 records comprising the
complete music of Brahms celebrating the 150th anniversary of his
birth. It is a mix of old and new recordings of varying artistic quality. Certainly this cannot be recommended for anyone but a library
or a Brahms fanatic; but if you are interested the most "basic" seg-
ment is Volume 1 with seven records including the acclaimed Karajan versions of the symphonies plus the complete *Hungarian
Dances* for orchestra and the Serenades Nos. 1 and 2 with Abbado
conducting. The "concerto box," Volume 2, has only one performance listed in this book.

Max Bruch   1838-1920

Concerto No. 1 in g for Violin, Op. 26

Five fine recordings by Mutter, Perlman, Ricci, Suk, and Ughi have
already been recommended under Mendelssohn: CONCERTO FOR
VIOLIN, with which they are all coupled. In addition, two outstanding versions are each coupled with Lalo: SYMPHONIE ES-

PAGNOLE. Zukerman is majestic and passionate *in excelsis* at full price, and Stern is a "golden oldie" on budget.

Mutter, Karajan, Berlin Philharmonic.
DG 2532 016 (D-LP); 3301 304 (CS); 400 031-2 (CD)

Perlman, Previn, London Symphony.
Angel S-36963 (LP, CS)

Ricci, Gamba, London Symphony. (B)
London Stereo Treasury STS 15402 (LP)

Stern, Ormandy, Philadelphia Orchestra. (B)
CBS MY 37811 (LP, CS)

Suk, Ančerl, Czech Philharmonic. (B)
Quintessence 7098 (LP, CS)

Ughi, Prêtre, London Symphony.
RCA ARC1-4955 (D-LP, CS)

Zukerman, Mehta, Los Angeles Philharmonic.
Columbia M 35132 (LP, CS)

Anton Bruckner   1824-1896

Symphony No. 4 in E-flat, "Romantic"

The classic Haitink reading, eloquent and unaffected, has been re-issued at budget price, and at the same price the even older Klemperer is solid and dramatic.. At full price the rather strident-sounding Karajan is superseded by the new digital Solti, an effective mix of tenderness and power.

Haitink, Concertgebouw. (B)
Philips Sequenza 6527 101 (LP); 7311 101 (CS)

Klemperer, Philharmonia Orchestra. (B)
Angel RL-32059 (LP, CS)

Solti, Chicago Symphony.
London LDR 71038 (D-LP, CS); 410 550-2 (CD)

Symphony No. 7 in E

Recommendations have not changed since the previous edition except for the Jochum which has been deleted. Haitink and Karajan run neck-and-neck for first place at full price, each with a coupling of Wagner's SIEGFRIED IDYLL. Rosbaud is the excellent dark horse on a single-disc budget, and Walter is classic on a double budget with older sound, but marvelously refurbished on the CD. Coupling is the *Te Deum*.

Haitink, Concertgebouw.
(2) Philips 6769 028 (LP); 7699 113 (CS)

Karajan, Berlin Philharmonic.
(2) DG 2707 102 (LP); 3370 023 (CS)

Rosbaud, SW German Symphony. (B)
Turnabout 34083 (LP); CT-4083 (CS)

Walter, Columbia Symphony. (B)
(2) Odyssey Y2 35328 (LP); (2) CBS Sony 35 DC 129/30 (CD)

Symphony No. 8 in c

Haitink's earlier version and Karajan's newest one get the top scores from critics. Haitink is coupled with SYMPHONY NO. 9 and takes three records, but at near-budget price that makes the set almost the same price as Karajan's two-disc version. Only Karajan comes on tape, however. Richard Freed of *Stereo Review* insists that Paita on Lodia (from Switzerland) is greater than anybody for both performance and sound, but the label is hard to find and the price is stratospheric.

Haitink, Concertgebouw. (B)
(3) Philips 6725 014 (D-LP)

Karajan, Berlin Philharmonic.
(2) DG 2707 085 (LP); 3370 019 (CS)

Symphony No. 9 in d

Haitink's older version is coupled with SYMPHONY NO. 8, recommended above. His 1983 single-disc version is also widely admired, though reviewers are split as to whether it is better than the 1966 recording. Karajan's newest reading has had very mixed reviews; *his* 1966 recording is thought by a majority to be superior and at budget price it is a much safer buy. All critics like Jochum's third and latest recording, and some prefer it to either Haitink or

Karajan. Giulini also has much support, and at the lowest price Walter is attractive (once again there is a CD).

Giulini, Chicago Symphony.
Angel S-37287 (LP, CS)

Haitink, Concertgebouw.
Philips 6514 191 (D-LP); 7337 191 (CS); 410 039-2 (CD)

Haitink, Concertgebouw. (B)
(3) Philips 6725 014 (D-LP)

Jochum, Dresden State Orchestra.
Angel S-37700 (LP, CS)

Karajan, Berlin Philharmonic. (B)
DG Privilege 2535 342 (LP); 3335 342 (CS)

Walter, Columbia Symphony.
CBS MP 39129 (LP, CS); CBS Sony 35 DC 114 (CD)

Emmanuel Chabrier 1841-1894

España

Maazel's long-famous sizzling performance of Rimsky-Korsakov's CAPRICCIO ESPAGNOL is included with Ravel's BOLERO on the reissued DG at rock-bottom price, a bargain impossible to beat if the couplings are satisfactory. At the normal (slightly higher) budget price, Bernstein's lively collection includes THE SORCERER'S APPRENTICE by Dukas, ORPHEUS IN THE UNDERWORLD OVERTURE by Offenbach, DANSE MACABRE and the *Bacchanale* by Saint-Saëns, and Ravel's PAVANE. If you don't need another "anthology" album, by far the best all-Chabrier disc is the acclaimed one conducted by Armin Jordan on an import label.

Bernstein, New York Philharmonic. (B)
CBS MY 37769 (LP, CS)

Jordan, Orchestre National de France.
Erato 75079 (D-LP)

Maazel, Berlin Philharmonic. (B)
DG Musikfest 413 250-1 (LP); 413 250-4 (CS)

Ernest Chausson   1855-1899

Poème for Violin and Orchestra, Op. 25

At full price Perlman is the usual first choice for the opulent approach, Kyung-Wha Chung for a more intimate interpretation, with Igor Oistrakh challenging Perlman at budget level. All three have exactly the same couplings: Ravel's *Tzigane,* and the HAVANAISE and INTRODUCTION AND RONDO CAPRICCIOSO of Saint-Saëns. Also good at budget price is Milstein, coupled with Saint-Saëns: CONCERTO FOR VIOLIN NO. 3.

Kyung-Wha Chung, Dutoit, Royal Philharmonic.
London CS 7073 (LP, CS)

Milstein, Fistoulari, Philharmonia Orchestra. (B)
Angel RL-32056 (LP, CS)

I. Oistrakh, Rozhdestvensky, Moscow Radio Symphony. (B)
Quintessence 7132 (LP, CS)

Perlman, Martinon, Orchestre de Paris.
Angel S-37118 (LP, CS)

Antonin Dvořák   1841-1904

Carnival Overture, Op. 92

Maazel has the most brilliant sound on his full-price recording, available on CD, with SYMPHONY NO. 9. The same coupling obtains on Giulini's vivid budget version. Fiedler and Szell are also excellent budgets, Fiedler with three other pieces conducted by William Steinberg (TILL EULENSPIEGEL'S MERRY PRANKS by Richard Strauss, THE SORCERER'S APPRENTICE by Dukas, and DANSE MACABRE by Saint-Saëns); and Szell with Dvořák's SLAVONIC DANCES and Smetana's THE MOLDAU and BARTERED BRIDE DANCES.

Fiedler, Boston Symphony. (B)
RCA AGL1-3967 (LP, CS)

Giulini, Philharmonia Orchestra. (B)
Seraphim S-60045 (LP, CS)

Maazel, Vienna Philharmonic.
DG 2532 079 (D-LP); 3302 079 (CS); 410 032-2 (CD)

Szell, Cleveland Orchestra. (B)
CBS MY 36716 or Odyssey Y 30049 (LP, CS)

Concerto in b for Cello, Op. 104

The recent digital-and-CD Lynn Harrell recording, with Ashkenazy conducting, looks like a winner on paper but got tepid to venomous reviews for the cellist's excessive interpretive point-making. Far more illuminating, if harder to find, is the noble digital-and-CD reading from Sweden by cellist Frans Helmerson and conductor Neeme Järvi, including a bonus of the lovely *Silent Woods*.

The great Rostropovich has recorded this work six times. The best all-around buy for performance, sound quality and price is his budget with Sir Adrian Boult. Fournier and Szell are excellent as well on another budget; some critics rate them above all others.

Fournier, Szell, Berlin Philharmonic. (B)
DG Privilege 2535 106 (LP); 3335 106 (CS)

Helmerson, Järvi, Gothenburg Symphony.
Bis 245 (D-LP, CS, CD)

Rostropovich, Boult, Royal Philharmonic. (B)
Seraphim S-60136 (LP, CS)

Quartet No. 12 in F, Op. 96, "American"

The classic Quartetto Italiano recording having recently been deleted, there is no great reason to pay full price when there are two such outstanding budgets as those by the Janáček and Concord Quartets. The former is coupled with Quartet No. 9, the latter with Borodin's QUARTET NO. 2. Virtually all critics have raved about the Concord Quartet's reading, which *Fanfare* for instance proclaimed "competitive with every other version regardless of price."

Janáček Quartet. (B)
London Stereo Treasury STS 15207 (LP)

Concord Quartet. (B)
Turnabout 37009 (LP); CT-7009 (CS)

Slavonic Dances, Op. 46, 72

All listed recordings contain highlights from among the best-loved of these short orchestral pieces, and all are budgets. The Reiner was already mentioned under Brahms: HUNGARIAN DANCES, and the Szell under Dvořák's CARNIVAL OVERTURE. Kertész and Kubelik are both coupled with works by Smetana, the former with THE MOLDAU and BARTERED BRIDE OVERTURE AND DANCES, the latter with THE MOLDAU and *From Bohemia's Fields and Meadows.*

Kertész, Israel Philharmonic. (B)
London Stereo Treasury STS 15409 (LP)

Kubelik, Bavarian Radio Symphony. (B)
DG Musikfest 413 251-1 (LP); 413 251-4 (CS)

Reiner, Vienna Philharmonic. (B)
London Stereo Treasury STS 15009 (LP)

Szell, Cleveland Orchestra. (B)
CBS MY 36716 or Odyssey Y 30049 (LP, CS)

Symphony No. 7 in d, Op. 70

Elsewhere in this book I have excused myself from listing the Carlos Paita recordings on the Lodia label as being too expensive and too difficult to find in stores. Besides, in most cases only one major reviewer was even making mention of these versions, and one might suspect a personal crusade. But in this case, with the *Penguin Guide, Stereo Review,* and *Gramophone* all naming Paita's Seventh as the best performance and most brilliant recording of it ever made, I can ill ignore it. Just remember Lodia records cost about twice as much as normal full price discs.

For the more practical purse the three budgets by Giulini, Monteux, and Szell will do nicely. Szell is available only in a low-price three record set of Dvořák's three last and greatest symphonies.

Giulini, London Philharmonic. (B)
Angel RL-32086 (LP, CS)

Monteux, London Symphony. (B)
London Stereo Treasury STS 15157 (LP)

Paita, Philharmonic Symphony.
Lodia 782 (LP, CS)

Szell, Cleveland Orchestra. (B)
(3) Columbia D3S 814 (LP)

Symphony No. 8 in G, Op. 88

Of recent full-price versions Marriner's has won widespread affection for its irresistibly sunny interpretation, warmly recorded. The budget versions by Karajan, Kertész, Szell, and Walter have all been chosen by their partisans, at some time or other, as "the best." Pick your favorite conductor and you should be happy. Note that Karajan's budget is generally considered superior to his full price recording which is also available; Kertész has a coupling of the Scherzo Capriccioso; Szell is available in the three-symphony set mentioned under SYMPHONY NO. 7 or on a separate single disc/cassette; Walter has a bonus of Brahms: VARIATIONS ON A THEME BY HAYDN, and is available on CD.

Karajan, Vienna Philharmonic. (B)
London Jubilee 41043 (LP, CS)

Kertész, London Symphony. (B)
London Stereo Treasury STS 15526 (LP)

Marriner, Minnesota Orchestra.
Philips 6514 050 (D-LP); 7337 050 (CS)

Szell, Cleveland Orchestra. (B)
(3) Columbia D3S 814 (LP)

Walter, Columbia Symphony. (B)
CBS MP 38889 (LP, CS); CBS Sony DC 113 (CD)

Symphony No. 9 in e, Op. 95, "From the New World"

Though most musicians would call the Seventh Dvořák's greatest symphony, the Ninth is unquestionably his most popular. In fact, a recent survey of American orchestras showed that it is programmed in concert more than any other symphony by anybody, including Beethoven.

Not surprisingly, there is a large number of recordings. The recent digital-and-CD recordings by Maazel and Solti have had the best reviews for orchestral playing and engineering, though both recordings have some detractors. The new digital Neumann version also has many admirers for its crisp, colorful, and idiomatic approach.

Beyond these three one may safely stay with the wide array of fine budgets as listed below. Be aware that there are *two* Kertész budget recordings, one from 1961, the other from 1967; only the newer one is listed. Giulini and Maazel each include the CARNIVAL OVERTURE, and Kertész has the *Othello Overture;* none of the others has couplings.

Giulini, Philharmonia Orchestra. (B)
Seraphim S-60045 (LP, CS)

Horenstein, Royal Philharmonic. (B)
Quintessence 7001 (LP, CS)

Kertész, London Symphony. (B)
London Jubilee 41022 (LP, CS)

Kubelik, Vienna Philharmonic. (B)
London Stereo Treasury STS 15007 (LP)

Maazel, Vienna Philharmonic.
DG 2532 079 (D-LP); 3302 079 (CS); 410 032-2 (CD)

Neumann, Czech Philharmonic.
Pro Arte PAD-157 (D-LP, CS)

Solti, Chicago Symphony.
London 410 116-1 (D-LP); 410 116-4 (CS); 410 116-2 (CD)

Szell, Cleveland Orchestra. (B)
CBS MY 37763 (LP, CS); or (2) Columbia MG 30371 (LP) (with Beethoven: SYMPHONY NO. 5 *and Schubert:* SYMPHONY NO. 8) *or (3) Columbia D3S 814 (LP) (with* SYMPHONIES NOS. 7 AND 8)

Walter, Columbia Symphony. (B)
Odyssey Y 30045 (LP, CS); CBS Sony 35 DC 89 (CD)

César Franck   1822-1890

Pièce héroïque

This is the most famous of Franck's fine organ works, of which the three famous *Chorales* are probably the greatest. All four works are on one budget record with the great Marcel Dupré, though the sound is not the best. Kinder on the ears but not on the purse is Michael Murray's digital record "Encores à la Française," with the *Pièce héroïque* and several other popular short organ works by other composers. Import shops may have André Isoir's excellent disc coupled with the *Cantabile* and *Grande pièce symphonique*.

Dupré. (B)
Mercury 75006 (LP)

Isoir.
Calliope 1920 (LP); 4920 (CS)

Murray.
Telarc 10069 (D-LP)

Sonata in A for Violin and Piano

There are three extremely fine full-price recordings. The oldest (1970) is by Perlman and Ashkenazy, and is still first choice of many critics. Coupling is the Brahms Horn Trio with Barry Tuckwell. Some prefer the more aristocratic and inward version by Kyung-Wha Chung and Radu Lupu (with Debussy's Sonata No. 3 for Violin and Piano); and the most recent version with Danczowska and Zimerman on DG has very strong reviews as well, though its coupling of Szymanowski's *Mythes* is hardly "basic library" material. The exciting "live" recording with Oistrakh and Richter is the best budget, coupled with Brahms's Sonata No. 3 for Violin and Piano.

Kyung-Wha Chung, Lupu.
London CS 7171 (LP)

D. Oistrakh, Richter. (B)
Quintessence 7133 (LP, CS)

Perlman, Ashkenazy.
London CS 6628 (LP)

Symphonic Variations for Piano and Orchestra

Most of the recordings of this work are on budget disc and tape. Three stand above the rest: Moravec is breathtakingly poetic in both this and the Schumann CONCERTO FOR PIANO; Curzon is exceptionally lyrical and thoughtful, coupled with one of the finest versions of Grieg: CONCERTO FOR PIANO (plus the delightful little *Scherzo* by Litolff); and Casadesus is the authoritative old classic (though the sound is rather hissy) with d'Indy's SYMPHONY ON A FRENCH MOUNTAIN AIR.

Casadesus, Ormandy, Philadelphia Orchestra.
Odyssey Y 31274 (LP, CS)

Curzon, Boult, London Philharmonic. (B)
London Stereo Treasury STS 15407 (LP, CS)

Moravec, Neumann, Czech Philharmonic. (B)
Quintessence 7153 (LP, CS)

Symphony in d

The classic recording by which all others are measured is the legendary Monteux, and no library should be without it. Unfortunately, RCA has recently almost doubled the price of the disc on the excuse of remastering the recording; the sonics have improved slightly, but the pressing has not.

All of the other listed recordings are budgets. Barenboim was recommended earlier under Berlioz: ROMAN CARNIVAL OVERTURE. Karajan's LES PRELUDES, and Andrew Davis offers Fauré's PELLEAS ET MELISANDE. The only performance to directly challenge Monteux is that by Cantelli; its 1954 sound is unbelievably good and RCA has spared us the favor of "improving" it.

Barenboim, Orchestre de Paris. (B)
DG Signature 410 833-1 (LP); 410 833-4 (CS)

Boult, New Symphony Orchestra of London. (B)
Quintessence 7050 (LP, CS)

Cantelli, NBC Symphony. (B)
RCA AGL1-4083 (LP, CS)

A. Davis, New Philharmonia. (B)
CBS MY 38471 (LP, CS)

Karajan, Orchestre de Paris. (B)
Angel RL-32133 (LP, CS)

Monteux, Chicago Symphony.
RCA ATL1-4156 (LP, CS)

Edvard Grieg   1843-1907

Concerto in a for Piano, Op. 16

The beautiful Bishop-Davis recording has recently been deleted, and I have perhaps added to the misery by dropping the sublime Lipatti-Galliera version for sonic reasons (see under Schumann: CONCERTO FOR PIANO). For consolation you might turn to the Curzon budget recording paired with Rachmaninoff: RHAPSODY ON A THEME OF PAGANINI: or the newer and sonically superior Zimerman disc with the classic coupling of Schumann: CONCERTO FOR PIANO.

Curzon, Fjeldstad, London Symphony. (B)
London Stereo Treasury STS 15047 (LP, CS)

Rubinstein, Wallenstein, RCA Symphony.
RCA ARL1-4409 (LP) or with Rachmaninoff: CONCERTO FOR PIANO NO. 2 *and Tchaikovsky:* CONCERTO FOR PIANO NO. 1 *on (2)* RCA VCS-7070 **(B)**

Zimerman, Karajan, Berlin Philharmonic.
DG 2532 043 (D-LP); 3302 043 (CS)

Peer Gynt Suites Nos. 1, 2, Op. 46, 55

The best combination of great playing and brilliant sound is Karajan's newer DG; the coupling of *Pelléas and Mélisande* by Sibelius is not one of our "basic" pieces, but it is a fine one and gorgeously performed. Karajan's budget disc does not include all of the music from the suites, but it is an attractive anthology album with additional excerpts from Tchaikovsky: NUTCRACKER, SWAN LAKE, and SLEEPING BEAUTY, and from Johann Strauss: DIE FLEDERMAUS.

Fiedler's bright recording, coupled with a lively NUTCRACKER SUITE by Tchaikovsky remains a good choice; and Bernstein offers a striking, if slightly eccentric, version coupled with FINLANDIA and VALSE TRISTE by Sibelius. For those who want the complete *Peer Gynt* incidental music, not just the Suites, the 1957 Beecham recording at budget price is the irreplaceable classic.

Beecham, Royal Philharmonic. (B)
Angel RL-32026 (LP, CS)

Bernstein, New York Philharmonic. (B)
CBS MY 36718 (LP, CS)

Fiedler, Boston Pops.
London SPC 21142 (LP, CS)

Karajan, Berlin Philharmonic.
DG 2532 068 (D-LP); 3302 068 (CS); 410 026-2 (CD)

Karajan, Vienna Philharmonic. (B)
London Stereo Treasury STS 15208 (LP)

Edouard Lalo   1823-1892

Symphonie espagnole for Violin and Orchestra, Op. 21

Perlman's rich and rhythmic version with Barenboim has sup-
planted the older Perlman-Previn version with most reviewers.
Coupling is the Berlioz *Rêverie et caprice.* Zukerman's performance is a shade less exciting than Perlman's, but the recorded
sound is warmer and the coupling of Bruch: CONCERTO FOR VIO-
LIN NO. 1 far more "basic."

Bruch is also the pairing on the "old standard" Stern version
now at budget price. The budget Menuhin still glitters and adds
the HAVANAISE and INTRODUCTION AND RONDO CAPRICCIOSO by
Saint-Saëns.

Menuhin, Goossens, Philharmonia Orchestra. (B)
Seraphim S-60370 (LP, CS)

Perlman, Barenboim, Orchestre de Paris.
DG 2532 011 (D-LP); 3302 011 (CS); 400 032-2 (CD)

Stern, Ormandy, Philadelphia Orchestra. (B)
CBS MY 37811 (LP, CS)

Zukerman, Mehta, Los Angeles Philharmonic.
Columbia M 35132 (LP, CS)

Franz Liszt   1811-1886

Concerti (2) for Piano and Orchestra

The Richter recording has long stood a head taller than all others in
this repertoire. The record has recently disappeared from the cata-

log and I am forced to presume that Philips will be reissuing it at budget price. Watch for that, or look for a remaindered copy of the original, Philips 835 474. Next best choice is Brendel at full price, with a bonus of the *Totentanz*. There is no safely recommendable budget. Vásáry would come closest, but though the Schwann Catalog is still showing a cassette number I could not find it in DG's own current catalog; the LP is definitely out of print.

Brendel, Haitink, London Philharmonic.
Philips 6500 374 (LP)

Hungarian Rhapsodies — Orchestral Versions (6)

Listings are limited to recordings which contain at least the most famous of these colorful works — No. 2. Dorati has already been recommended under Dvořák: SLAVONIC DANCES. Karajan has three recordings; the best deal is the one listed, with couplings of LES PRELUDES and *Mazeppa*. Stokowski was in his element with No. 2, and his budget disc has equally ebullient readings of Enesco's RUMANIAN RHAPSODY NO. 1, and Smetana's BARTERED BRIDE OVERTURE. It is true that real Hungarians seem to get into this music more than others; a good example of the power of love and commitment can be heard in the recording of Nos. 2, 3, 4, and 6 by the provincial Szeged Symphony conducted by Tamás Pál, available in import shops.

Dorati, Detroit Symphony.
London CS 7119 (LP, CS)

Karajan, Berlin Philharmonic. (B)
DG Privilege 2535 110 (LP); 3335 110 (CS)

Pál, Szeged Symphony.
Hungaroton 12062 (LP, CS)

Stokowski, RCA Victor Symphony. (B)
RCA AGL1-3880 (LP, CS)

Les Préludes (Symphonic Poem No. 3)

A just and simple solution is to stick with the Boult recommended under Franck: SYMPHONY, or the Karajan listed above under HUNGARIAN RHAPSODIES — both budgets.

Boult, New Symphony Orchestra of London. (B)
Quintessence 7050 (LP, CS)

Karajan, Berlin Philharmonic. (B)
DG Privilege 2535 110 (LP); 3335 110 (CS)

Sonata in b for Piano

The most famous recording of this work is the budget disc by Sir Clifford Curzon, available according to the London Records catalog but, like Curzon's Mozart piano concerto disc (q.v.), not appearing in the Schwann Catalog. Apparently Mr. Schwann's computer does not accept Curzon entries, among other things (Tchaikovsky's *Overture 1812* was missing entirely from the August, 1984 issue). If this recording really disappears altogether, the best alternative is Argerich's full-price version.

Argerich.
DG 2530 193 (LP)

Curzon. (B)
London Stereo Treasury STS 15552 (LP, CS)

Jules Massenet   1842-1912

Thais: Méditation

Massenet was the master of French *suavité,* and the only composer to raise sentimentality to the level of art. This lush piece for violin and orchestra has been jerking tears for decades. The late Michael Rabin could do just about anything on the violin and this budget record ("Michael Rabin — In Memoriam") shows every aspect of his talent, from the sultriness of the *Méditation* to the flashing lightning of Paganini's *Moto Perpetuo.* Included is the INTRODUCTION AND RONDO CAPRICCIOSO of Saint-Saëns.

Rabin, F. Slatkin, Hollywood Bowl Symphony. (B)
Seraphim S-60199 (LP, CS)

Modest Mussorgsky   1839-1881

A Night on Bald Mountain

No shortage of good recordings here! For Leibowitz, Maazel and Slatkin, see PICTURES AT AN EXHIBITION. Barenboim is discussed under Borodin: PRINCE IGOR, Rostropovich and Solti under Glinka: RUSSLAN AND LUDMILA. Bernstein's record is one of the most apt and striking he ever made, with THE SORCERER'S APPREN-TICE of Dukas, TILL EULENSPIEGEL'S MERRY PRANKS of Richard Strauss, and the DANSE MACABRE of Saint-Saëns. Stokowski, like Leibowitz, doctors the score but is exciting anyway; his couplings are Stravinsky's FIREBIRD SUITE and Tchaikovsky's MARCHE SLAVE.

Fiedler has an enjoyable anthology in beautiful sound with bonuses of Tchaikovsky's OVERTURE 1812, Bernstein's CANDIDE OVERTURE, Bach's *Toccata and Fugue in d* in an orchestral tran-scription, Khachaturian's *Sabre Dance* from *Gayne,* and Sousa's *The Stars and Stripes Forever.*

Barenboim, Chicago Symphony. (B)
DG Privilege 2536 379 (LP); 3336 379 (CS)

Bernstein, New York Philharmonic.
Columbia MS 7165 (LP)

Fiedler, Boston Pops.
DG 2584 019 (LP)

Leibowitz, Royal Philharmonic. (B)
Quintessence 7059 (LP, CS)

Maazel, Cleveland Orchestra.
Telarc 10042 (D-LP, CD)

Rostropovich, Orchestre de Paris.
Angel S-37464 (LP, CS)

L. Slatkin, St. Louis Symphony. (B)
Turnabout 34633 (LP); CT-2109 (CS)

Solti, London Symphony.
London CS 6785 (LP, CS)

Stokowski, London Symphony.
London SPC 21026 (LP)

Pictures at an Exhibition (orch. Ravel)

Maazel's famous digital recording is now available also on CD; it was a landmark of the "early digital era" (how time flies) and is still the favorite of many listeners. Some critics dissent, however, scoring the performance as humorless and unsubtle. The more recent digital-and-CD Solti recording has superseded Maazel in the eyes and ears of some reviewers, though Solti too has been accused of insensitivity. Maazel is coupled with A NIGHT ON BALD MOUNTAIN, Solti with Ravel's *Tombeau de Couperin*. Abbado is also digital and available on CD, with a coupling of Ravel's LA VALSE. Most critics like Abbado's *Pictures* but nobody rates it first choice. That designation more often goes (at lease among full-price versions) to one of three analog recordings: Giulini (with Prokofiev: SYMPHONY NO. 1), Karajan (with Ravel: BOLERO), or Muti (with Stravinsky: FIREBIRD SUITE).

One of the most thrilling older performances is that by Reiner; RCA has remastered it beautifully but its full price seems unfair. If lower cost and solid musical qualities mean more to you than fancy engineering, there are four excellent true budgets to choose from: Leibowitz (with A NIGHT ON BALD MOUNTAIN and DANSE MACABRE by Saint-Saëns); Mackerras (with the *Prelude to Khovanshchina);* Slatkin (with A NIGHT ON BALD MOUNTAIN); and Szell — of which more in a moment. In my earlier edition I called Slatkin and the St. Louis Symphony "less well-known artists," and referred to their record as a "sleeper." In the interval they have become very well-known indeed as one of America's most successful recording teams. Their budget disc remains highly competitive, even with the reissued classic Reiner.

Returning to Szell, his version if not the very best is certainly excellent, but what makes his record one of the great bargains in the catalog is the coupling with the complete original piano solo version of *Pictures* in the legendary 1958 recording by Sviatoslav Richter. For the piano version alone Ashkenazy's new full-price digital version (coupled only with four shorter piano pieces by other Russian composers) naturally has far better sound than Richter, but though excellent does not usurp the older artist's artistic throne.

Abbado, London Symphony.
DG 2532 057 (D-LP); 3302 057 (CS); 410 032-2 (CD)

Ashkenazy (piano solo).
London LDR 71124 (D-LP, CS)

Giulini, Chicago Symphony.
DG 2530 783 (LP); 3300 783 (CS)

Karajan, Berlin Philharmonic.
DG 139 010 (LP); 923 018 (CS)

Leibowitz, Royal Philharmonic. (B)
Quintessence 7059 (LP, CS)

Maazel, Cleveland Orchestra.
Telarc 10042 (D-LP, CD)

Mackerras, New Philharmonia. (B)
Vanguard Cardinal 10116 (LP); CA-471188 (CS)

Muti, Philadelphia Orchestra.
Angel S-37539 (LP, CS)

Reiner, Chicago Symphony.
RCA ATL1-4268 (LP, CS)

Slatkin, St. Louis Symphony. (B)
Turnabout 34633 (LP); CT-2109 (CS)

Solti, Chicago Symphony.
London LDR 10040 (D-LP, CS); 400 051-2 (CD)

Szell, Cleveland Orchestra (orch.); Richter (piano solo). (B)
Odyssey Y 32223 (LP, CS)

Jacques Offenbach   1819-1880

Gaîté Parisienne (arr. Rosenthal)

Manuel Rosenthal created this ballet from Offenbach tunes in the
late 1930s. His and Previn's recordings are the only ones to give the
score absolutely complete. Previn has the better sonics, Rosenthal
the more vivacious and authoritative interpretation. Both budgets
are good with abridged versions, and both have delightful (if, for
this book's purpose, "non-basic") couplings. Fiedler leads
Respighi's *La Boutique fantasque* ("The Fantastic Toyshop," based
on Rossini melodies), and Fistoulari conducts the ballet *Les Syl-
phides,* an orchestration made from Chopin piano music.

Fiedler, Boston Pops. (B)
RCA AGL1-2701 (LP, CS)

Fistoulari, Royal Philharmonic. (B)
Quintessence 7029 (LP, CS)

Previn, Pittsburgh Symphony.
Philips 6514 367 (D-LP); 7337 367 (CS); 411 039-2 (CD)

Rosenthal, Monte Carlo Opera Orchestra.
Angel S-37209 (LP, CS)

Orpheus in the Underworld: Overture

Bernstein's peppy version is available on the single-disc budget described under Chabrier: ESPANA, or in the double budget discussed under Glinka: RUSSLAN AND LUDMILA OVERTURE. At full price the Maazel disc is wonderfully bubbly in a mostly Johann Strauss program including the *Blue Danube Waltz,* but this is a live New Year's Eve (1980) concert in Vienna with applause included which may or may not bother you.

Bernstein, New York Philharmonic. (B)
CBS MY 37769 (LP, CS) or (2) Columbia MG 35188 (LP)

Maazel, Vienna Philharmonic.
DG 2532 002 (D-LP); 3302 002 (CS)

Amilcare Ponchielli   1834-1886

La Gioconda: Dance of the Hours

The ultra-low price Fricsay recording described under Borodin: PRINCE IGOR is undoubtedly a "best buy." For a similar ballet program with different selections and newer sound Kunzel's "Dances from the Opera" album is quite pleasurable at the lower end of the full-price spectrum.

Fricsay, Berlin Radio Symphony. (B)
DG Musikfest 413 255-1 (LP); 413 255-4 (CS)

Kunzel, Cincinnati Pops.
Vox 9019 (D-LP, CS)

Nikolai Rimsky-Korsakov 1844-1908

Capriccio espagnol, Op. 34

Maazel has a real knack for highly-colored Russian Romantic music. His full-price Cleveland recording has gorgeous sound and stunning couplings of the RUSSIAN EASTER OVERTURE and *Le Coq d'or Suite;* though the sound is older, some think the performances even better on his Berlin Philharmonic budget described under Chabrier: ESPANA. The Barenboim and Szell budgets are discussed under Borodin: PRINCE IGOR, and the full-price Rostropovich under Glinka: RUSSLAN AND LUDMILA OVERTURE.

Barenboim, Chicago Symphony. (B)
DG Privilege 2536 379 (LP); 3336 379 (CS)

Maazel, Berlin Philharmonic. (B)
DG Musikfest 413 250-1 (LP); 413 250-4 (CS)

Maazel, Cleveland Orchestra.
London CS 7196 (LP)

Rostropovich, Orchestre de Paris.
Angel S-37464 (LP, CS)

Szell, Cleveland Orchestra. (B)
(2) Columbia M2X 787 (LP)

Russian Easter Overture, Op. 36

The Barenboim and Markevitch budgets are recommended under Borodin: PRINCE IGOR; the full-price Maazel under CAPRICCIO ESPAGNOL.

Barenboim, Chicago Symphony. (B)
DG Privilege 2536 379 (LP); 3336 379 (CS)

Maazel, Cleveland Orchestra.
London CS 7196 (LP)

Markevitch, London Symphony. (B)
Philips Festivo 6570 191 (LP); 7310 191 (CS)

Scheherazade, Op. 35

Beecham, Haitink, and Previn have been the favorites in this work for some time. Beecham's magical standard-setter dates from 1958 and is still available on budget; the sound is not brilliant by today's standards, but is quite acceptable. Haitink has recently been deleted and may show up again from Philips on budget or CD. Previn's digital version has beautiful sound and emphasizes the score's lushness.

Kondrashin's brilliantly recorded analog-and-CD version has the critics split over his rather personal interpretation, but most find it enjoyably imaginative. The old Monteux is a good budget alternative. Colorful and atmospheric as the 1961 Ansermet budget is, I think Beecham is still better at the same price, and Ansermet's coupling of Borodin's POLOVTSIAN DANCES is below par.

Beecham, Royal Philharmonic. (B)
Angel RL-32027 (LP, CS)

Kondrashin, Concertgebouw.
Philips 9500 681 (LP); 7300 776 (CS); 400 021-2 (CD)

Monteux, London Symphony. (B)
London Stereo Treasury STS 15158 (LP, CS)

Previn, Vienna Philharmonic.
Philips 6514 231 (D-LP); 7337 231 (CS)

Camille Saint-Saëns   1835-1921

Carnival of the Animals

The old London Symphony version featuring pianists Julius Katchen and Gary Graffman, with whimsical narration by Beatrice Lillie, is incomparably light and amusing and is now available at budget price. For better sound and orchestral playing, try Böhm's full-price version with the brothers Kontarsky at the pianos and Hermione Gingold telling the story. Both recordings are coupled with Prokofiev's PETER AND THE WOLF.

Previn's digital-and-CD recording has the best sound of all, but some reviewers think the *Carnival* a bit low on *joie de vivre*, and not every listener will want Ravel's *Mother Goose Suite*,

wonderful as it is, in place of the more traditional Prokofiev coupling. Incidentally, the pianists listed in the Schwann Catalog as
"V. & P. Jennings" are really Joseph Villa and Patricia Prattis Jennings. For an "authentic" *Carnival,* there is the sparkling original
version for chamber orchestra without narration by an ensemble
including the French String Trio and pianists Michel Béroff and
Jean-Philippe Collard. Coupling is the *Trumpet Septet* with
Maurice André.

Béroff, Collard, Trio à Cordes Français, Ensemble.
Angel S-37874 (LP, CS)

Gingold, A. & A. Kontarsky, Böhm, Vienna Philharmonic.
DG 2530 588 (LP)

Lillie, Katchen, Graffman, Henderson, London Symphony. (B)
London Jubilee 411 650-1 (LP); 411 650-4 (CS)

Villa, Jennings, Previn, Pittsburgh Symphony.
Philips 9500 973 (D-LP); 7300 973 (CS); 400 016-2 (CD)

Concerto No. 1 in a for Cello, Op. 33

There are now two digital recordings, Ma and Maazel outpointing
Harrell and Marriner with a majority of critics. Neither has a
"basic" coupling, Ma's being the Lalo Cello Concerto. The classic
recording is DuPré-Barenboim on Angel, but the sound is dated
and not every one likes DuPré's rather careless rhapsodic style —
not a clear choice at full price. Rostropovich-Giulini look promis-
ing on paper, especially with the only "basic" coupling; but most
critics think others are better in the Saint-Saëns, and the flipside
Dvořák CONCERTO FOR CELLO is rated by many as the least successful of Rostropovich's five recordings.

Ma, Maazel, Orchestre National de France.
CBS IM 35848 (D-LP, CS, CD)

Concerto No. 2 in g for Piano, Op. 22

Rogé and Dutoit are the current leaders here with the traditional
coupling of the composer's next-best-known concerto, No. 4. Rubinstein is the "classic" account, but the old record is still at full
price and coupled with Falla's NIGHTS IN THE GARDENS OF SPAIN,

of which there is a more recommendable Rubinstein version at lower price.

Rogé, Dutoit, Royal Philharmonic.
London CS 7253 (LP, CS)

Concerto No. 3 in b for Violin, Op. 61

Cho-Liang Lin is a fine player and his digital recording with an excellent Mendelssohn CONCERTO FOR VIOLIN is a better first choice at full price than those by Kyung-Wha Chung and Perlman, excellent as they are, but with "non-basic" couplings. The lesser-known Pierre Amoyal has been rated by reviewers as good as the more famous soloists; if you already have a satisfactory Mendelssohn, you might choose this disc with the HAVANAISE and INTRODUCTION AND RONDO CAPRICCIOSO. Milstein's solidly romantic version, paired with Chausson's POEME, is the best budget; the *Penguin Guide* does find Milstein "a bit short on charm and gentleness" — but then, so was Saint-Saëns!

Amoyal, Handley, New Philharmonia.
RCA ARL1-3438 (LP, CS)

Cho-Liang Lin, Thomas, Philharmonic Orchestra.
CBS IM 39007 (D-LP, CS, CD)

Milstein, Fistoulari, Philharmonia Orchestra. (B)
Angel RL-32056 (LP, CS)

Danse macabre, Op. 40

Barenboim is recommended under Berlioz: ROMAN CARNIVAL OVERTURE; Leibowitz under Mussorgsky: PICTURES AT AN EXHIBITION; Steinberg under Dvořák: CARNIVAL OVERTURE (with Fiedler); the budget Bernstein under Chabrier: ESPANA; and the full-price Bernstein under Mussorgsky: A NIGHT ON BALD MOUNTAIN. The only new recording to consider is Dutoit's, an all Saint-Saëns program with the three other tone poems and a march. This is a very idiomatic, well-played and well-recorded album, but for the beginning collector the couplings may not be "basic" enough.

Barenboim, Orchestre de Paris. (B)
DG Signature 410 833-1 (LP); 410 833-4 (CS)

Bernstein, New York Philharmonic. (B)
CBS MY 37769 (LP, CS)

Bernstein, New York Philharmonic.
Columbia MS 7165 (LP)

Dutoit, Philharmonia Orchestra.
London CS 7204 (LP)

Leibowitz, Paris Symphony. (B)
Quintessence 7059 (LP, CS)

Steinberg, Boston Symphony. (B)
RCA AGL1-3967 (LP, CS)

Havanaise; Introduction and Rondo Capriccioso

Only recordings containing both of these lively works for violin
and orchestra are listed here; one or the other of the pieces may
show up as fillers on various records recommended elsewhere in
this book.

Perlman is the usual first choice at full price, with Kyung-
Wha Chung preferred by those who like a smaller-scaled performance. Igor Oistrakh is the best budget. All three are coupled with
the Chausson POEME and Ravel's *Tzigane*. Amoyal is recommended above under CONCERTO FOR VIOLIN NO. 3, Menuhin under
Lalo: SYMPHONIE ESPAGNOLE.

Amoyal, Handley, New Philharmonia.
RCA ARL1-3438 (LP, CS)

Kyung-Wha Chung, Dutoit, Royal Philharmonic.
London CS 7073 (LP, CS)

Menuhin, Goossens, Philharmonia Orchestra. (B)
Seraphim S-60370 (LP, CS)

I. Oistrakh, Rozhdestvensky, Moscow Radio Symphony. (B)
Quintessence 7132 (LP, CS)

Perlman, Martinon, Orchestre de Paris.
Angel S-37118 (LP, CS)

Symphony No. 3 in c, Op. 78, "Organ"

This is one of the most difficult symphonies to record well. It cries
out for the "sonic spectacular" treatment, but the problem of bal-

ancing a full orchestra with a pipe organ is difficult, and it seems that non-French conductors have trouble balancing the lyrical and stentorian poles of the score.

The recent digital Karajan recording has unsatisfactory balances and the unidiomatic performance, as *High Fidelity* remarks, "veers from languid schmaltz to brutal vehemence." Barenboim's mid-70s recording solved the sonic problem rather well by recording the orchestra and organ in diffferent locations and mixing them later; but despite high praise from some quarters, many reviewers feel the performance is insensitively blatant. Ormandy's digital recording was previously listed here for sonics, but its eminence in that respect has faded and it was always short on inner poetry and vitality. The distortion-prone Paray recording and the murky Martinon no longer seem satisfactory, despite distinguished interpretations.

The most substantive of recent issues is that by Dutoit. The reading is stylish and well-shaped and most critics find the sonics superb, though there are a few dissenters. Munch is, overall, the most elegant and exuberant (i.e., French); I did not list it in the old edition because I felt a 1959 recording should not be at full price, but RCA's recent remastering has restored it to such aural splendor that it seems worth any price. The only budget worth bothering with is Ansermet's; the early stereo sound is quite decent, and the conductor finds more poetry in the music than anyone.

Ansermet, Segon, Suisse Romande.
London Stereo Treasury STS 15154 (LP)

Dutoit, Hurford, Montreal Symphony.
London LDR 71090 (D-LP, CS); 410 201-2 (CD)

Munch, Zamkochian, Boston Symphony.
RCA ARP1-4440 (LP, CS)

Bedřich Smetana   1824-1884

Bartered Bride: Overture and Dances

All the best choices are budgets. Bernstein (see under Glinka: RUSSLAN AND LUDMILA OVERTURE) and Stokowski (see under Liszt: HUNGARIAN RHAPSODIES) give the Overture only; Szell (see under Borodin: PRINCE IGOR and elsewhere) has only the Dances. Kertész (see under Dvořák: SLAVONIC DANCES) is the only one with both selections on one disc.

Bernstein, New York Philharmonic. (B)
(2) Columbia MG 35188 (LP)

Kertész, Israel Philharmonic. (B)
London Stereo Treasury STS 15409 (LP)

Stokowski, RCA Victor Symphony. (B)
RCA AGL1-3880 (LP, CS)

Szell, Cleveland Orchestra. (B)
CBS MY 36716 or Odyssey Y 30049 (LP, CS); or (2) Columbia M2X 787 (LP)

The Moldau

The Kertész, Stokowski, and Szell recordings listed under BARTERED BRIDE above all contain this beloved tone poem (I will not repeat the catalog numbers below). In addition, there is Kubelik's super-low Musikfest budget mentioned under Dvořák: SLAVONIC DANCES. And if you want to get away from "anthology" albums and more into Smetana there is Kubelik's slightly higher budget on Privilege with three more of the tone poems.

Kubelik, Boston Symphony. (B)
DG Musikfest 413 251-1 (LP); 413 251-4 (CS)

Kubelik, Boston Symphony. (B)
DG Privilege 2535 132 (LP); 3335 132 (CS)

Johann Strauss II 1825-1899

Waltzes, Polkas, Overtures

There are dozens of good-to-excellent recordings of the popular short works of "The Waltz King." I can only suggest here a few of the more prominent conductors and the albums which contain the best-loved examples from Strauss's nearly 500 compositions. Just a few hints: the budget Boskovsky is the "most basic" of that conductor's many idiomatic Strauss records, with the six most famous waltzes all together; the digital Karajan record is the most recommendable CD; and the Maazel was previously recommended under Offenbach: ORPHEUS IN THE UNDERWORLD OVERTURE — almost all the rest of the album is by the Strauss family.

Boskovsky, Vienna Philharmonic. (B)
London Jubilee 41036 (LP, CS)

Dorati, London Philharmonic. (B)
London Stereo Treasury STS 15545 (LP, CS)

Fiedler, Boston Pops.
DG 2584 008 (LP); 3374 008 (CS) or, with different selections
London SPC 21144 (LP, CS)

Horenstein, Vienna State Opera Orchestra / Vienna Symphony. (B)
Quintessence 7051 and 7061 (LP, CS)

Karajan, Berlin Philharmonic.
DG 2532 025 (D-LP); 3302 025 (CS); 400 025-2 (CD)

Karajan, Vienna Philharmonic. (B)
London Stereo Treasury STS 15163 (LP, CS)

Maazel, Vienna Philharmonic.
DG 2532 002 (LP); 3302 002 (CS)

Ormandy, Philadelphia Orchestra. (B)
RCA AGL1-3786 (LP, CS)

Reiner, Chicago Symphony and **Fiedler, Boston Pops. (B)**
RCA LSC-5005 (LP); RK-1190 (CS)

Szell, Cleveland Orchestra. (B)
Odyssey Y 30053 (LP)

Peter Ilyich Tchaikovsky   1840-1893

Capriccio italien, Op. 45

None of the high-priced "sonic spectacular" versions has the unqualified endorsement of a majority of critics surveyed. Much more favorably received is the analog Rostropovich, full of temperament, with good couplings of the NUTCRACKER SUITE and the *Andante Cantabile*.

The rest of the best are budgets. Szell's is part of his double set mentioned under Borodin: PRINCE IGOR and elsewhere. Ormandy's record, with MARCHE SLAVE and OVERTURE 1812, was a best seller for years at full price. Dorati's record, with just the OVERTURE 1812, has been a best seller since the first days of stereo, and its sound still amazes — a real classic of the catalog. The surprise is Alwyn, a virtually unknown conductor whose readings of OVER-TURE 1812, MARCHE SLAVE, and the *Capriccio italien* are both musical and exciting with excellent sound.

Alwyn, London Symphony. (B)
London Stereo Treasury STS 15221 (LP, CS)

Dorati, Minneapolis Symphony. (B)
Mercury 75001 (LP, CS)

Ormandy, Philadelphia Orchestra. (B)
RCA AGL1-5219 (LP, CS)

Rostropovich, Berlin Philharmonic.
DG 2531 112 (LP); 3301 112 (CS)

Szell, Cleveland Orchestra. (B)
(2) Columbia M2X 787 (LP)

Concerto No. 1 in b-flat for Piano, Op. 23

The legendary Cliburn recording of 1958 has sold over a million copies, and few have challenged it for power and passion. I suppose one cannot blame RCA for keeping it at full price. More recent in the full-price category is the very poetic account by Ashkenazy, available singly or in the collection described under Beethoven: CONCERTO FOR PIANO NO. 5. Gilels is splendid in a recent digital-and-CD version, but Mehta and the New York Philharmonic are not so I am not listing it; there is more to a piano concerto than the piano.

Three budgets command attention. Argerich-Dutoit is outstanding and preferred by most critics over the newer and more expensive Argerich-Kondrashin. Graffman-Szell are exciting and incisive, with couplings of three Rachmaninoff Preludes. Rubinstein is best obtained in the double-record set coupled with his famous readings of the Grieg CONCERTO FOR PIANO and Rachmaninoff's CONCERTO FOR PIANO NO. 2.

Argerich, Dutoit, Royal Philharmonic. (B)
DG Privilege 2535 295 (LP); 3335 295 (CS)

Ashkenazy, Maazel, London Symphony.
London CS 6360 (LP, CS); or with other famous concerti on (3) London CSP 12 (LP, CS) **(B)**

Cliburn, Kondrashin.
*RCA LSC-2252 (LP); RK-1002 (CS) or "high-tech" version on
RCA ARP1-4441 (LP, CS)*

Graffman, Szell, Cleveland Orchestra. (B)
CBS MY 37263 (LP, CS)

Rubinstein, Leinsdorf, Boston Symphony. (B)
(2) RCA VCS-7070 (LP)

Concerto in D for Violin, Op. 35

Many critics still call the old Heifetz recording, coupled with Mendelssohn: CONCERTO FOR VIOLIN, the most exciting ever. Of the
newest digital recordings Kyung-Wha Chung is the most admired, with the same coupling. Other excellent full-price choices
are Milstein and Zukerman, also with the Mendelssohn, and Perl-
man-Ormandy with *Sérénade mélancolique* (or in the three-
record "concerto box" described under Mendelssohn).

Among budgets David Oistrakh has no coupling, but is rated
by many reviewers as a second only to Heifetz in excitement; Stern
has previously been recommended under the Mendelssohn; and
the older Perlman version, with Wallenstein conducting, has a bonus of MARCHE SLAVE.

Heifetz, Reiner, Chicago Symphony.
*RCA LSC-3304 (LP); RK-1284 (CS); or "high-tech" version on
RCA ARP1-4567 (LP, CS)*

Kyung-Wha Chung, Dutoit, Montreal Symphony.
London LDR 71058 (D-LP, CS); 410 011-2 (CD)

Milstein, Abbado, Vienna Philharmonic.
DG 2530 359 (LP)

D. Oistrakh, Ormandy, Philadelphia Orchestra. (B)
Odyssey Y 30312 (LP, CS)

Perlman, Ormandy, Philadelphia Orchestra.
Angel SZ-37640 (LP); or (3) Angel SCZ-3912 (LP, CS)

Perlman, Wallenstein, London Symphony. (B)
Quintessence 7056 (LP, CS)

Stern, Ormandy, Philadelphia Orchestra. (B)
CBS MY 36724 (LP, CS)

Zukerman, Dorati, London Symphony.
Columbia MS 7313 (LP)

Francesca da Rimini, Op. 32

There is pretty general agreement that Rostropovich is best at full price, Giulini at budget. Both are coupled with ROMEO AND JULIET, and both lead performances of controlled passion. There is a marvelous Munch budget on Quintessence, but the coupling of the Bizet SYMPHONY is singularly inappropriate and the performance of it does not have much endorsement.

Giulini, Philharmonia Orchestra. (B)
Seraphim S-60311 (LP, CS)

Rostropovich, London Philharmonic.
Angel S-37528 (LP, CS)

Marche Slave, Op. 31

The Alwyn and Ormandy are recommended above under CAPRICCIO ITALIEN, the Stokowski under Mussorgsky: A NIGHT ON BALD MOUNTAIN, and the Freccia under the Perlman-Wallenstein CONCERTO FOR VIOLIN. In addition, Karajan at full price is musically sensitive with fine sound and pairings of OVERTURE 1812 and ROMEO AND JULIET; and the Boult budget is taken up mostly with Horenstein's powerful reading of SYMPHONY NO. 5.

Alwyn, London Symphony. (B)
London Stereo Treasury STS 15221 (LP, CS)

Boult, London Philharmonic. (B)
Quintessence 7002 (LP, CS)

Freccia, London Philharmonic. (B)
Quintessence 7056 (LP, CS)

Karajan, Berlin Philharmonic.
DG 139 029 (LP); 923 045 (CS)

Ormandy, Philadelphia Orchestra.
RCA AGL1-5219 (LP, CS)

Stokowski, London Symphony.
London SPC 21026 (LP)

Nutcracker, Op. 71 (Complete)

Ansermet and Dorati are both so wonderful it is impossible to choose between them; Dorati has the greater orchestra and newer sound, Ansermet good sound and a much lower price.

Ansermet, Suisse Romande. (B)
(2) London Stereo Treasury STS 15433/4 (LP, CS)

Dorati, Concertgebouw.
(2) Philips 6747 257 (LP); 7505 076 (CS)

Nutcracker (Excerpts)

The Karajan budget was recommended under Grieg: PEER GYNT. Ormandy has sumptuous sound and is available on a single record or in a budget box with highlights from the other two great Tchaikovsky ballets, SLEEPING BEAUTY and SWAN LAKE.

Karajan, Vienna Philharmonic. (B)
London Stereo Treasury STS 15208 (LP)

Ormandy, Philadelphia Orchestra.
RCA ARL1-0027 (LP, CS); or (3) RCA CRL3-1261 (LP) **(B)**

Nutcracker Suite, Op. 71a

Ansermet and Dorati are obvious choices, each with the standard Suite plus the "Suite No. 2." The other recordings listed have different couplings. The Karajan and Maazel are best in the digital-and-CD category, both coupled with ROMEO AND JULIET. For full-price analogs, Fiedler has already been recommended under Grieg: PEER GYNT and Rostropovich under CAPRICCIO ITALIEN.

There is a good Fiedler budget with excerpts from SWAN LAKE; and there are two good budgets with Boult — the Quintessence with SWAN LAKE and the Seraphim with SLEEPING BEAUTY highlights.

Ansermet, Suisse Romande. (B)
London Stereo Treasury STS 15569 (LP, CS)

Boult, New Symphony Orchestra of London. (B)
Quintessence 7010 (LP, CS)

Boult, Royal Philharmonic. (B)
Seraphim S-60176 (LP, CS)

Dorati, Concertgebouw.
Philips 9500 697 (LP); 7300 788 (CS)

Fiedler, Boston Pops.
London SPC 21142 (LP)

Fiedler, Boston Pops. (B)
RCA AGL1-5233 (LP, CS)

Karajan, Berlin Philharmonic.
DG 410 873-1 (D-LP); 410 873-4 (CS); 410 873-2 (CD)

Maazel, Cleveland Orchestra.
Telarc 10068 (D-LP, CD)

Rostropovich, Berlin Philharmonic.
DG 2531 112 (LP); 3301 112 (CS)

Overture 1812, Op. 49

Alwyn, Dorati, and Ormandy were previously listed under CA-
PRICCIO ITALIEN, Fiedler under Mussorgsky: A NIGHT ON BALD
MOUNTAIN, Karajan under MARCHE SLAVE, and Markevitch under
Borodin: PRINCE IGOR; all are recordings that have been around
for some time. Among newer high-tech issues Muti's digital version is the most recommendable for a combination of good sonics
and a performance that is both kinetically thrilling and musically
respectable. Kunzel is certainly the top choice for those to whom
audiophilic considerations are paramount; musically the recording cannot compare with the others for as *Gramophone*'s critic said
"the stars of this record are the cannon."

Alwyn, London Symphony. (B)
London Stereo Treasury STS 15221 (LP, CS)

Dorati, Minneapolis Symphony. (B)
Mercury 75001 (LP, CS)

Fiedler, Boston Pops.
DG 2584 019 (LP)

Karajan, Berlin Philharmonic.
DG 139 029 (LP); 923 045 (CS)

Kunzel, Cincinnati Symphony.
Telarc 10041 (D-LP, CD)

Markevitch, Concertgebouw. (B)
Philips Festivo 6570 191 (LP); 7310 191 (CS)

Muti, Philadelphia Orchestra.
Angel DS-37777 (D-LP, CS)

Ormandy, Philadelphia Orchestra. (B)
RCA AGL1-5219 (LP, CS)

Romeo and Juliet

Giulini and Rostropovich are discussed above under FRANCESCA DA RIMINI, the digital Karajan and Maazel recordings under NUT-CRACKER SUITE, and the analog Karajan under MARCHE SLAVE. Ozawa's unique record is one of the most beautiful he has ever made: the lovers are depicted very differently by three great composers, by means of Tchaikovsky's tone poem, excerpts from Prokofiev's ballet ROMEO AND JULIET, and highlights from the "dramatic symphony" *Roméo et Juliette* by Berlioz.

Giulini, Philharmonia Orchestra. (B)
Seraphim S-60311 (LP, CS)

Karajan, Berlin Philharmonic.
DG 139 029 (LP); 923 045 (CS)

Karajan, Berlin Philharmonic.
DG 410 873-1 (D-LP); 410 873-4 (CS); 410 873-2 (CD)

Maazel, Cleveland Orchestra.
Telarc 10068 (D-LP, CD)

Ozawa, San Francisco Symphony.
DG 2530 308 (LP); 3300 284 (CS)

Rostropovich, London Philharmonic.
Angel S-37528 (LP, CS)

Sleeping Beauty, Op. 66 (Complete)

Here Ansermet is the clear choice for both price and performance, even over Dorati, whose *Sleeping Beauty* has not had the same glowing reception as his NUTCRACKER.

Ansermet, Suisse Romande. (B)
(3) London Stereo Treasury STS 15496/8 (LP)

Sleeping Beauty (Excerpts)

Boult is recommended above under NUTCRACKER SUITE, the budget Karajan under Grieg: PEER GYNT. The full-price analog Karajan and Rostropovich recordings are both outstanding, each coupled with highlights from SWAN LAKE. For extended excerpts from *Sleeping Beauty* alone, Ormandy is best at full price (singly or in the budget box described under NUTCRACKER EXCERPTS), Monteux at budget price.

Boult, Royal Philharmonic. (B)
Seraphim S-60176 (LP, CS)

Karajan, Berlin Philharmonic.
DG 2530 195 (LP); 3300 205 (CS)

Karajan, Vienna Philharmonic. (B)
London Stereo Treasury STS 15179 (LP)

Ormandy, Philadelphia Orchestra.
RCA ARL1-0169 (LP, CS); or (3) RCA CRL3-1261 (LP) **(B)**

Rostropovich, Berlin Philharmonic.
DG 2531 111 (LP); 3301 111 (CS)

Swan Lake, Op. 20 (Complete)

A third win among the big three ballets for Ansermet. Though London charges full price in this case, the music is squeezed onto two discs instead of the three of the other (lesser?) versions.

Ansermet, Suisse Romande.
(2) London CSA 2204 (LP)

Swan Lake (Excerpts)

Boult and Fiedler have been previously recommended under NUTCRACKER SUITE, Karajan-Berlin and Rostropovich under SLEEPING BEAUTY EXCERPTS, and Karajan-Vienna under Grieg: PEER GYNT and elsewhere. For extended excerpts from *Swan Lake* alone, the situation is almost just as it was for SLEEPING BEAUTY: Ormandy at full price singly or in the budget three-ballet box, and Monteux at budget price; except that there is an all-*Swan Lake* highlights budget record from our champion, Ernest Ansermet.

Ansermet, Suisse Romande. (B)
London Stereo Treasury STS 15598 (LP, CS)

Boult, New Symphony Orchestra of London. (B)
Quintessence 7010 (LP, CS)

Fiedler, Boston Pops. (B)
RCA AGL1-5233 (LP, CS)

Karajan, Berlin Philharmonic.
DG 2530 195 (LP); 3300 205 (CS)

Karajan, Vienna Philharmonic. (B)
London Stereo Treasury STS 15208 (LP)

Monteux, London Symphony. (B)
Philips Festivo 6570 187 (LP)

Ormandy, Philadelphia Orchestra.
RCA ARL1-0030 (LP, CS); or (3) RCA CRL3-1261 (LP) **(B)**

Rostropovich, Berlin Philharmonic.
DG 2531 111 (LP); 3301 111 (CS)

Symphonies Nos. 4 in f, Op. 36; 5 in e, Op. 64; 6 in b, Op. 74, "Pathétique"

Because most conductors who are good in one of the great Tchaikovsky symphonies tend to be good in them all, I am treating
them here as an entity, with exceptions listed separately at the end.

Ashkenazy and Mravinsky at full and budget price respectively are, not surprisingly, the most Russian in their interpretations — vigorous, passionate, melancholy by turn, always compelling. Karajan is dramatic, polished, lushly recorded, Olympian in
his viewpoint. Bernstein divides critics: to some his readings are
ideally intense, to others they are overemphatic or even hysterical.
They are available in a budget-priced box. Muti's performances
crackle much in the Toscanini manner, sacrificing some charm in
the process; they have just been digitally remastered and are available in a box of all six Tchaikovsky symphonies, priced as four.

Ashkenazy, Philharmonia Orchestra.
*(#4) London CS 7144 (LP, CS); (#5) CS 7107 (LP, CS); (#6)
CS 7170 (LP, CS)*

Bernstein, New York Philharmonic. (B)
(3) Columbia D3S 781 (LP)

Karajan, Berlin Philharmonic.
*(#4) DG 2530 883 (LP); 3300 883 (CS); (#5) 2530 699 (LP);
3300 699 (CS); (#6) 2530 774 (LP); 3300 774 (CS)*

Mravinsky, Leningrad Philharmonic. (B)
*(#4) DG Privilege 2535 235 (LP); 3335 235 (CS); (#5) 2535 236
(LP); (#6) 2535 237 (LP); 3335 237 (CS); also, Nos. 4 and 5 on
separate cassette 410 569-4*

Muti, Philadelphia Orchestra. (B)
(6) Angel SFD-3966 (LP, CS)

In addition to these, there are some notable individual performances. Of Maazel's Vienna recordings from the '60s, only the direct and gripping No. 4 is now available, reissued at budget price. For No. 5, the budget Horenstein has already been recommended under Boult's MARCHE SLAVE. There is a wider choice for No. 6: of Abbado's series, once widely admired, only the Sixth is still available. Of Giulini's two attempts at this symphony, the older budget one is to be preferred as one of the conductor's noblest performances on disc. There is a budget of Karajan's 1964 account which many critics feel is the equal of or even superior to his newer, more expensive one. All three symphonies used to be available by Markevitch; now there is only a budget of No. 6. Like Ashkenazy and Mravinsky he is very Russian and exciting, though some think he overdoes the aggressiveness on occasion.

Abbado, Vienna Philharmonic.
(#6) DG 2530 350 (LP)

Giulini, Philharmonia Orchestra. (B)
(#6) Seraphim S-60031 (LP, CS)

Horenstein, New Philharmonia. (B)
(#5) Quintessence 7002 (LP, CS)

Karajan, Berlin Philharmonic. (B)
(#6) DG Privilege 2535 341 (LP); 3335 341 (CS)

Maazel, Vienna Philharmonic. (B)
(#4) London Jubilee 41059 (LP, CS)

Markevitch, London Symphony. (B)
(#6) Philips Festivo 6570 047 (LP); 7310 047 (CS)

Richard Wagner 1813-1883

Orchestral Selections

All of these recordings feature orchestral highlights (no singing, except occasionally for a few "Ho-jo-to-hos" in the *Ride of the Valkyries*) from the Wagner music dramas. Exactly which ones you want will depend on your favorite conductors and which pieces are on each program.

The most comprehensive collection is Szell's three-record budget box endorsed by all critics surveyed, and characterized by one as "beyond adequate praise." Of the high-tech versions Tennstedt's digital-and-CD recording of excerpts from DER RING DES NIBELUNGEN has had the best marks, and comparisons included Solti's similar format with the Vienna Philharmonic. Critics say Solti's older analog recording (listed below) is preferable. Karajan's two Angel albums are established favorites, and Haitink's single disc has lovely sound, musicianly performances, and pleasing sequencing.

Among several fine budgets, Horenstein and Kubelik include the SIEGFRIED IDYLL. Klemperer's three majestic anthologies are now desirable bargains on Angel Red Line. Stokowski is famous for his extremely lush approach, best heard on his RCA Gold Seal collection and on the Odyssey "symphonic synthesis" of TRISTAN UND ISOLDE, coupled with a blazing rendition of Falla's EL AMOR BRUJO with soloist Shirley Verrett. Reiner's record has highlights from only two of the music dramas, but is one of the most thrilling and exciting of all.

Haitink, Concertgebouw.
Philips 6500 932 (LP); 7300 391 (CS)

Horenstein, Royal Philharmonic. (B)
Quintessence 7047 (LP, CS)

Karajan, Berlin Philharmonic.
Angel S-37097 (LP, CS); and S-37098 (LP, CS)

Klemperer, Philharmonia Orchestra. (B)
Angel RL-32039 (LP, CS); RL-32057 (LP, CS); RL-32058 (LP, CS)

Kubelik, Berlin Philharmonic. (B)
DG Privilege 2535 212 (LP); 3335 212 (CS)

Reiner, Chicago Symphony. (B)
RCA AGL1-1278 (LP, CS)

Solti, Chicago Symphony.
London CS 7078 (LP, CS)

Stokowski, Symphony of the Air. (B)
RCA AGL1-1336 (LP)

Stokowski, Philadelphia Orchestra. (B)
Odyssey Y 32368 (LP, CS)

Szell, Cleveland Orchestra. (B)
(3) Columbia D3M 32317 (LP); also partially repackaged as single discs MY 36715 (LP, CS) and MY 38486 (LP, CS)

Tennstedt, Berlin Philharmonic.
Angel DS-37808 (D-LP); CDC-47007 (CD)

Siegfried Idyll

The Horenstein and Kubelik budgets are recommended above under ORCHESTRAL SELECTIONS. Haitink and the full-price Karajan have this piece as filler on their recordings of Bruckner: SYMPHONY NO. 7. The budget Karajan and the digital Ashkenazy are both highly praised performances and are both coupled with Schönberg: VERKLARTE NACHT. Solti's classic reading is included as an "encore" in the budget box "An Introduction to the Ring," discussed under DER RING DES NIBELUNGEN.

Ashkenazy, English CO.
London 410 111-1 (D-LP); 410 111-4 (CS)

Haitink, Concertgebouw.
(2) Philips 6769 028 (LP); 7699 113 (CS)

Horenstein, Royal Philharmonic. (B)
Quintessence 7047 (LP, CS)

Karajan, Berlin Philharmonic.
(2) DG 2707 102 (LP); 3370 023 (CS)

Karajan, Berlin Philharmonic. (B)
DG Signature 2543 510 (LP); 3343 510 (CS)

Kubelik, Berlin Philharmonic.
DG Privilege 2535 212 (LP); 3335 212 (CS)

Solti, Vienna Philharmonic. (B)
(3) London RDN-S-1 (LP)

For listening beyond the core repertoire of the "Mainstream Romantics," try these:

Brahms
Fantasias for Piano, Op. 116
Intermezzi for Piano, Op. 117
Piano Pieces, Op. 118, 119
Quintet in b for Clarinet and Strings, Op. 115
Quintet in f for Piano and Strings, Op. 34
Trio in E-flat for Horn, Violin, and Piano, Op. 40

Delibes
Coppélia Suite
Sylvia: Suite

Liszt
Faust Symphony
Mephisto Waltz

Tchaikovsky
Serenade in C for Strings, Op. 48

The
Late Romantics

Claude Debussy
1862-1918

Images pour orchestre

This evocative suite of three "orchestral pictures" consists of *Gigues, Ibéria,* and *Rondes de printemps,* usually, but not necessarily, in that order. *Ibéria* ("Spain") is the most famous and is often given separately in concert or on recordings. Currently the most recommendable recordings are those with all three selections.

Composer-critic Eric Salzman called composer-conductor Pierre Boulez "the man who rescued Debussy from Hollywood." Boulez's performances are unique for a clarity that peels away the romantic excesses many other conductors have applied to this composer. Some critics feel Boulez is too analytical and heartless, but if his approach matches your taste there is a budget box of three records with the *Images* plus LA MER, the NOCTURNES, PRELUDE A L'APRES-MIDI D'UN FAUNE, and others.

Haitink's full price Debussy recordings have been highly regarded in some circles but the Schwann Catalog is showing only an import three-record box at the moment. There is a new Haitink NOCTURNES to be discussed later, but for the older performances it may be better to wait for budget reissues, if any.

Previn's performances of the *Images,* coupled with the PRELUDE, was the first Angel digital recording and won the Gramophone Awards for best sound and best orchestral record in 1979. It is still a preferred version, though some critics think it a bit tentative and low-powered. They consider Tilson Thomas more atmospheric and colorful; but his sonics are not up to Previn's. (Thomas also has the PRELUDE.)

Boulez, Cleveland Orchestra. (B)
(3) Columbia D3M 32988 (LP)

Previn, London Symphony.
Angel DS-37674 (D-LP, CS); CDC-47001 (CD)

Thomas, Boston Symphony.
DG 2530 145 (LP)

La Mer

The only full-price version one need consider for first choice is Karajan's, mainly for the beautiful orchestral playing. Couplings are the PRELUDE and one of the most exciting readings of BOLERO by Ravel.

Several budget recordings are all more idiomatic in *La Mer.* There is the Boulez box described above under IMAGES, and there is also a budget single disc of this performance coupled with the PRELUDE and *Jeux.* Giulini's 1963 performance, coupled with NOCTURNES, is universally admired — a real classic of the catalog, and preferred to his later expensive DG version. Ansermet too is classic and quite atmospheric, if less well-played, but with more music: both the PRELUDE and Ravel's RAPSODIE ESPAGNOLE. Szell is excellent with bonuses of Ravel's DAPHNIS ET CHLOE SUITE NO. 2 and PAVANE. If you prefer his lush treatment there is a double budget that includes the PRELUDE, NOCTURNES, the orchestral version of *Clair de lune,* and the *Danses sacrée et profane.*

Ansermet, Suisse Romande. (B)
London Stereo Treasury STS 15109 (LP)

Boulez, New Philharmonia Orchestra. (B)
(3) Columbia D3M 32988 (LP); or single disc CBS MY 37261 (LP, CS)

Giulini, Philharmonia Orchestra. (B)
Angel RL-32033 (LP, CS)

Karajan, Berlin Philharmonic.
Angel S-37438 (LP, CS)

Ormandy, Philadelphia Orchestra. (B)
(2) Columbia MG 30950 (LP)

Szell, Cleveland Orchestra. (B)
Odyssey Y 31928 (LP, CS)

Nocturnes

Boulez is discussed in the preceding listings, Giulini and Ormandy specifically under LA MER. Monteux is a classic budget record with the PRELUDE, Ravel's PAVANE and RAPSODIE ESPAGNOLE — but only two movements of the *Nocturnes.* Five of six critical publications surveyed gave first place in this music to Haitink's 1980 recording, now available on CD. Sound and interpretation were both extolled, but *High Fidelity* dissented, calling the performance "disconcertingly static." Coupled with *Jeux.*

Boulez, New Philharmonia Orchestra. (B)
Columbia D3M 32988 (LP)

Giulini, Philharmonia Orchestra. (B)
Angel RL-32033 (LP, CS)

Haitink, Concertgebouw.
Philips 9500 674 (LP); 7300 769 (CS); 400 023-3 (CD)

Monteux, London Symphony. (B)
London Stereo Treasury STS 15356 (LP, CS)

Ormandy, Philadelphia Orchestra. (B)
(2) Columbia MG 30950 (LP)

Piano Music

The beginning collection must include at least *Clair de lune,* which is the third of four movements from the *Suite Bergamasque.* The best single record for sampling Debussy's solo piano works is that by Tamás Vásáry. For the orchestral version, the Ormandy budget set is preferred (see under LA MER, etc.).

Vásáry.
DG 139 458 (LP)

Prélude à l'après-midi d'un faune

All ten leading possibilities for this work are contained on recordings previously recommended, and it seems more redundant than usual to list them again. Check for Ansermet, Boulez, Haitink, Karajan, and Ormandy under LA MER; for Monteux under NOCTURNES; for the analog Previn under Glinka: RUSSLAN AND LUDMILA OVERTURE; and for the digital Previn and the Thomas under IMAGES.

Quartet in g, Op. 10

This work is almost always coupled with the Ravel QUARTET IN F, and almost all the existing recordings are good. My scoreboard shows the version by the Melos Quartet receiving most votes for first choice overall. Reviewers noted the ensemble's perfect ensemble and pitch, refinement, poetry, sensitivity, and sophistication, plus beautiful tone and engineering. Notices were nearly as rapturous for the digital recording by the Galimir Quartet (Felix Galimir, founder of this group, made the first recording of the Ravel in

1935 under the composer's direction). The most recent recording, that by the Orlando Quartet (from Holland, not Florida), has not had time at this writing to accumulate many reviews, but the one I saw was highly favorable and this performance is currently the only one available on CD. Although I would rate these three the most desirable of all, hardly any you can buy will really disappoint.

Galimir Quartet.
Vanguard 25009 (D-LP)

Melos Quartet.
DG 2531 203 (LP); 3301 203 (CS)

Orlando Quartet.
Philips 6514 387 (D-LP); 7337 387 (CS); 411 050-2 (CD)

Frederick Delius   1862-1934

On Hearing the First Cuckoo in Spring

Sir Thomas Beecham's name will always be associated with that of Delius as the first champion of his music. No reviewer has a sufficient vocabulary of praise for Beecham's immortal recording that includes several other of the composer's dreamy tone pictures, available (forever, one hopes) at budget prices. For newer sound Marriner makes the best choice, with some different couplings.

Beecham, Royal Philharmonic. (B)
Seraphim S-60185 (LP, CS)

Marriner, Academy SMF.
Argo ZRG 875 (LP, CS)

Paul Dukas   1865-1935

The Sorcerer's Apprentice (L'Apprenti Sorcier)

The budget Bernstein is recommended under Chabrier: ESPANA, the full-price Bernstein under Mussorgsky: A NIGHT ON BALD

MOUNTAIN; it is the same famous performance of *The Sorcerer's Apprentice* and the price you pay for it will be based on the desirability of the couplings on the two discs. Steinberg is listed earlier under the Fiedler record of Dvořák: CARNIVAL OVERTURE. The remaining choice is the celebrated Ansermet record containing also Honegger's PACIFIC 231 and Ravel's BOLERO and LA VALSE; these are great readings, but one of these days London ought to put this long-lived record in the budget category.

Ansermet, Suisse Romande.
London CS 6367 (LP)

Bernstein, New York Philharmonic. (B)
CBS MY 37769 (LP, CS)

Bernstein, New York Philharmonic.
Columbia MS 7165 (LP)

Steinberg, Boston Symphony. (B)
RCA AGL1-3967 (LP, CS)

Edward Elgar   1857-1934

Enigma Variations, Op. 36

The best budgets are by Barbirolli, a 1963 recording with Elgar's *Cockaigne Overture,* and by Sargent with Britten's YOUNG PERSON'S GUIDE. Barbirolli is the greater performance, Sargent has a more "basic" coupling. For better sound at higher price the choices are Marriner with three of the POMP AND CIRCUMSTANCE marches, and Previn with Vaughan Williams: FANTASIA ON A THEME BY TALLIS and *The Wasps Overture.*

Barbirolli, Philharmonia Orchestra. (B)
Angel RL-32127 (LP, CS)

Marriner, Concertgebouw.
Philips 9500 424 (LP); 7300 642 (CS)

Previn, London Symphony.
Angel SZ-37627 (LP, CS)

Sargent, Philharmonia Orchestra. (B)
Seraphim S-60173 (LP, CS)

Pomp and Circumstance March in D, Op. 39, No. 1

This is only the most famous of five marches by Elgar gathered under the title *Pomp and Circumstance*. Marriner's version is noted above under ENIGMA VARIATIONS. The distinguished composer Sir Arthur Bliss becomes an excellent conductor on the budget disc of all five marches, plus his own *Things to Come Suite* and *Welcome to the Queen*. More modern sound is heard on Sir Adrian Boult's very idiomatic recording of the five marches plus the two great ones in the Elgarian tradition by Sir William Walton: *Crown Imperial* and *Orb and Sceptre*.

Bliss, London Symphony. (B)
London Stereo Treasury STS 15112 (LP)

Boult, London Philharmonic.
Angel S-37436 (LP, CS)

Marriner, Concertgebouw.
Philips 9500 424 (LP); 7300 642 (CS)

Gabriel Fauré 1845-1924

Pelléas et Mélisande, Op. 80

Marriner's neat and well-played digital-and-CD recording is coupled with the *Fantaisie for Flute and Piano, Masques et bergamasques,* and the *Pavane* (Fauré's, not Ravel's). Baudo's good budget disc also has *Masques et bergamasques,* along with the *Dolly* Suite. A more "basic" recording, with newer sound, is the Andrew Davis, recommended earlier under Franck: SYMPHONY IN D MINOR.

Requiem, Op. 48

Andrew Davis is at his best in French Romantic music; his Fauré *Requiem* is not afraid to be more voluptuous than the others, and the work can take it. The sound is rich, soloists Popp and Nimsgern excellent. Fournet is musical and stylish but much cooler; his sound and soloists (Ameling and Kruysen) are perhaps even better than Davis's. The Willcocks budget has only adequate soloists, but the King's College Choir are wonderful singers in their utterly un-

French-Romantic way. All three recordings have Fauré's *Pavane* as bonus.

A. Davis, Philharmonia Orchestra, Ambrosian Singers.
Columbia M 35153

Fournet, Rotterdam Philharmonic, Netherlands Radio Choir.
Philips 6500 968 (LP); 7300 417 (CS)

Willcocks, King's College Choir. (B)
Seraphim S-60096 (LP, CS)

Vincent d'Indy
1851-1931

Symphony on a French Mountain Air, Op. 25

Robert Casadesus's lively performance with Ormandy remains the classic performance and the most "basic" introductory recording with its coupling of Franck's SYMPHONIC VARIATIONS.

Casadesus, Ormandy, Philadelphia Orchestra. (B)
Odyssey Y 31274 (LP)

Gustav Mahler
1860-1911

Das Lied von der Erde

The passage of time only confirms the eminence of two of the oldest recordings. Klemperer's version with the great singers Christa Ludwig and Fritz Wunderlich continues to be cited by critics with awe, and continues to be a best-seller despite fading sound and a full price two-disc format. The fourth side is a Mahler song recital by Ms. Ludwig. Bruno Walter's last and only stereo recording of this work is the other classic performance and manages to fit all the music on a single budget disc. It has even been sonically refurbished and issued on a CD. Soloists are Mildred Miller and Ernst Haefliger.

Klemperer, Philharmonia Orchestra.
(2) Angel SB-3704 (LP)

Walter, New York Philharmonic. (B)
CBS MP 39027 (LP, CS); CBS Sony 35 DC 115 (CD)

Symphony No. 1 in D

Bernstein's traversal of all nine of Mahler's symphonies was one of the historic recording events of the 1960s. Although many contemporary critics feel that his highly emotional manner tends to overpower the music, and neither the orchestral playing nor the sonics are up to current standards, these performances are undeniably special and have been packaged at attractive prices. The listed box contains also the "basic" SYMPHONY NO. 9 as well as No. 6; it is the safest, most economical introduction to Bernstein's Mahler.

Among newer issues, Abbado's digital-and-CD version has had almost universal praise for its radiance and cohesiveness. A new Muti digital has appeared just as we go to press, and the first reviews seem highly favorable. The full-price analogs by Ozawa and Solti still claim many adherents, and the powerful Giulini is now even more attractive at budget price. Walter wrings the heart in his even older budget, also rehabbed for CD.

Abbado, Chicago Symphony.
DG 2532 020 (D-LP); 3302 020 (CS); 400 033-2 (CD)

Bernstein, New York Philharmonic. (B)
(4) Columbia M4X 31427 (LP)

Giulini, Chicago Symphony. (B)
Angel RL-32037 (LP, CS)

Muti, Philadelphia Orchestra.
Angel DS-38078 (D-LP, CS); CDC 47032 (D)

Ozawa, Boston Symphony.
DG 2530 993 (LP); 3300 993 (CS)

Solti, London Symphony.
London CS 6401 (LP)

Walter, Columbia Symphony. (B)
CBS MY 37235 (LP, CS); CBS Sony 35 DC 90 (CD)

Symphony No. 2 in c, "Resurrection"

Critical opinion is all over the board, but mostly admiring, regarding Solti's new digital-and-CD recording with soloists Buchanan and Zakai. *Ovation* summed it up as "a great, unusually risky and touching performance." Many critics still find Bernstein's 1974 account supreme; *Stereo Review* calls it "wildly visionary."

Bernstein, London Symphony, Edinburgh Festival Chorus.
(2) Columbia M2 32681 (LP, CS)

Solti, Chicago Symphony and Chorus.
(2) London LDR 72006 (D-LP); 410 202-2 (CD)

Symphony No. 4 in G

Mahler's most popular symphony seems to bring out the best in conductors. It has had perhaps more good recordings than any other work of music. My earlier guide listed eleven versions; by digging through additional reviews and applying even more rigorous standards, I have reduced the recommendations to those three that have achieved the most universal and continuing support.

Solti, an acknowledged master of the Mahler style, has taken unusual pains with his Fourth. He has an exquisite soloist in Kiri Te Kanawa, and the newest sonics. Haitink's reissued analog with soprano Elly Ameling strives for chamber-music textures and in the process, as *Gramophone* noted, "avoids pitfalls over which more ambitious versions unwittingly stumble." The Szell budget with Judith Raskin continues to be one of the best-loved readings; critics always remark on its careful attention to detail and its concentrated ecstatic atmosphere.

Haitink, Concertgebouw. (B)
Philips Sequenza 6527 203 (LP); 7311 203 (CS)

Solti, Chicago Symphony.
London 410 188-1 (D-LP); 410 188-4 (CS); 410 188-2 (CD)

Szell, Cleveland Orchestra. (B)
CBS MY 37225 (LP, CS)

Symphony No. 8 in E-flat, "Symphony of a Thousand"

Solti's 1972 classic has been heaped with honors. Ozawa's more recent digital-and-CD version has the best soloists and sound; critics seem to be split by the Atlantic, with most Americans rating the interpretation one of the best or even first choice, and the British finding others, especially Solti or the now deleted Haitink, far preferable. Bernstein loyalists will want his majestic, forceful version, but at full price one must think twice about the harsh sound which is particularly debilitating to this massive work. Maurice Abravanel recorded all the Mahler symphonies after Bernstein with generally less success, but his Eighth is comparable with the best and is a most desirable budget set.

Abravanel, Utah Symphony. (B)
(2) Vanguard 276/7 (LP)

Bernstein, London Symphony.
(2) Columbia M2S 751 (LP)

Ozawa, Boston Symphony.
(2) Philips 6769 069 (D-LP); 7654 069 (CS); 410 607-2 (CD)

Solti, Chicago Symphony.
(2) London CSA 1295 (LP, CS)

Symphony No. 9 in D

Bernstein's angst-ridden version is covered above under SYMPHONY NO. 1. Nearly all reviewers are in agreement that the 1981 Karajan recording is one of the greatest legacies of the Berlin Philharmonic; *Gramophone,* for example, called it "one of the seven wonders of the modern musical world." It is a reading of unparalleled concentration and intensity, and Karajan's own choice for the finest recording he has ever made. Then, as if to top the achievement, Karajan recorded the symphony *again* in 1982 before a live audience. This spectacular version is available only on CD.

There are other fine performances by Giulini, Haitink, Levine, and Solti, but surely at full price one would wish to give priority to the Karajan as a "basic library" first choice. If you just can't afford it, then get the lyrical and meditative Walter set at budget price.

Karajan, Berlin Philharmonic.
(2) DG 2707 125 (LP); 3370 038 (CS)

Karajan, Berlin Philharmonic.
(2) DG 410 726-2 (CD)

Walter, Columbia Symphony. (B)
(2) Odyssey Y2 30308 (LP)

Sergei Rachmaninoff   1873-1943

Concerto No. 2 in c for Piano, Op. 18

What is missing from the listings here is almost more interesting than what is not. The recent Licad-Abbado digital-and-CD recording has received some of the most diametrically opposing reviews from major critics that I have ever seen. *Fanfare*, for instance, raved about Ms. Licad's "singing pianism" and *Gramophone* waxed rhapsodic over her "splendid artistry." *High Fidelity*, on the other hand, excoriated her record as a "sad debut disc," claiming she "seems only overwhelmed by the score." I asked Don Manildi, host of the syndicated radio program *The Romantic Piano*, to break the tie for me. He voted "no," and the record is not listed. Missing also is the very popular and exciting budget recording by Earl Wild with Horenstein conducting. Though at this writing it and other Wild recordings recommended in my earlier guide are still shown in the Schwann Catalog, it is my understanding that they are actually not available because Quintessence has lost licensing rights to all of the pianist's recordings on the label. Surely they will reappear elsewhere soon, but where I cannot tell you. In addition Janis-Dorati and the irreplaceable box with the composer's own performance have been deleted!

That leaves Ashkenazy-Previn at the top of the full-price field, either in the single disc coupled with the much less popular Concerto No. 1, or in the three-record "concerto box" described under Beethoven: CONCERTO FOR PIANO NO. 5. Of the great Rubinstein's three recordings, the best deal — and the best conducting — is the double budget set mentioned under Grieg: CONCERTO FOR PIANO. Cheapest of all, and coupled most conveniently with the RHAPSODY ON A THEME OF PAGANINI, is the exhilaratingly virtuosic recording by Abby Simon with Leonard Slatkin conducting.

Ashkenazy, Previn, London Symphony.
London CS 6774 (LP, CS); or (3) CSP 12 (LP, CS) **(B)**

Rubinstein, Reiner, Chicago Symphony. (B)
RCA VCS-7070 (LP)

Simon, L. Slatkin, St. Louis Symphony. (B)
Turnabout 34658 (LP); CT-2148 (CS)

Concerto No. 3 in d for Piano, Op. 30

Oddly, there is currently a better selection of recordings of this work than for the more popular No. 2. For sheer power it would be hard to top the 1978 Carnegie Hall recital by Vladimir Horowitz with Ormandy conducting. RCA has made it available on LP, cassette, 8-track, and CD. The sound is on the dry side, but perhaps to make up for that RCA has generously priced the recording a bit lower than normal full price (though I cannot in good conscience list it as a budget.)

Then, as if to demonstrate how irrational the music business is, RCA has issued the 1958 Cliburn-Kondrashin recording (twenty years older than the Horowitz, you will note) in dubiously "improved" sound at a price $3.00 higher! It is a thunderous performance, but few would rank it above Horowitz so why pay a premium?

Ashkenazy currently has two performances in print. That with Fistoulari conducting is at budget price, is the most poetic and delicate of all versions, and has much better recorded piano sound than the full-price version with Ormandy on the podium.

There are three recommendable budgets: Berman-Abbado, dazzlingly Russian with somewhat shallow sound; Simon-Slatkin, tasteful and virtuosic with transparent sound; and Weissenberg-Prêtre, with rather icy pianism but a wonderfully compensating clarity, and generally considered better than Weissenberg-Bernstein at full price.

Ashkenazy, Fistoulari, London Symphony. (B)
London Jubilee 41023 (LP, CS)

Berman, Abbado, London Symphony. (B)
CBS MY 37809 (LP, CS)

Horowitz, Ormandy, New York Philharmonic.
RCA CRL1-2633 (LP, CS, CD, 8-track)

Simon, L. Slatkin, St. Louis Symphony. (B)
Turnabout 34682 (LP); CT-2272 (CS)

Weissenberg, Prêtre, Chicago Symphony.
RCA AGL1-3366 (LP, CS)

Rhapsody on a Theme of Paganini, Op. 43

Rubinstein's enchanting performance is available at budget price with Falla: NIGHTS IN THE GARDENS OF SPAIN. If you prefer the same performance coupled with Grieg: CONCERTO FOR PIANO you must pay full price! Simon and Slatkin triumph again on the budget disc recommended under CONCERTO NO. 2. And at full price Ashkenazy leads with a coupling of the less popular Concerto No. 4.

Ashkenazy, Previn, London Symphony.
London CS 6776 (LP, CS)

Rubinstein, Reiner, Chicago Symphony (with Falla). (B)
RCA AGL1-5205 (LP, CS)

Rubinstein, Reiner, Chicago Symphony (with Grieg).
RCA ARL1-4409 (LP)

Simon, L. Slatkin, St. Louis Symphony. (B)
Turnabout 34658 (LP); CT-2148 (CS)

Symphony No. 2 in e, Op. 27

At full price the battle lines are drawn fairly evenly among three conductors, with British critics leaning towards Previn's rich and almost floridly romantic interpretation, and the American reviewers vacillating between Ashkenazy's straightforward, radiantly played version, and the more passionately Russian one by Temirkanov. Ormandy is the best budget, lushly played and recorded but short on subtlety.

Ashkenazy, Concertgebouw.
London LDR 71063 (D-LP, CS); 400 081-2 (CD)

Ormandy, Philadelphia Orchestra. (B)
RCA AGL1-4365 (LP, CS)

Previn, London Symphony.
Angel S-36954 (LP, CS)

Temirkanov, Royal Philharmonic.
Angel S-37520 (LP, CS)

Richard Strauss   1864-1949

Also sprach Zarathustra, Op. 30

I am almost tempted to say that for your first recording of any Strauss tone poem you should simply buy any of the budget discs conducted by Rudolf Kempe. It seems posterity will remember the late maestro mainly, if not exclusively, for his absolutely apt way with the music of Richard Strauss. But then we must take into account the bigger "name" conductors and their legions of fans, and in most cases they do have something substantial to offer.

For this work — which nobody ever included among the most popular classical works until a few bars of it were immortalized in the film *2001: A Space Odyssey* — the reviewers tend to divide (excluding Kempe and Solti) between Karajan and Ormandy on nationalistic lines, the British preferring the former, Americans the latter. Ormandy is digital. The Karajan situation is rather confusing: there is a 1974 Berlin analog recording with no coupling which the *Penguin Guide* calls "arguably the most electrifying recording ever made"; there is an early-'60s budget disc from Vienna with couplings of DON JUAN and TILL EULENSPIEGEL'S MERRY PRANKS; and there is a new digital-and-CD Berlin version coupled only with DON JUAN for which at this writing I have not seen a single review! (I am listing all three just to be safe.)

Solti's full-price recording has the same music as the Karajan-Vienna budget disc, but more up-to-date sound and a more incisive performance. The 1954 Reiner was listed in my earlier book when it was on the budget Victrola label. One of the greatest, if grimmest, versions, it can no longer be wholeheartedly recommended since RCA has tripled the price on the excuse of remastering the sound: it isn't *that* much better.

Karajan, Berlin Philharmonic.
DG 2530 402 (LP); 3300 375 (CS)

Karajan, Vienna Philharmonic. (B)
London Jubilee 41017 (LP, CS)

Karajan, Berlin Philharmonic.
DG 410 959-1 (D-LP); 410 959-4 (CS); 410 959-2 (CD)

Ormandy, Philadelphia Orchestra.
Angel DS-37744 (D-LP)

Solti, Chicago Symphony.
London CS 6978 (LP, CS)

Death and Transfiguration, Op. 24
(Tod und Verklärung)

Neither of Karajan's available recordings has a "basic" coupling, but if you must have this conductor get the newer, digital one with an intense performance of the *Metamorphosen*. What Karajan's *Death and Transfiguration* lacks in dramatic conviction is found aplenty in Kempe's model version at half the price, coupled with TILL EULENSPIEGEL and the "Dance of the Seven Veils" from *Salome*.

Reiner's superb reading from 1956 can be recommended this time at budget price (coupling is TILL EULENSPIEGEL), as can Szell with TILL and DON JUAN. Szell has more music, Reiner has better sound. Another conductor who has had good success with Richard Strauss is Maazel. He has recorded this work three times and all are excellent; the newest, a digital available on CD and coupled with DON JUAN and TILL, is probably a better first choice at full price than Karajan.

Karajan, Berlin Philharmonic.
DG 2532 074 (D-LP); 3302 074 (CS); 410 892-2 (CD)

Kempe, Dresden State Orchestra. (B)
Seraphim S-60297 (LP, CS)

Maazel, Cleveland Orchestra.
CBS IM 35826 (D-LP, CS, CD)

Reiner, Vienna Philharmonic. (B)
London Stereo Treasury STS 15582 (LP, CS)

Szell, Cleveland Orchestra. (B)
CBS MY 36721 (LP, CS)

Don Juan, Op. 20

Karajan-Vienna, Karajan-Berlin (digital), and Solti are discussed under ALSO SPRACH ZARATHUSTRA; Maazel and Szell under DEATH AND TRANSFIGURATION. I will not list them all again here, but they are recommended. Kempe is a bit of a problem this time. There are two recordings on different labels. The Seraphim has better sound but is coupled with one of Strauss's lesser works, the tone poem *Macbeth*. The Quintessence has two couplings, the *Salome* excerpt which is duplicated on Kempe's recording of DEATH AND TRANSFIGURATION, and Respighi's PINES OF ROME which one would be more likely to want coupled as it usually is with the same composer's FOUNTAINS OF ROME. So I will say that Kempe's *Don Juan* is excellent and leave it at that.

Don Quixote, Op. 35

The buyer is in luck: almost all existing recordings are budgets, including the best two at any price. Rostropovich and Karajan are very lively, if sometimes overdriven; the sound is excellent. Tortelier and Kempe recorded this work twice. The classic 1958 version is now out of the US catalogs, but the 1974 recording is almost equally poetic and eloquent, the sonics good but occasionally cramped. Both recordings tend to over-spotlight the cello soloist.

Rostropovich, Karajan, Berlin Philharmonic. (B)
Angel RL-32106 (LP, CS)

Tortelier, Kempe, Dresden State Orchestra. (B)
Seraphim S-60363 (LP)

Ein Heldenleben, Op. 40

There are excellent full price versions by Mehta, Ozawa, Reiner, and Solti — but there is little need to invest in them at the outset with two such superior budgets as Haitink and Kempe available. Haitink's 1971 record is one of the finest he has ever made of anything, with a splendid balance of all the contrasts inherent in this score. Even one reviewer who tends to rate Karajan first in everything admits that here Haitink makes his idol sound "a little superficial." Kempe's powerful performance is just as cheap and would be the unquestioned first choice had not Haitink invaded his turf with such surprising effectiveness. Of all available recordings, only Reiner can challenge Haitink and Kempe for excitement. At RCA's ridiculously high price, the challenge may as well go unmet.

Haitink, Concertgebouw. (B)
Philips Sequenza 6527 128 (LP); 7311 128 (CS)

Kempe, Dresden State Orchestra. (B)
Seraphim S-60315 (LP, CS)

Till Eulenspiegel's Merry Pranks, Op. 28

The eight most recommendable recordings have all been described and I shall not list them again. See ALSO SPRACH ZARATHUSTRA for Karajan-Vienna and Solti; DEATH AND TRANSFIGURATION for Kempe, Maazel, Reiner, and Szell; the Fiedler listing of Dvořák: CARNIVAL OVERTURE for Steinberg; and Mussorgsky: A NIGHT ON BALD MOUNTAIN for Bernstein.

The "Late Romantics" are further represented by these selections:

Debussy
Preludes for Piano, Books 1 and 2
Sonata No. 3 in g for Violin and Piano

Mahler
Songs of a Wayfarer

Strauss, R.
Salome: Dance of the Seven Veils

The
Modern
Romantics

The very cosmopolitan group of gentlemen I have chosen to call "Modern Romantics" might more properly be called "Romantic Moderns," but the reverse order seemed more euphonious, which is a good word to describe them. These are the composers who have strayed least far from the familiar practices of the nineteenth century by preserving in their style, no matter how many "new" harmonies and techniques they employ, an essentially lyrical approach.

Benjamin Britten   1913-1976

Young Person's Guide to the Orchestra, Op. 34

You must decide here whether you want the purely musical version, or the one with Eric Crozier's superimposed narration which explains, ostensibly for children, what is happening in the music. Previn is distinguished by brilliant playing, realistic sound, and a welcome absence of histrionics as he both conducts and narrates. The three other best choices lack narration. The composer's own 1964 reading is an irreplaceable document and a fine performance as well, but the beginning collector may not want the overside *Variations on a Theme by Frank Bridge,* especially at full price. Ormandy has much better sound and virtuoso playing, though less subtlety and authority. Sir Malcolm Sargent made the first recording of this work, and his later stereo version (1958) is still the best budget, recommended earlier under Elgar: ENIGMA VARIATIONS. Ormandy and Previn are paired with Prokofiev: PETER AND THE WOLF.

Britten, London Symphony.
London CS 6671 (LP)

Ormandy, Philadelphia Orchestra.
RCA ARL1-2743 (LP, CS, CD)

Previn, London Symphony.
Angel S-36962 (LP, CS)

Sargent, BBC Symphony. (B)
Seraphim S-60173 (LP, CS)

Georges Enesco

1881-1955

Rumanian Rhapsody No. 1, Op. 11

Dorati is the acknowledged champion for full-price versions, Stokowski for budgets. Simple! Both are described further under Liszt: HUNGARIAN RHAPSODIES.

Dorati, Detroit Symphony.
London CS 7119 (LP, CS)

Stokowski, RCA Victor Symphony. (B)
RCA AGL1-3880 (LP, CS)

Manuel de Falla

1876-1946

El amor brujo

The popular "Ritual Fire Dance" comes from this unique ballet with passages for mezzo-soprano. Stokowski's budget record with Shirley Verrett is especially famous; see under Wagner: ORCHESTRAL SELECTIONS. Giulini's version with Victoria de los Angeles is highly atmospheric and polished with welcome couplings of Ravel's PAVANE and RAPSODIE ESPAGNOLE: a wonderful record, but I wish Angel would drop it to budget status. Dutoit's digital-and-CD recording is tops for sound and has the most apt coupling: Falla's other great ballet, THE THREE-CORNERED HAT. Huguette Tourangeau, however, is less attractive than her rival soloists.

Dutoit, Montreal Symphony.
London LDR 71060 (D-LP, CS); 410 008-2 (CD)

Giulini, Philharmonia Orchestra.
Angel S-36385 (LP)

Stokowski, Philadelphia Orchestra. (B)
Odyssey Y 32368 (LP, CS)

Nights in the Gardens of Spain

No piano concerto has a more enticing title than this! Rubinstein's classic budget recording is recommended under Rachmaninoff:

RHAPSODY ON A THEME OF PAGANINI. Spanish pianist Alicia De Larrocha has made a specialty of this work; her newest of three recordings with Frühbeck de Burgos conducting is digital and available on CD, coupled with piano rhapsodies by fellow Spaniards Albéniz and Turina.

De Larrocha, Frühbeck de Burgos, London Philharmonic.
London 410 289-1 (D-LP); 410 289-4 (CS); 410 289-2 (CD)

Rubinstein, Ormandy, Philadelphia Orchestra. (B)
RCA AGL1-5025 (LP, CS)

The Three-Cornered Hat

Dutoit's brilliant new complete recording is recommended above under EL AMOR BRUJO; soloist in this work is Colette Boky. For excerpts only, Previn's recording is the consensus favorite; see under Glinka: RUSSLAN AND LUDMILA OVERTURE.

Dutoit, Montreal Symphony.
London LDR 71060 (D-LP, CS); 410 008-2 (CD)

Previn, London Symphony.
Angel S-37409 (LP, CS)

Gustav Holst   1874-1934

The Planets

Boult's 1967 recording is regarded widely as the musically definitive version, although it differs in many ways from the composer's own approach as preserved on a historic disc. The sonics are not up to current standards, of course, but the performance, as one critic aptly summarized, is "brilliantly literal." Excellent orchestral playing and superb sonics have won Haitink's version rave reviews in America, while the British tend to think it not very exciting. A point to consider is that Haitink uses the revised score of 1969, incorporating Holst's changes and corrections.

Marriner's sound is, if anything, even better than Haitink's, with an interpretation strong on poetry, short on sensuousness. Karajan's digital recording is available on CD; critics are very divided over the approach, some rating it above all others (especially for the stunning playing), some insisting it pays little attention to musical values and has no sense of mystery. An opposite controversy surrounds Rattle's digital (but not CD) version — some think the orchestral playing is not polished enough, others think the conductor plumbs new depths in the score. Both Karajan and Rattle have too many staunch admirers for me to leave them out, and their advanced sonics compel me to bump the older Solti recording, recommended in my earlier book, since that version has a similar ratio of proponents and detractors.

Boult, Philharmonia Orchestra.
Angel S-36420 (LP, CS)

Haitink, London Philharmonic.
Philips 6500 072 (LP); 7300 058 (CS)

Karajan, Berlin Philharmonic.
DG 2532 019 (D-LP); 3302 019 (CS); 400 028-2 (CD)

Marriner, Concertgebouw.
Philips 9500 425 (LP); 7300 643 (CS)

Rattle, Philharmonia Orchestra.
Angel DS-37817 (D-LP)

Aram Khachaturian   1903-1978

Gayne (Excerpts)

This Armenian-Soviet composer's most famous ballet, also spelled *Gayaneh,* is the source of the popular "Sabre Dance." The composer himself has conducted two single-disc performances, both coupled with highlights from his second-best-known ballet *Spartacus,* though the selections in each case are slightly different. Both versions are full of fire and spectacle; the newer one, naturally, has clearer sound and gets the nod here. Stanley Black's budget disc has good sound (just a bit dry) and quite an excellent idiomatic performance, with couplings of *Spartacus* highlights plus the attractive *Masquerade Suite.*

Black, London Symphony. (B)
London Stereo Treasury STS 15588 (LP, CS)

Khachaturian, London Symphony.
Angel S-37411 (LP, CS)

Maurice Ravel   1875-1937

Alborada del gracioso

"The Jester's Morning Song" was originally part of *Miroirs,* a suite for solo piano. We are concerned here only with the later and more popular orchestral version.

Dutoit's digital-and-CD recording, coupled with BOLERO, RAPSODIE ESPAGNOLE, and LA VALSE, is the critical favorite by far of the newest editions, with stunning sound, superlative readings, and an obviously "all-basic" program. You must be careful when grabbing in the bin for this, since there is *another* Dutoit digital recording of this piece on the same label, but with different Ravel couplings. I am not listing this alternate since its couplings are done as well or better by other artists.

Full-price analog recordings worth investigating are those by Boulez and Maazel. Boulez approaches Ravel much as he does Debussy (q.v.), with microscopic analysis. Some find this treatment definitive, others think it calculated and pretentious. Couplings are DAPHNIS ET CHLOE SUITE NO. 2, the PAVANE, and RAPSODIE ESPAGNOLE. One might justly suspect that Maazel's famous album (with BOLERO, the PAVANE, and LA VALSE) sells because of its notoriously erotic cover, but the musical contents are just as stimulating.

There are two very superior bargains in the budget category. Paul Paray was a true master of the French style, and his brilliant single disc with BOLERO, the PAVANE, RAPSODIE ESPAGNOLE, and LA VALSE is exceptionally distinguished. If you really like Ravel, Skrowaczewski provides the collector's dream with a four-record budget set of all Ravel's orchestral works (actually, about one-third of DAPHNIS ET CHLOE is omitted) with excellent sound and fine performances.

Boulez, Cleveland Orchestra.
Columbia M 30651 (LP)

Dutoit, Montreal Symphony.
London LDR 71059 (D-LP, CS); 410 010-2 (CD)

Maazel, New Philharmonia.
Angel S-36916 (LP, CS)

Paray, Detroit Symphony. (B)
Mercury 75033 (LP)

Skrowaczewski, Minnesota Orchestra. (B)
(4) Vox SVBX-5133 (LP, CS)

Boléro

Heading the long list of critics who had nothing but contempt for this work was the composer himself, who, while ruefully acknowledging it as his only masterpiece, added that "unfortunately, it contains no music." This has had not the slightest effect on conductors, who love to conduct it, or on audiences, who love to hear it. It is one of the most-recorded classical compositions, and has legions of devoted admirers even among people who usually hate classical music, including but not limited to those who enjoyed the movie *10*.

If you are especially intent on obtaining an outstanding *Boléro*, two recordings still top the list. The Karajan version on Angel, previously recommended for its LA MER by Debussy, has bone-rattling playing and superb sound. Paray's BOLERO has been called "the perfect performance"; it is included on the record described above under ALBORADA DEL GRACIOSO.

Fine alternates include several versions recommended elsewhere for their couplings: Ansermet (see Dukas: SORCERER'S APPRENTICE); Dutoit, Maazel-New Philharmonia, and Skrowaczewski (see ALBORADA DEL GRACIOSO); Karajan on DG (see Mussorgsky: PICTURES AT AN EXHIBITION); and Maazel-Berlin (see Chabrier: ESPANA).

To these must be added the Skrowaczewski single-disc budget (same performance as in the box) coupled with the PAVANE, RAPSODIE ESPAGNOLE, and LA VALSE, and now available on CD. I have been chary of listing the Martinon recordings as I did in the past because their somewhat murky sound is no longer fully acceptable. Nevertheless this conductor was a superlatively idiomatic interpreter of most French music, and his *Boléro* coupled with RAPSODIE ESPAGNOLE, LA VALSE, and one other piece deserves a place of honor. I would restore most of his Ravel and Debussy records if Angel would put them on the budget Red Line label.

Ansermet, Suisse Romande. (B)
London CS 6367 (LP)

Dutoit, Montreal Symphony.
London LDR 71059 (D-LP, CS); 410 010-2 (CD)

Karajan, Berlin Philharmonic.
DG 139 010 (LP); 923 018 (CS)

Karajan, Berlin Philharmonic.
Angel S-37438 (LP, CS)

Maazel, New Philharmonia.
Angel S-36916 (LP, CS)

Maazel, Berlin Philharmonic. (B)
DG Musikfest 413 250-1 (LP); 413 250-4 (CS)

Martinon, Orchestre de Paris.
Angel S-37147 (LP, CS, 8-track)

Paray, Detroit Symphony. (B)
Mercury 75033 (LP)

Skrowaczewski, Minnesota Orchestra. (B)
(4) Vox SVBX-5133 (LP, CS)

Skrowaczewski, Minnesota Orchestra. (B)
Turnabout 34595 (LP); Mobile Fidelity MFCD-802 (CD)

Concerto in G for Piano

The early stereo version by Arturo Benedetti Michelangeli belongs in the small and select category of "legendary recordings." It is the first choice of every reviewer surveyed for this book. All agreed with *Stereo Review* that the performance has "never been surpassed." Coupling is the Rachmaninoff Piano Concerto No. 4.

The nearest rival is Argerich, whom one critic at least rated as a tie with Michelangeli. Her sound is newer, and the coupling of Prokofiev's CONCERTO FOR PIANO NO. 3 is both superb and "more basic." The most logical coupling, however, is Ravel's other piano concerto, that in D "for the left hand," and among these recordings Collard has the best reviews, even winning the coveted Rosette from *Penguin Guide*.

Among budget recordings of the Concerto in G, Katchen's very poetic reading is the standard, coupled with Bartók's CONCERTO FOR PIANO NO. 3.

Argerich, Abbado, Berlin Philharmonic.
DG 139 349 (LP)

Collard, Maazel, Orchestre National de France.
Angel SZ-37730 (LP)

Katchen, Kertész, London Symphony. (B)
London Stereo Treasury STS 15494 (LP)

Michelangeli, Gracis, Philharmonia Orchestra.
Angel S-35567 (LP)

Daphnis et Chloé

Live concerts are more likely to present the shortened "Suite No. 2," but the complete ballet fits on one record and there is no very good reason not to enjoy all of it. The recent digital-and-CD complete version by Dutoit has received about every critical accolade imaginable, including the *Penguin Guide* Rosette and the *Opus* "100 Inspired Recordings" list. *Stereo Review* called it "a dream performance...the finest recording yet offered of this music."

The only justification for listing another recording would be price, so I will add the 1959 Monteux reissue, the former undisputed champion and fellow Rosette recipient. The sound is still lush and spacious, and this recording's 25 years at the top of the list is an achievement not to be ignored.

If you will be satisfied with the shorter version of the music, check the recordings by Boulez and Skrowaczewski recommended under ALBORADA DEL GRACIOSO, or by Szell under Debussy: LA MER.

Boulez, Cleveland Orchestra.
Columbia M 30651 (LP)

Dutoit, Montreal Symphony.
London LDR 71028 (D-LP, CS); 400 055-2 (CD)

Monteux, London Symphony. (B)
London Stereo Treasury STS 15090 (LP)

Skrowaczewski, Minnesota Orchestra. (B)
(4) Vox SVBX-5133 (LP, CS)

Szell, Cleveland Orchestra. (B)
Odyssey Y 31928 (LP, CS)

Pavane pour une infante défunte

With one exception, every most-recommended version is available on a recording listed elsewhere earlier in the book: Bernstein (see Chabrier: ESPANA); Boulez, Maazel, Paray, and the Skrowaczewski budget box (see ALBORADA DEL GRACIOSO); Giulini (see Falla: EL AMOR BRUJO); Monteux (see Debussy: NOCTURNES); the Skrowaczewski single disc (see BOLERO); and Szell (see Debussy: LA MER). The only necessary addition is Gerhardt's attractive anthology of svelte French favorites including the "other" *Pavane* by Fauré, Ravel's *Tombeau de Couperin* and *Introduction and Allegro*, and Nos. 1 and 2 from the TROIS GYMNOPEDIES by Satie. This recording was warmly recommended in my previous edition at full price, and is doubly attractive now in the budget category.

Bernstein, New York Philharmonic. (B)
CBS MY 37769 (LP, CS)

Boulez, Cleveland Orchestra.
Columbia M 30651 (LP)

Gerhardt, National Philharmonic. (B)
RCA AGL1-4948 (LP, CS)

Giulini, Philharmonia Orchestra.
Angel S-36385 (LP)

Maazel, New Philharmonia.
Angel S-36916 (LP, CS)

Monteux, London Symphony. (B)
London Stereo Treasury STS 15356 (LP, CS)

Paray, Detroit Symphony. (B)
Mercury 75033 (LP)

Skrowaczewski, Minnesota Orchestra. (B)
(4) Vox SVBX-5133 (LP, CS)

Skrowaczewski, Minnesota Orchestra. (B)
Turnabout 34595 (LP); Mobile Fidelity MFCD-802 (CD)

Szell, Cleveland Orchestra. (B)
Odyssey Y 31928 (LP, CS)

Quartet in F

All recommended recordings are coupled with Debussy's QUAR-TET; look under that heading for detailed descriptions.

Rapsodie espagnole

Every recommended recording is available with couplings already listed: Ansermet (see Debussy: LA MER); Boulez, Dutoit, Paray, and the Skrowaczewski budget box (see: ALBORADA DEL GRACIO-SO); Dorati (see Liszt: HUNGARIAN RHAPSODIES); Giulini (see Falla: EL AMOR BRUJO); Martinon and the Skrowaczewski single disc (see BOLERO); and Monteux (see Debussy: NOCTURNES). Please refer to these listings for more information.

La Valse

Once again all recommendations can be found on previously listed recordings, and catalog numbers will not be appended here. Pre-

ferences include Abbado (see Mussorgsky: PICTURES AT AN EXHI-
BITION); Ansermet (see Dukas: SORCERER'S APPRENTICE); Dutoit,
Maazel, Paray, and the Skrowaczewski budget box (see ALBORADA
DEL GRACIOSO); and Martinon and the Skrowaczewski single disc
(see BOLERO).

Ottorino Respighi   1879-1936

Ancient Airs and Dances

When Respighi orchestrated these Italian Baroque pieces they
were considered antiquarian oddities. Nowadays they are easily
heard in their original versions, but Respighi's work is still justifi-
ably popular in its own right. Dorati's recording from the '60s, now
at budget price, is the impeccably delightful standard. For just the
most popular suite, the Third, get Karajan's anthology described
under Albinoni: ADAGIO.

Dorati, Philharmonia Hungarica. (B)
Mercury 75009 (LP, CS)

Karajan, Berlin Philharmonic.
DG 2530 247 (LP); 3300 317 (CS)

Fountains of Rome; Pines of Rome

Another tripartite Respighi publication is the set of three tone
poems sometimes known as the "Roman triptych." The third one,
Feste Romane (Roman Festivals), is this time the least popular and
many recordings give only the two listed in the heading above.

For all three together, Dutoit at full price has the best performance and exquisite digital sound that greatly enhances these
ultra-colorful pieces. On budget Freccia has excellent analog
sound and a further bonus of a short piece by one of Respighi's contemporaries, Alfredo Catalani.

For the more usual coupling of just the *Pines* and *Fountains*,
Karajan's full-price analog recording is the best known for sonics
and interpretation. Reiner's early stereo version is superb for both
poetry and excitement, and even at RCA's inflated price (for half-
speed remastering) is still worth getting. In the budget category

Munch and Ormandy are the classic readings, each with its vociferous adherents.

Dutoit, Montreal Symphony.
London LDR 71091 (D-LP, CS); 410 145-2 (CD)

Freccia, New Philharmonia. (B)
Quintessence 7058 (LP, CS)

Karajan, Berlin Philharmonic.
DG 2531 055 (LP); 3301 055 (CS)

Munch, New Philharmonia. (B)
London Jubilee 41024 (LP, CS)

Ormandy, Philadelphia Orchestra. (B)
CBS MY 38485 (LP, CS)

Reiner, Chicago Symphony.
RCA ATL1-4040 (LP, CS)

Joaquin Rodrigo   1902-

Concierto de Aranjuez

The irreplaceable classic recording is still that by guitarist Narciso Yepes with the magnificent conducting of Ataulfo Argenta on a budget label. It is even more magical than Yepes's own later and more expensive DG recording. But with the current popularity of digital and compact disc recording it is necessary to give some other good, if higher-priced, alternatives. Both Julian Bream and John Williams have recorded this work three times, and in each case the most recent versions are to be preferred for overall interpretation and sonics. Williams leads in impeccable technique, Bream in passionate commitment. There is another recent digital-and-CD version with guitarist Carlos Bonell, conducted by Dutoit, but though *Penguin Guide* gives it the Rosette and calls it the "clear first choice," most other critics have blasted it for such alleged faults as weak guitar playing, insipid interpretation, and bloated sonics. I have decided to leave it out. Williams and Yepes are coupled with Rodrigo's number two hit, the *Fantasia para un gentil-hombre;* Bream with the *Invocación.*

Bream, Gardiner, Chamber Orchestra of Europe.
RCA RCD1-4900 (D-LP, CS, CD)

Williams, Frémaux, Philharmonia Orchestra.
CBS IM 37848 (D-LP, CS, CD)

Yepes, Argenta, National Orchestra of Spain. (B)
London Stereo Treasury STS 15199 (LP, CS)

Erik Satie   1866-1925

Trois Gymnopédies

These simple little pieces, once ignored by the critics, have caught
the public fancy and become immensely popular. They exist in
both piano solo and orchestral versions. There is a "best basic"
choice for each. Aldo Ciccolini's name is almost synonymous with
Satie's piano music and the first volume of his multi-disc series
contains these works and the next-best-known ones in authoritative performances. For the full-orchestra versions, Gerhardt's
record (see Ravel: PAVANE) is now even more desirable at budget
price that it was in my old book. He includes only Nos. 1 and 2,
but those are the ones you really want anyhow.

Ciccolini.
Angel S-36482 (LP, CS)

Gerhardt, National Philharmonic. (B)
RCA AGL1-4948 (LP, CS)

Jan Sibelius   1865-1957

Concerto in d for Violin, Op. 47

There is possibly no better bargain in the catalog than Jascha Heifetz's classic 1960 recording of this work, coupled with Prokofiev's
excellent Violin Concerto No. 2 on a budget label. Heifetz made
the first recording of the Sibelius Concerto in 1935, and no one yet
has matched him for the effortless technique and interpretive
depth displayed in this later reading. By any measure this is the

best choice for a first purchase, even with competition such as Kremer, David Oistrakh, Perlman, Stern, and Zukerman—all of whom have one or more drawbacks in terms of interpretation, sonics, price, or couplings.

Heifetz, Hendl, Chicago Symphony. (B)
RCA AGL1-5241 (LP, CS)

Finlandia, Op. 26

Ashkenazy's recent digital-and-CD recording has by far the best sound and is a powerful, deeply-felt reading. Couplings are SYM-PHONY NO. 4 and the seldom-heard *Luonnotar*. Karajan's hair-raising way with *Finlandia* is legendary; of his various recordings the one listed below is best for sound and the couplings of other Sibelius tone poems, SWAN OF TUONELA, *En Saga,* and *Tapiola.* On budget labels, Barbirolli and Bernstein stand out. Sir John's orchestra is below the top standard as is the mid-'60s sound, but the performances are excellent in an all-Sibelius program including VALSE TRISTE, the *Karelia* Suite, *Pohjola's Daughter,* and *Lemminkäinen's Return.* Bernstein's exciting *Finlandia* is on a record previously recommended under Grieg: PEER GYNT SUITES.

Ashkenazy, Philharmonia Orchestra.
London LDR 71019 (D-LP); 400 056-2 (CD)

Barbirolli, Hallé Orchestra. (B)
Seraphim S-60208 (LP, CS)

Bernstein, New York Philharmonic. (B)
CBS MY 36718 (LP, CS)

Karajan, Berlin Philharmonic.
Angel S-37408 (LP, CS)

Swan of Tuonela

This haunting little tone-picture must have just the right aura of melancholy resignation to succeed. Those who do it best are Bernstein on his record listed above and under Grieg: PEER GYNT SUITES, and Karajan on his Angel album described under FINLANDIA.

Bernstein, New York Philharmonic. (B)
CBS MY 36718 (LP, CS)

Karajan, Berlin Philharmonic.
Angel S-37408 (LP, CS)

Symphony No. 2 in D, Op. 43

In recent years Sir Colin Davis has won quite a reputation as a Sibelian with his recordings of all the symphonies. At full price his Second is the best choice, with lovely sound. (Beware: both Ashkenazy and Karajan are unbelievably off-form in this work.) But you can do just as well, maybe better, with the budgets. Of Barbirolli's four (!) recordings his 1962 reading is both the best and the cheapest. He puts a little Mediterranean passion into the composer's craggy arctic landscape, while Monteux adopts a brooding and grandly tragic interpretation. At this writing Szell's famous Concertgebouw performance, long the first choice of many critics, has been dropped from the catalogs. I would say "watch for a budget reissue," but it already was a budget. Come now, Philips people, surely this is a mistake.

Barbirolli, Royal Philharmonic. (B)
Quintessence 7008 (LP, CS)

C. Davis, Boston Symphony.
Philips 9500 141 (LP); 7300 518 (CS)

Monteux, London Symphony. (B)
London Stereo Treasury STS 15098 (LP)

Symphony No. 4 in a, Op. 63

The composer's dark, anguished Fourth is not his most popular symphony, but many think it his greatest. Certainly it is the most totally typical of his distinctive sound-world. Sibelius uttered the understatement of the century when he said it has "nothing of the circus about it." Being an unorthodox and elusive work, it has eluded some of the greatest conductors. Davis's recording is rated the one flop in his fine series and has been dropped. Karajan's lushly romantic view is entirely inappropriate. Listening to either of his recordings is, as the *Penguin Guide* puts it, "as if one were observing the iciness of a Finnish winter landscape from the comfort of a smooth-running, well-heated limousine." Bernstein's vividly emotional reading has been dropped, and Rozhdestvensky's thoughtful, concentrated one soon will be. Ormandy is actually quite satisfyingly intense, but his sonics are inferior. That leaves the recent digital-and-CD Ashkenazy recording already recommended for its FINLANDIA. Critics are wildly divided over the symphony's interpretation, comments ranging from "dull" *(Ovation)* to "insightful" (*Stereo Review* — who named it Record of the Year in 1981). Whoever is right, everyone agrees the sound is great, the *Finlandia* is wonderful, and there is plenty of music crowded onto the disc/cassette/CD. Be thankful for small favors.

Ashkenazy, Philharmonia Orchestra.
London LDR 71019 (D-LP); 400 056-2 (CD)

Symphony No. 5 in E-flat, Op. 82

Ashkenazy and Karajan do much better in this work, but are outclassed by Colin Davis whose recording "remains unchallenged" in its responsiveness to "those sudden shafts of darkness and radiant breakthroughs of sunlight" (*High Fidelity*). In fact, they are outclassed by young Simon Rattle, whose recent digital-and-CD version has had wide praise for its fidelity to the score and interpretive intensity. Rattle is coupled with *Night Ride and Sunrise,* one of Sibelius's less consequential pieces, and Davis with a good if not great performance of the Symphony No. 7.

C. Davis, Boston Symphony.
Philips 6500 959 (LP); 7300 415 (CS)

Rattle, Philharmonia Orchestra.
Angel DS-37883 (D-LP, CS); CDC-47006 (CD)

Valse triste

Enough of controversy! Get Barbirolli on the recording recommended under FINLANDIA, or Bernstein (see under Grieg: PEER GYNT, etc.). Both good, both cheap.

Barbirolli, Hallé Orchestra. (B)
Seraphim S-60208 (LP, CS)

Bernstein, New York Philharmonic. (B)
CBS MY 36718 (LP, CS)

Ralph Vaughan Williams   1872-1958

Fantasia on "Greensleeves"

Barbirolli's record, a longtime standard of the catalog, is still considered definitive by many. Rich and eloquent, it is coupled with an equally fine FANTASIA ON A THEME BY TALLIS and two Elgar pieces for strings. The record, however, is more than twenty years old and is still being sold at full price. Marriner with both Fantasias has better sound and nearly as fine readings for the same cost, plus two other Vaughan Williams works, the *Variants of "Dives and Lazarus"* and the gorgeous romance for violin and orchestra *The Lark Ascending*. At budget price Bernstein has both Fantasias and his famous version of Barber's ADAGIO FOR STRINGS, a thoughtful British-American program of soulful music for string orchestra. (N.B.: there is a newer Marriner record on the same label with *Greensleeves,* but the couplings are much less interesting and the sound actually inferior to the older record, listed here.)

Barbirolli, London Sinfonietta.
Angel S-36101 (LP)

Bernstein, New York Philharmonic. (B)
CBS MY 38484 (LP, CS)

Marriner, Academy SMF.
Argo ZRG 696 (LP); 15696 (CS)

Fantasia on a Theme by Tallis

All the best versions have been recommended earlier — Barbirolli, Bernstein, and Marriner under FANTASIA ON "GREENSLEEVES" above, and Previn under Elgar: ENIGMA VARIATIONS. I won't repeat the catalog numbers here.

Symphony No. 2, "London"

In one of its more inexplicable "artistic" decisions, RCA has deleted its great Previn recording of the composer's most popular symphony while retaining Previn versions of four others — three at budget price, one at full price! The disc was universally admired for its powerful, poetic, well-structured interpretation and rich sound. If it does come back, get it. Meanwhile, Sir Adrian Boult's fine edition, from his complete series, is still available at full price. It suffers only by comparison with the even more satisfying Previn.

Boult, London Philharmonic.
Angel S-36838 (LP, CS)

Investigate the "Modern Romantics" in greater depth with these works:

Britten
Serenade for Tenor, Horn, and Strings, Op. 31

Ravel
Ma Mère l'Oye (ballet)
Le Tombeau de Couperin
Tzigane for Violin and Orchestra

Sibelius
Karelia Suite, Op. 11

Walton
Belshazzar's Feast

The
Mainstream
Moderns

The distinction between "Romantic" and "Mainstream Modern" composers is certainly not black-and-white, but all of these latter composers more or less consciously sought to make definite breaks with the Romantic tradition. Some, like Carl Orff, went back to *pre*-Romantic sources for inspiration; others, like Béla Bartók, altered and augmented Romantic principles until they were scarcely recognizable; and still others, like Arnold Schönberg (though not in the work included in this "basic library"), deliberately overthrew all convention and invented their own musical theories and systems.

Béla Bartók   1881-1945

Concerto for Orchestra

This orchestral "showpiece" cries out for magnificent sonics, and in this category the new digital Solti is undisputed winner, though opinions vary on the merits of the interpretation. Some prefer Solti's earlier (1966) version, placed by *Opus* in their "100 Inspired Recordings" list and now available at budget price.

Several other critics prefer the budget Reiner to either of Solti's versions for its powerfully brilliant yet balanced interpretation. The sound, however, is not as good as either Solti. Two other excellent budget versions are those by Ančerl and Boulez and if the others are not to hand you will probably be satisfied with either for a first listen.

Both Solti recordings are coupled with the *Dance Suite;* the other versions lack couplings.

Ančerl, Czech Philharmonic. (B)
Quintessence 7152 (LP, CS)

Boulez, New York Philharmonic. (B)
CBS MY 37259 (LP, CS)

Reiner, Chicago Symphony. (B)
RCA AGL1-2909 (LP)

Solti, Chicago Symphony.
London LDR 71036 (D-LP, CS); 400 052-2 (CD)

Solti, London Symphony. (B)
London Jubilee 41037 (LP, CS)

Concerto No. 3 for Piano

Katchen's deeply probing performance on a budget disc has already been recommended under Ravel: CONCERTO IN G. The recent Ashkenazy-Solti recording is generally recognized as the finest version ever recorded and it may be said to effectively replace the former (since 1960) champion, Anda-Fricsay, especially with the same coupling of Piano Concerto No. 2.

Ashkenazy, Solti, London Philharmonic.
London CS 7167 (LP, CS)

Katchen, Kertész, London Symphony.
London Stereo Treasury STS 15494 (LP)

Music for Strings, Percussion and Celesta

Critics are unanimous that Reiner's authoritative version is superbly organized, faithful to the score, immensely powerful and exciting, fully idiomatic, sonically impressive despite its age, and dirt cheap. Not to mention a bonus of the *Hungarian Sketches*. At full price one might be interested in Marriner's analog disc. Although critics disagree on the conductor's approach, it is the only performance using a chamber-sized orchestra as the composer intended. The coupling is the *Divertimento for Strings,* one of Bartók's most immediately attractive scores.

Marriner, Academy SMF.
Argo ZRG 657 (LP)

Reiner, Chicago Symphony. (B)
RCA AGL1-4087 (LP, CS)

Quartets (6)

The 1963 Juilliard budget boxed set has shown up on most "great recordings" lists for twenty years and is still considered an essential component of any basic library of chamber music and/or 20th-century music. The new Juilliard digital set (with new personnel) surpasses the older issue only in sound. Most critics still prefer the 1963 version, which is also cheaper and available if desired on three individual discs. It is doubtless the natural first choice, but mention must be made of the recent set by the Tokyo Quartet which has won wide approval for its lively, committed performances and splendid sound. Some feel that the Tokyo group unnecessarily prettifies the music; but as *High Fidelity*'s critic wrote, "for listeners who prefer a less aggressive, more restrained conception of this music, it may even represent an ideal choice."

Juilliard Quartet. (B)
(3) Columbia D3S 717 (LP); or individually at full price as M 31196, M 31197, M 31198

Tokyo Quartet.
(3) DG 2740 235 (LP)

Alban Berg   1885-1935

Concerto for Violin

There are currently available two great recordings, one at full price, one at budget. Perlman's recent account, coupled with the Stravinsky Violin Concerto, offers outstanding playing from both soloist and orchestra and excellent recording quality. Suk's luminous reading won the Grand Prix du Disque in 1967 and the sonics still hold up. Coupling is Berg's Chamber Concerto.

Perlman, Ozawa, Boston Symphony.
DG 2531 110 (LP); 3301 110 (CS)

Suk, Ančerl, Czech Philharmonic. (B)
Quintessence 7179 (LP, CS)

Paul Hindemith   1895-1963

Mathis der Maler (Symphony)

Alas, the superb Horenstein recording listed in my earlier guide has been deleted by Nonesuch. Ormandy's recording is good and coupled with the basic SYMPHONIC METAMORPHOSIS OF THEMES BY WEBER, but it is a long way from definitive and at full price this aging album is no bargain.

Ormandy, Philadelphia Orchestra.
Columbia MS 6562 (LP)

Symphonic Metamorphosis of Themes by Weber

Szell's recording of Hindemith's "orchestral showpiece," coupled with Janáček's SINFONIETTA, may by now fairly be considered a classic, though the conductor's claque of detractors complain that it is too mechanical. In any case it is a better deal than Shaw's only average reading on Telarc coupled with Orff's CARMINA BURANA; this double set is not up to the label's highest engineering standards and currently lists for $25.

Ormandy, Philadelphia Orchestra.
Columbia MS 6562 (LP)

Szell, Cleveland Orchestra.
Columbia MS 7166 (LP)

Arthur Honegger   1892-1955

Pacific 231

The title refers to a real railway train whose rhythms inspired this tone-picture. Ansermet's record, with its all-basic couplings described under Dukas: SORCERER'S APPRENTICE, is getting old but is still the standard.

Ansermet, Suisse Romande.
London CS 6367 (LP)

Leos Janáček   1854-1928

Sinfonietta

Szell's recording was recommended under Hindemith: SYMPHON-IC METAMORPHOSIS. All other recommended recordings are coupled with Janáček's tone poem *Taras Bulba*. Kubelik, Neumann, and Rattle all have strong points, but the full-price field is clearly led by the extraordinary digital Mackerras recording. This conductor is a master of Janáček's style, and the orchestral playing and sonics here are quite beyond the usual. Mackerras leads the best *Taras Bulba* of them all and has the only CD availability. The budget Ancerl cannot compete in engineering but contains wonderfully idiomatic readings.

Ancerl, Czech Philharmonic. (B)
Quintessence 7184 (LP, CS)

Mackerras, Vienna Philharmonic.
London LDR 71021 (D-LP); 410 138-2 (CD)

Szell, Cleveland Orchestra.
Columbia MS 7166 (LP)

Zoltán Kodály   1882-1967

Háry János: Suite

Two fine budgets make a first choice easy in this delightful music, both coupled with Prokofiev's LIEUTENANT KIJE SUITE. Leinsdorf's recording is the only one to include the vocal parts in the Prokofiev. Szell's is the more idiomatic performance.

Leinsdorf, Philharmonia Orchestra. (B)
Seraphim S-60209 (LP)

Szell, Cleveland Orchestra. (B)
CBS MY 38527 (LP, CS)

Darius Milhaud   1892-1974

La Création du monde

The composer's own budget recording is, naturally, very authoritative. The orchestra is a fairly mediocre one but they get the music across, and the overside ballet *Le Boeuf sur le toit* has really incomparable energy and wit. Bernstein's full-price recording with both these pieces plus the *Saudades do Brasil* has much newer sound and a better orchestra, but lacks something in true French sparkle.

Bernstein, Orchestre National de France.
Angel S-37442 (LP, CS)

Milhaud, Orchestre du Théâtre des Champs-Élysées.
Nonesuch 71122 (LP)

Carl Nielsen   1865-1931

Symphony No. 5, Op. 50

The greatest Danish composer's greatest symphony has fallen on
hard times. The sublime Horenstein recording on Nonesuch has
gone the same way as that of Hindemith's MATHIS DER MALER. The
only decent alternative at the moment is the three-record budget
set of Nos. 4, 5, and 6 plus one tone poem, and unfortunately
Blomstedt's Fifth is the least distinguished of the three. An inex-
cusable situation.

Blomstedt, Danish Radio Symphony. (B)
(3) Seraphim SIC-6098 (LP)

Carl Orff   1892-1982

Carmina Burana

Here is another work in the "sonic spectacular" category. Sound
buffs are directed to the Mata recording; it got mixed reviews, but
the reservations were minor. Shaw's version may tempt some because it is on the famous audiophile label Telarc, but be warned
that not only is this not one of Telarc's best-recorded efforts, it is
available only in a very expensive two-record set (or CD) and the
orchestra is inferior to Mata's.

The overall first choice of most critics for a decade has been
Kegel's Philips recording which currently shows up in the Schwann
Catalog on cassette only. Perhaps it is slated for a budget LP reissue.
Beware of Kegel's older effort available on a DG budget — it is
distinctly inferior to the Philips edition, famed for its solid musical
qualities, excitement, and excellent sound.

Jochum's aging DG version must be passed over at full price in favor of the Ozawa, which is unique for its handling of the grandiose aspects of the score and has recently been sonically refurbished and re-released at budget price. Ozawa also replaces the previously preferred budget choice by Smetacek.

Kegel, Leipzig Radio Symphony and Chorus.
Philips 7300 444 (CS)

Mata, London Symphony and Chorus.
RCA ARC1-4550 (D-LP, CS, CD)

Ozawa, Boston Symphony and NE Conservatory Chorus. (B)
RCA AGL1-5260 (LP, CS)

Francis Poulenc   1899-1963

Concerto in g for Organ, Strings, Timpani

Prêtre's 1961 recording with organist Maurice Duruflé has long been the standard, coupled with the GLORIA, but by now ought to qualify for budget status. Especially at full price the disc has strong competition from Shaw's digital version with organist Michael Murray — the choral work is good in the GLORIA, Murray is a fine soloist, both performances have life and power.

Prêtre, French Radio Orchestra.
Angel S-35953 (LP)

Shaw, Atlanta Symphony.
Telarc 10077 (D-LP)

Gloria in G

To the versions recommended in the preceding listing should be added Bernstein, whose *Gloria* is rough in spots and often overemphasized, but whose flipside SYMPHONY OF PSALMS by Stravinsky is one of the most powerful and exciting.

Bernstein, New York Philharmonic.
Columbia M 34551 (LP, CS)

Serge Prokofiev 1891-1953

Alexander Nevsky, Op. 78

I have been unable to turn up anything but raves for Abbado's idiomatic, energetic, intense, brilliantly recorded version with soloist Elena Obraztsova. All other recordings have significant drawbacks — Slatkin's chorus is weak, Schippers is sloppy and dimly recorded, Previn is too genteel, and Reiner's great old record is sung in (ugh!) English.

Abbado, London Symphony.
DG 2531 202 (LP); 3301 202 (CS)

Concerto No. 3 in C for Piano, Op. 26

Martha Argerich has become the name most associated with this work; her recording has already been recommended under Ravel: CONCERTO IN G. John Browning is a close runner-up and his lower-priced recording is coupled with Ravel's other concerto (in D, "for the left hand"). Graffman's version, straightforward yet very exciting, has been a favorite for years. The sound is worse than the others, but at least CBS has put the record (which includes the Piano Concerto No. 1) on its budget "Great Performances" series.

Argerich, Abbado, Berlin Philharmonic.
DG 139 349 (LP)

Browning, Leinsdorf, Philharmonia Orchestra. (B)
Seraphim S-60224 (LP)

Graffman, Szell, Cleveland Orchestra. (B)
CBS MY 37806 (LP, CS)

Lieutenant Kijé Suite, Op. 60

The Leinsdorf and Szell budgets were previously recommended under Kodály: HARY JANOS SUITE. Rossi's budget disc features less than stellar forces, but the 1959 sound is surprisingly good and overside is a priceless PETER AND THE WOLF with Boris Karloff. At full price Marriner's beautifully recorded version is coupled with the LOVE FOR THREE ORANGES SUITE and the SYMPHONY NO. 1.

Leinsdorf, Philharmonia Orchestra. (B)
Seraphim S-60209 (LP)

Marriner, London Symphony.
Philips 9500 903 (LP); 7300 903 (CS)

Rossi, Vienna State Opera Orchestra.
Vanguard 174 (LP)

Szell, Cleveland Orchestra. (B)
CBS MY 38527 (LP, CS)

Love for Three Oranges: Suite, Op. 33b

See above under LIEUTENANT KIJE for Marriner's recording.

Peter and the Wolf, Op. 67

Critics often sniff at the version narrated by Beatrice Lillie with Skitch Henderson conducting the London Symphony, but it is probably the one that will most amuse both you and your children. It is also now reduced in price. It and the more "serious" full-price performance by Karl Böhm and the Vienna Philharmonic, with Hermione Gingold telling the story, were previously recommended under Saint-Saëns: CARNIVAL OF THE ANIMALS.

Two other full-price versions were listed under Britten: YOUNG PERSON'S GUIDE TO THE ORCHESTRA. Conductor Previn does the narration himself on the Britten side, but his then-wife Mia Farrow handles the tale of Peter. Ormandy's performance of the Britten dispensed with the narration but his overside Prokofiev is narrated by rock star David Bowie, whose charmingly sober and understated approach will come as a pleasant surprise to anyone harboring pop-culture stereotypes.

Speaking of stereotypes, the name of Boris Karloff will forever be associated with Frankenstein and other terrifying monsters of the films; but behind his gruesome facade he was one of the kindliest of men, and his story-spinning on the Rossi disc (recommended above for its LIEUTENANT KIJE SUITE) is both elegant and soothing. What a unique, marvelous voice — if only the story of *Peter and the Wolf* contained the word "antipasto!" Footnote: the budget versions narrated by Michael Flanders and Sir Ralph Richardson (with Efrem Kurtz and Sir Malcolm Sargent conducting, respectively) are perfectly fine but may appeal less to American than British listeners, and both are coupled with the SYMPHO-

NY NO. 1 which it seems to me is more apt when included with other music.

Bowie, Ormandy, Philadelphia Orchestra.
RCA ARL1-2743 (LP, CS, CD)

Farrow, Previn, London Symphony.
Angel S-36962 (LP, CS)

Gingold, Böhm, Vienna Philharmonic.
DG 2530 588 (LP)

Karloff, Rossi, Vienna State Opera Orchestra. (B)
Vanguard 174 (LP)

Lillie, Henderson, London Symphony. (B)
London Jubilee 411 650-1 (LP); 411 650-4 (CS)

Romeo and Juliet, Op. 64

Maazel's recording of the complete ballet (three discs) has come to be accepted as the classic version. Its sharp precision is thought by most to be more idiomatic than the more romantically opulent version by Previn. There are highlights discs by each, and Maazel is again preferable for a more logical and varied program of selections.

Among newer versions of highlights the recent Muti digital recording, available on CD, has had extravagant praise from most critics with only minor reservations (except *High Fidelity* who called it "unbearably overdriven" and "a parody of digital recording"). There is also at full price Ozawa's unique analog disc described under Tchaikovsky: ROMEO AND JULIET.

The most attractive budget disc of excerpts is that by Skrowaczewski with 65 minutes of music comprised of Prokofiev's own "Suite No. 2" (the most popular set of selections with most listeners) plus Stravinsky's LE SACRE DU PRINTEMPS, which ordinarily takes up a whole record by itself, often at twice the price of this disc. With stunning sonics, this is an extraordinary bargain. (Note that the cassette is coupled with LOVE FOR THREE ORANGES SUITE.)

Maazel, Cleveland Orchestra (complete).
(3) London CSA 2312 (LP, CS)

Maazel, Cleveland Orchestra (highlights).
London CS 6865 (LP)

Muti, Philadelphia Orchestra (highlights.)
Angel DS-37776 (D-LP, CS); CDC-47004 (CD)

Ozawa, San Francisco Symphony (excerpts).
DG 2530 308 (LP); 3300 284 (CS)

Skrowaczewski, Minnesota Orchestra (Suite No. 2). (B)
Candide 31108 (LP); CT-2293 (CS)

Symphony No. 1 in D, Op. 25, "Classical"

There is an abundance of fine recordings. Among full-price choices, Giulini was previously recommended under Mussorgsky: PICTURES AT AN EXHIBITION and Marriner under LIEUTENANT KIJE SUITE.

Among budgets, Marriner's earlier recording is described under Bizet: SYMPHONY NO. 1, and Previn under Mendelssohn: SYMPHONY NO. 4. Add to these Kurtz's authoritative performance interestingly coupled with the SYMPHONY NO. 1 by Prokofiev's compatriot Shostakovich, and Martinon's excellent version coupled most generously with Prokofiev's SYMPHONY NO. 5.

Giulini, Chicago Symphony.
DG 2530 783 (LP); 3300 783 (CS)

Kurtz, Philharmonia Orchestra. (B)
Seraphim S-60330 (LP, CS)

Marriner, London Symphony.
Philips 9500 903 (LP); 7300 903 (CS)

Marriner, Academy SMF. (B)
London Jubilee 41065 (LP, CS)

Martinon, French Radio Orchestra. (B)
Turnabout 34599 (LP); CT-2159 (CS) (cassette includes two additional works)

Previn, London Symphony. (B)
RCA AGL1-2703 (LP, CS)

Symphony No. 5, Op. 100

This work's recording history seems to be in a state of transition. Notable performances by Szell, Bernstein, Ansermet, Leinsdorf, Maazel, Previn and others have all disappeared from the catalogs; while new ones, such as those by Bernstein (again) and Slatkin, have not had time to establish themselves as I write this (I have no Slatkin reviews, and wildly mixed ones on Bernstein II).

The current safest bets are the budget Martinon recommended above under SYMPHONY NO. 1, and the compelling Karajan, happily just switched to budget status by DG (no coupling though).

Karajan, Berlin Philharmonic. (B)
DG Signature 410 992-1 (LP); 410 992-4 (CS)

Martinon, French Radio Orchestra. (B)
Turnabout 34599 (LP); CT-2159 (CS) (cassette includes two additional works)

Arnold Schönberg   1874-1951

Verklärte Nacht, Op. 4 (Transfigured Night)

For the full-orchestra version Ashkenazy and Karajan were recommended under Wagner: SIEGFRIED IDYLL, which is the coupling for both of them. If you wish to investigate the lesser-known original version for string sextet try the excellent digital Nonesuch disc—a captivating performance with very helpful program notes, and a bonus of the String Trio, Op. 45.

Ashkenazy, English CO.
London 410 111-1 (D-LP); 410 111-4 (CS)

Karajan, Berlin Philharmonic.
DG Signature 2543 510 (LP); 3343 510 (CS)

Santa Fe Chamber Players.
Nonesuch 79028 (D-LP)

Dmitri Shostakovich   1906-1975

Symphony No. 1 in F, Op. 10

The performance by Kurtz on a budget disc is the only one to follow the composer's instructions rigorously, right down to the metronome markings. It was recommended earlier under Prokofiev: SYMPHONY NO. 1. More famous is Bernstein's vivid reading, available both at full price and budget with different couplings. I am listing the budget, with the Cello Concerto (Rostropovich soloing), because Bernstein's other coupling of the Symphony No. 9 is available with newer sound and at slightly lower price on Susskind's record. The lesser-known conductor turns in first-class performances of both symphonies.

Bernstein, New York Philharmonic. (B)
CBS MP 38750 (LP, CS)

Kurtz, Philharmonia Orchestra. (B)
Seraphim S-60330 (LP, CS)

Susskind, Cincinnati Symphony.
Vox 9003 (LP, CS)

Symphony No. 5, Op. 47

The recording situation relative to Shostakovich's most popular symphony has become more complicated since 1981, when I listed only the budget version by the composer's son Maxim as the critics' choice for a "definitive" reading. Since then Bernstein's historic 1959 recording has become available at budget price, and the same conductor has issued a newer (1979) digital performance, available on CD. My survey of numerous reviews showed the critics splitting almost evenly over which edition is the greater. A choice may boil down to the fact that the earlier one is cheaper, the newer one more vivid-sounding.

Three other recent digital versions by Haitink, Maazel, and Rostropovich have all received extremely mixed reviews. I will not confuse the issue by listing them here, but if you have a penchant for any of these conductors you may wish to seek them out. Maxim Shostakovich's budget disc remains the consensus favorite for overall interpretation, though the orchestra is far from the world's best. The record is still available but may disappear soon because of licensing changes; grab it fast, or wait for a presumed appearance on another label.

Bernstein, New York Philharmonic. (B)
CBS MY 37218 (LP, CS)

Bernstein, New York Philharmonic.
CBS IM 35854 (D-LP, CS, CD)

M. Shostakovich, USSR Symphony. (B)
Quintessence 7202 (LP, CS)

Symphony No. 10 in e, Op. 93

The Shostakovich Fifth is far and away the composer's most popular symphony; most musicians think his Tenth is the greatest. The great majority of critics have expressed unbounded admiration for Karajan's digital recording, with *Ovation* summing it up as "a true testament to Karajan's distinguished and enduring artistry." If you are hesitant about spending full price for this work, the budget version by Andrew Davis is a fine performance — just less exciting and overwhelming than Karajan.

A. Davis, London Philharmonic. (B)
Seraphim S-60255 (LP)

Karajan, Berlin Philharmonic.
DG 2532 030 (D-LP); 3302 030 (CS); 413 361-2 (CD)

Igor Stravinsky   1882-1971

Firebird: Suite

A forewarning: there is more than one edition of the score of each of the three famous Stravinsky ballets. Overlapping this fact, two of the three are heard in both complete and "suite" versions. I will indicate in each set of listings which is the most "basic" version/edition for the beginning collector's purposes, weighing this against the other standards for recommendation.

As for *The Firebird,* the Suite is far more often heard than the complete score and I will concentrate on the shorter version in the listings. The Suite itself comes in three editions, dating from 1911, 1919, and 1945. The 1919 edition is the standard for recordings. It is scored for a smaller orchestra than the original version and contains two additional sections of music.

For an exciting performance with excellent sound at full price I am listing Muti this time, coupled with Mussorgsky: PICTURES AT AN EXHIBITION, in preference to the older Abbado which has the "non-basic" *Jeu de cartes* on the overside. Muti gives the 1919 edition, as does Stokowski on his equally thrilling, if less naturally recorded, disc (no cassette) paired with Mussorgsky: A NIGHT ON BALD MOUNTAIN and Tchaikovsky: MARCHE SLAVE.

Pierre Monteux conducted the premieres of both PETROUCHKA and LE SACRE DU PRINTEMPS. The standard complete 1911 edition of PETROUCHKA is the coupling for his performance of the standard *Firebird Suite,* on a budget disc in still-vivid early stereo sound. Bernstein is also famous for his Stravinsky. There are two budget recordings of identical performances of the standard *Firebird Suite* coupled with (take note) the less popular 1947 edition of the complete PETROUCHKA. I am listing the single disc/cassette edition; the other is a two-record set (no cassette) augmented by a superfluous lecture on PETROUCHKA by the conductor.

Stravinsky's own performances of his works are universally regarded as among the most significant documentations in recording history. Unfortunately, perhaps, Stravinsky tended to prefer the editions that other conductors (and the audiences) have liked less well — his *Firebird* is the 1945 version. Even worse, the orchestral playing tends to the scrappy side, and the composer-led versions that most critics consider the best are sonically worse besides being currently out of print. And worst of all, the surviving recordings, true to CBS's unstated motto that "there is madness in our method," exist in several different single and multi-disc formats at wildly varying and confusing prices. The two-record budget set listed is, I hope, the best compromise choice for the beginning collector. A close second is the three-record set in which you get, for a bit higher but still-budget price, the complete PETROUCHKA, which I think preferable to the Suite on the two-disc set. There is also a budget cassette containing the 1945 *Firebird Suite,* the 1947 PETROUCHKA SUITE, and the 1943 LE SACRE DU PRINTEMPS.

Bernstein, New York Philharmonic. (B)
CBS MY 37221 (LP, CS)

Monteux, Paris Conservatory Orchestra. (B)
London Stereo Treasury STS 15197 (LP)

Muti, Philadelphia Orchestra.
Angel S-37539 (LP, CS)

Stokowski, London Symphony.
London SPC 21026 (LP)

Stravinsky, Columbia Symphony. (B)
(2) Columbia MG 31202 (LP) or (3) D3S 705 (LP) or MGT 39015 (CS)

Petrouchka (Complete)

The Bernstein and Stravinsky recordings are on discs recommended above under FIREBIRD SUITE. Both use the scaled-down 1947 edition of the score, as does Temirkanov on his budget recording — one of the most colorful and exciting accounts available. I am not listing the digital Abbado recording because it has had a lukewarm reception from most major critics (except the *Penguin Guide*). But if you should wind up with a copy, be informed that the edition used is that of 1947, not 1911 as stated on the record jacket.

The real 1911 version is available on the famous Boulez recording (full price), and the fine budgets by Monteux and Mackerras.

Bernstein, New York Philharmonic. (B)
CBS MY 37221 (LP, CS)

Boulez, New York Philharmonic.
Columbia M 31076 (LP, CS)

Mackerras, London Symphony. (B)
Vanguard Cardinal 10113 (LP); CA-471177 (CS)

Monteux, Paris Conservatory Orchestra.
London Stereo Treasury STS 15197 (LP)

Stravinsky, Columbia Symphony. (B)
(2) Columbia MG 31202 (LP) or D3S 705 (LP) or MGT 39015 (CS)

Temirkanov, Leningrad Philharmonic. (B)
Quintessence 7147 (LP, CS)

Pulcinella: Suite

This ballet inspired by melodies of Pergolesi comes from Stravinsky's "neo-classical" period and until recently was not so often heard. But it is steadily becoming more popular and now has several fine recordings, both complete and in suite form. The best introduction is Marriner's precise and beautifully recorded Suite, coupled with another beautiful but lesser-known Stravinsky ballet, *Apollo* (often listed by its French title *Apollon musagète*).

Marriner, Academy SMF.
Argo ZRG 575 (LP)

Le Sacre du printemps (The Rite of Spring)

There is less confusion with this work as to which version to buy. There is no suite of *The Rite of Spring* — it is always presented complete. And almost all recordings (note exception below under Solti) use Stravinsky's 1943 edition, which isn't terribly different from the 1913 original anyway.

Mention must be made of Maazel's digital-and-CD recording even though critics are divided as to its interpretive merits, because the orchestral playing and the sound quality are both quite superior. In fact the compact disc, according to *Ovation,* "may well be the best sound ever produced by a recording."

More clearly recommendable as performances, with excellent analog sound at full price, are Abbado and Solti. The latter is the only one to use the original 1913 score.

Nearly all critics agree that the Boulez performance is one of the best recordings. *Time* magazine called it one of "the ten best classical discs of the '70s," and *Opus* placed it on their list of the "100 Inspired Recordings" of all time. The sound is not comparable to those mentioned above, but at budget price the recording is very competitive.

The other recommendations are also budgets. Monteux conducted the premiere of *Le Sacre* in 1913 and his 1958 stereo version is acknowledged as the best of his three recordings over the years — a true classic of the record catalog. The Czech conductor Zdeněk Košler has come up with a sleeper performance that *Ovation* called "one of the finest ever" and *Fanfare* said "comes closest to the best concert performance...that by Stravinsky himself." (Don't think you are hallucinating when you read the blurbs on the lower left of the jacket back — they refer to a different record of Schubert symphonies and somehow wandered onto the wrong disc.) Two more recommendable budgets are Stravinsky's own performance, listed above under FIREBIRD SUITE, and Skrowaczewski's generously filled recording described under Prokofiev: ROMEO AND JULIET (and remember the cassette of this adds PETROUCHKA).

Abbado, London Symphony.
DG 2530 635 (LP)

Boulez, Cleveland Orchestra. (B)
CBS MY 37764 (LP, CS)

Košler, Czech Philharmonic. (B)
Quintessence 7226 (LP, CS)

Maazel, Cleveland Orchestra.
Telarc 10054 (D-LP, CD)

Monteux, Paris Conservatory Orchestra. (B)
London Stereo Treasury STS 15318 (LP, CS)

Skrowaczewski, Minnesota Orchestra. (B)
Candide 31108 (LP); CT-2212 (CS)

Solti, Chicago Symphony.
London CS 6885 (LP, CS)

Stravinsky, Columbia Symphony. (B)
(2) Columbia MG 31202 (LP) or D3S 705 (LP) or MGT 39015 (CS)

Symphony of Psalms

The most powerful and exciting recording is that by Bernstein, recommended earlier for its somewhat less impressive GLORIA by Poulenc. The other indispensable recording is Stravinsky's own using his revised version of the score and coupled with his Symphony in C.

Bernstein, London Symphony, English Bach Festival Chorus.
Columbia M 34551 (LP, CS)

Stravinsky, CBS Symphony, Toronto Festival Chorus.
Columbia MS 6548 (LP)

Heitor Villa-Lobos   1887-1959

Bachiana Brasileira No. 5

Virtually every available recording of this brief but haunting modern classic has something to recommend it — except "basic" couplings. Stokowski's recording, with soprano soloist Anna Moffo, is probably the best overall first choice in terms of performance, sound quality, and compatible bonus music (Rachmaninoff's *Vocalise* and Canteloube's *Songs of the Auvergne*). RCA has also kindly reduced the price of this fine recording to budget level.

Moffo, Stokowski, American Symphony. (B)
RCA AGL1-4877 (LP)

In your excavations of the "Mainstream Moderns," the next level will yield:

Bartók
Concerto for Violin and Orchestra (1938)

Berg
Lyric Suite for String Quartet

Poulenc
Songs (selections)

Prokofiev
Concerto No. 2 in g for Violin and Orchestra, Op. 63
Sonata No. 7 in B-flat for Piano, Op. 83

Schönberg
Five Pieces for Orchestra, Op. 16

Shostakovich
Concerto No. 1 for Piano, Trumpet, and Orchestra, Op. 35

Stravinsky
Apollo (Apollon musagète)
L'Histoire du soldat: Suite

Varèse
Ionisation

Webern
Five Movements for String Quartet, Op. 5

The
Americans

There is no very good reason to put the American composers into a separate little section, except to dramatize which native sons have achieved world rank comparable to their contemporaries. The following works are those which I think bid fair to achieve permanent inclusion in any list of basic concert music.

Samuel Barber   1910-1981

Adagio for Strings

Two fine anthology albums have already been recommended: for Bernstein's budget see under Vaughan Williams: FANTASIA ON "GREENSLEEVES"; for the full-price Previn, see Glinka: RUSSLAN AND LUDMILA OVERTURE. The Bernstein performance is also available in a two-disc budget anthology of exclusively American music including Copland's APPALACHIAN SPRING, Gershwin's AN AMERICAN IN PARIS, Ives's *Fourth of July* and *Washington's Birthday*, and Piston's *The Incredible Flutist*. Morton Gould's recent digital record at budget price is a unique bargain, coupled with Gershwin: AN AMERICAN IN PARIS and his own popular *American Salute*.

Bernstein, New York Philharmonic. (B)
CBS MY 38484 (LP, CS)

Bernstein, New York Philharmonic. (B)
(2) Columbia MG 31155 (LP)

Gould, National Philharmonic. (B)
Sinfonia 627 (D-LP, CS)

Previn, London Symphony.
Angel S-37409 (LP, CS)

Leonard Bernstein   1918-

Candide: Overture

Bernstein is, not surprisingly, definitive in his own composition, included in the double budget set "Curtain Raisers" described earlier under Glinka: RUSSLAN AND LUDMILA OVERTURE. Fiedler's "Best of the Boston Pops Volume 1" is described under Mussorgsky: A NIGHT ON BALD MOUNTAIN.

Bernstein, New York Philharmonic. (B)
(2) Columbia MG 35188 (LP)

Fiedler, Boston Pops.
DG 2584 019 (LP)

Ernest Bloch

Schelomo — Rhapsody for Cello and Orchestra

The full-price analog by Rostropovich and Bernstein is predictably emotional. They dig into this music and give it the ecstatic sweep it must have. Coupling is the Schumann Cello Concerto. At budget price Piatigorsky is almost as impassioned with Munch, but the sound is fairly mediocre. Overside is the Walton Cello Concerto, a piece commissioned by Piatigorsky and of course played with authority. Nelsova and Abravanel are a third choice, but only by a hair, and the sonics fall somewhere between the other two. The flip has Bloch's *Israel* Symphony.

Nelsova, Abravanel, Utah Symphony. (B)
Vanguard Cardinal 10007 (LP)

Piatigorsky, Munch, Boston Symphony. (B)
RCA AGL1-4086 (LP, CS)

Rostropovich, Bernstein, ORTF.
Angel S-37256 (LP)

Aaron Copland

1900-

Appalachian Spring

Copland is a good conductor as well as composer and he is best at leading the ballet music. Since *Appalachian Spring* is America's greatest ballet, Copland's complete recording of the original chamber-orchestra version is naturally indispensable. Most other recordings are of the abbreviated Suite for full orchestra, and Copland is available here too in a budget box containing BILLY THE KID, FANFARE FOR THE COMMON MAN, RODEO, *Dance Panels, Lincoln Portrait, Our Town,* and *El Salón México.*

Leonard Bernstein is perhaps a lesser composer, but he is a greater conductor and has had the graciousness to give everything in himself to honor his compatriot with great performances. His classic reading of the Suite is available in three different budget recordings: the double set recommended earlier under Barber: ADAGIO FOR STRINGS (MG 31155); another all-Copland double set with BILLY THE KID, RODEO, and *El Salón México* (MG 30071); and a single disc with *Danzon Cubano, El Salón México,* and FANFARE FOR THE COMMON MAN (MY 37257). Sorry for the confusion, but this is just one of numerous examples of the CBS penchant for repackaging the same material endlessly.

One more recording has special appeal: the direct-to-digital version of the chamber-music original with Dennis Russell Davies conducting. There is a very generous bonus of the chamber-orchestra version of Ives: THREE PLACES IN NEW ENGLAND (the Copland single disc has no coupling), and this superb-sounding record which once had an extravagantly high price has reappeared on a new label at much lower cost but with no diminution of quality.

Bernstein, New York Philharmonic. (B)
(2) Columbia MG 30071 (LP, CS) or (2) Columbia MG 31155 (LP) or CBS MY 37257 (LP, CS)

Copland, Columbia CO.
Columbia M 32736 (LP, CS)

Copland, London Symphony. (B)
(3) Columbia D3M 33720 (LP)

Davies, Saint Paul CO.
Pro Arte PAD-140 (D-LP, CS)

Billy the Kid

Choose from the Copland budget box or the Bernstein double budget as listed below and described under APPALACHIAN SPRING. Copland also comes on a single disc with RODEO. And in yet another CBS repackaging feat, another Bernstein budget single pops up with a coupling of just RODEO. Gould's budget, also coupled with RODEO, is worthy of comparison with any of the others.

Bernstein, New York Philharmonic. (B)
(2) Columbia MG 30071 (LP, CS) or CBS MY 36727 (LP, CS)

Copland, London Symphony.
Columbia M 30114 (LP) or (3) Columbia D3M 33720 (LP) (B)

Gould, Orchestra. (B)
RCA AGL1-4410 (LP, CS)

Fanfare for the Common Man

This is an awfully small piece to get a separate listing, but as it has become almost a second national anthem to some people I am highlighting it. To the Bernstein and Copland budgets listed below and described under APPALACHIAN SPRING, add Ormandy's full-throated version coupled with the full-orchestra edition of Ives: THREE PLACES IN NEW ENGLAND and Copland's *A Lincoln Portrait.* The latter piece strikes some listeners as unbearably melo-dramatic and chauvinistic, but the narration here by the late Adlai Stevenson is so dignified and naturally affecting that it can occa-sionally melt a jaded heart. The alternate Ormandy record listed is a potpourri of Americana (marches, etc.) including Ives: VARIA-TIONS ON "AMERICA."

Bernstein, New York Philharmonic. (B)
CBS MY 37257 (LP, CS)

Copland, London Symphony. (B)
(3) Columbia D3M 33720 (LP)

Ormandy, Philadelphia Orchestra.
Columbia MS 6648 (LP) or MS 7289 (LP)

Rodeo

All repetitions here, with two each by Bernstein and Copland as variously discussed under APPALACHIAN SPRING and BILLY THE KID, plus the Gould (see also BILLY THE KID).

Bernstein, New York Philharmonic. (B)
(2) Columbia MG 30071 (LP, CS) or CBS MY 36727 (LP, CS)

Copland, London Symphony.
Columbia M 30114 or (3) Columbia D3M 33720 (LP) **(B)**

Gould, Orchestra. (B)
RCA AGL1-4410 (LP, CS)

George Gershwin   1898-1937

An American in Paris

Bernstein's exuberant and idiomatic 1960 performance is a standard of the catalog and still first choice of many critics. It is available on the double budget recommended under Barber: ADAGIO FOR STRINGS (see that listing also for the budget digital recording by Gould) or on a single budget disc coupled with RHAPSODY IN BLUE. Fiedler's budget gives Bernstein's a real run for the money, coupled with a brilliant RHAPSODY IN BLUE featuring pianist Earl Wild.

Bernstein, New York Philharmonic. (B)
(2) Columbia MG 31155 (LP) or CBS MY 37242 (LP, CS)

Fiedler, Boston Pops. (B)
RCA AGL1-5215 (LP, CS)

Gould, National Philharmonic. (B)
Sinfonia 627 (D-LP, CS)

Rhapsody in Blue

The simplest, safest bet is to stick with either the Bernstein single budget disc or the Fiedler budget recommended above under AN AMERICAN IN PARIS.

Bernstein, Columbia Symphony. (B)
CBS MY 37242 (LP, CS)

Wild, Fiedler, Boston Pops. (B)
RCA AGL1-5215 (LP, CS)

Ferde Grofé   1892-1972

Grand Canyon Suite

At full price Abravanel's recording stands out for sonic quality and a sensitive musical treatment that this warhouse doesn't always get. The coupling is Copland's *El Salón México,* similarly well-done. An older classic is Bernstein's budget version, with a coupling of Grofé's equally enjoyable *Mississippi Suite,* conducted by André Kostelanetz.

Abravanel, Utah Symphony.
Angel S-37314 (LP, CS)

Bernstein, New York Philharmonic. (B)
CBS MY 37759 (LP, CS)

Charles Ives   1874-1954

Symphony No. 2

Fifty years after this piece was written Leonard Bernstein conducted the world premiere with the New York Philharmonic. His superbly enthusiastic recording thus has a unique authority, and it has a bonus of Ives's *Fourth of July.* Tilson Thomas's recent digital record has better sound, but no coupling. It is a "straighter" reading viewing Ives more from the traditional symphonic standpoint than as the much-vaunted "Peck's bad boy" of music.

Bernstein, New York Philharmonic.
Columbia MS 6889 (LP)

Thomas, Concertgebouw.
CBS IM 37300 (D-LP, CS)

Three Places in New England

The Davies chamber version recorded is detailed under Copland: APPALACHIAN SPRING, and Ormandy's full-orchestra version under Copland: FANFARE FOR THE COMMON MAN.

Davies, Saint Paul CO.
Pro Arte PAD-140 (D-LP, CS)

Ormandy, Philadelphia Orchestra.
Columbia MS 6684 (LP)

Variations on "America" (orch. William Schuman)

For the orchestral version get Ormandy's album "America," previously mentioned under Copland: FANFARE FOR THE COMMON MAN. For the original organ solo version select the E. Power Biggs anthology described under Bach: ORGAN MUSIC.

Biggs.
Columbia MS 7269 (LP)

Ormandy, Philadelphia Orchestra.
Columbia MS 7289 (LP)

A shameless attack of musical chauvinism may lead you to acclaim these additional examples of American music:

Bernstein
West Side Story: Dance Music

Carter
Sonata for Flute, Oboe, Cello, and Harpsichord

Copland
El Salón México

Gershwin
Concerto in F for Piano and Orchestra

Ives
Sonata No. 2 for Piano "Concord, Mass., 1840-1860"
The Unanswered Question

Piston
The Incredible Flutist

Thomson, V.
The Plow That Broke the Plains

Opera

Having hosted opera broadcasts on three radio stations over several years, I am well aware how sharply the subject divides listeners. More than any other type of "classical" music opera tends to be either violently hated or as vehemently loved. This is not the place for a philosophical discussion on why this is so. I will say only that there is no effective shortcut, at least on recordings, to learning to like opera. It does require some study and real effort, maybe a short non-credit course, or, more enjoyably, an introduction with recorded excerpts and explanations by an enthusiastic friend.

Most opera anthologies on record have as their purpose the showcasing of one or two artists instead of the music itself and are therefore more suited to the specialist than to the general or beginning student. Highlights discs from individual operas are better alternatives, though they provide at best a disjointed and unbalanced representation of an opera's continuity and integrity. Also, many operas do not lend themselves at all well to excerpting, and I have seldom been more than half-satisfied with the selections made for these discs.

Of the 88 composers treated in this book, 73 wrote operas, and most of the rest composed oratorios or songs that are essentially in the operatic tradition. Even Chopin wrote a handful of art-songs, and Bach's *St. Matthew Passion* is more operatic than some operas. Mahler wrote no operas, but completed an unfinished one by Weber, and was more famous during his lifetime as an opera conductor than as a composer. I point these things out to emphasize that opera is virtually inescapable if you intend to delve into classical music. Many of the musical works in the preceding sections of this book are actually orchestral excerpts or arrangements from operas. Opera for many people must be an acquired taste, but it seems to me terribly sad to deliberately deprive oneself of this vast and magnificent literature which pervades every period of Western music. (And much non-Western music too — the Chinese *love* opera!)

So make an effort for your own enrichment, but resign yourself to the fact that there is no bargain-basement way to acquire a collection of recorded opera that is anything more than a pitiful jumble of vocal potsherds. If you find yourself liking parts of an opera, do it the justice of listening to all of it; if operas were meant only to be strings of "highlights" that's how they would be written.

As an introduction I have selected 30 of the most famous operas representing all the major genres, nationalities, and composers. Highlights recordings are included when available. Because opera usually requires far more performers than any other musical form, it is correspondingly more difficult to find a recording that is without some blemish. The choices reflect those that seem to have had the widest critical acceptance — a recording with one rave review but three negative ones is not likely to be listed.

Ludwig van Beethoven   1770-1827

Fidelio

It's nice to be able to start out with a performance that has total consensus. The weakest thing any critic has said about Klemperer's recording is that it is "by far the best" of all available versions. No soloist is less than excellent, and the conductor's vision is as noble and monumental as the music.

Since the old highlights disc of this set is no longer available, the budget-minded are directed to Fricsay's set with outstanding singing from Rysanek and Fischer-Dieskau. A shade less magnificently integrated than Klemperer's, this set is nevertheless more than worth its modest price, especially as the opera is fitted onto two discs instead of the normal three.

Fricsay, Bavarian State Opera. (B)
(2) DG Privilege 2726 088 PSI (LP)

Klemperer, Philharmonia Orchestra.
(3) Angel SCL-3625 (LP)

Vincenzo Bellini   1801-1835

Norma

Maria Callas was the most justly famous heroine of this opera over the past 50 years, and she remains supreme on records. There are two available sets, both conducted by Tullio Serafin. The 1960 stereo version, alas, finds the soprano in bad voice. The 1954 budget set is monophonic, but easier on the ear regardless — and costs about half as much.

Serafin, La Scala Opera. (M) (B)
(3) Seraphim IC-6037 (LP, CS)

Alban Berg   1885-1935

Wozzeck

Of my previous choices for this, the one undisputed masterpiece of twentieth-century opera, the mono Mitropoulos has been deleted, and the Böhm may be said to have been superseded by the new digital recording conducted by Christoph von Dohnányi. All critics surveyed gave this version high marks for musical accuracy, dramatic viability, and beautiful sonics. Of all performances *Ovation* called it "by far the best now available," and *Opus* has already put it in the category of "100 Inspired Recordings."

Dohnányi, Vienna Philharmonic.
(2) London LDR 72007 (D-LP)

Georges Bizet   1838-1875

Carmen

Scholars and critics furiously rage together over the textual problems of this beloved work. The "original" version, still not agreed upon precisely, had spoken passages where Bizet's amanuensis Guiraud later inserted sung recitative. Though there is much to be said in favor of the earlier *opéra-comique* format, the fully-sung version is still the one you are most likely to hear in concert.

Best in the latter category is Beecham's imperishable account with de los Angeles, Gedda, and Blanc in the lead roles. It was the first stereo recording of the opera and remains unique for its idiomatic élan and special magic.

The two other and newer choices were available when my earlier guide was issued, but I felt at that time that they had not achieved a clear consensus of support from reviewers. Each still has detractors, but they seem to have settled fairly comfortably into a niche as the twin stars of modern recordings. Solti's version with Troyanos, Te Kanawa, Van Dam, and Domingo is generally credited with having made the most sense of the many textual problems, and with providing an especially thoughtful and carefully worked-out interpretation. Abaddo, with Berganza, Cotrubas, Milnes, and (again) Domingo has the more forceful orchestral work. Both sets of singers are excellent, as are the sonics; a choice may depend on your favorite cast.

Abbado, London Symphony.
*(3) DG 2709 083 (LP); 3371 040 (CS); highlights on
DG 2531 171 (LP); 3301 171 (CS)*

Beecham, ORTF.
(3) Angel SCL-3613 (LP); highlights on Angel RL-32077 (LP, CS)

Solti, London Philharmonic.
(3) London OSA 13115 (LP, CS)

Gaetano Donizetti   1797-1848

Lucia di Lammermoor

The reigning Lucia of our time is Joan Sutherland, whose 1971 recording under Richard Bonynge is generally regarded as the one to beat. The score is given without cuts (a *sine qua non* these days) and the supporting cast of Pavarotti, Milnes and Ghiaurov is at least the equivalent of that found on any other set.

Although heavily cut and sonically dated, the 1953 Callas-DiStefano-Gobbi version, conducted by Serafin, preserves an artistically peerless performance at low price.

Bonynge, Royal Opera House.
*(3) London OSA 13103 (LP, CS); highlights on
London OS 26332 (LP)*

Serafin, Florence Festival. (M) (B)
(2) Seraphim IB-6032 (LP)

George Gershwin   1898-1937

Porgy and Bess

Yes, Virginia, there is a great American opera. After years of man-handling, this masterpiece receives its musical and theatrical due from the Houston Grand Opera under the baton of John DeMain, with Clamma Dale and Donnie Albert in the title roles. There is now a highlights disc (as there was not in 1981), but you might also be interested in a budget record of selections with the wonderful singing of Leontyne Price and William Warfield, conducted by Skitch Henderson.

DeMain, Houston Grand Opera.
(3) RCA ARL3-2109 (LP, CS); highlights on RCA ARL1-4680 (LP, CS)

Henderson, RCA Victor Orchestra.
RCA AGL1-5234 (LP, CS)

Charles Gounod   1818-1893

Faust

Queen Victoria would not be amused at the recording fate of her favorite opera. Although the Cluytens reading is universally regarded as the best, that is only because it has abysmal competition. Despite big-name singers such as de los Angeles, Gedda, Gorr, Blanc, and Christoff, few of them seem much at home in their parts, and the sonics are unexceptional.

Cluytens, Paris Opera.
(4) Angel SDL-3622 (LP); highlights on Angel S-35827 (LP, CS)

Ruggero Leoncavallo   1857-1919

Pagliacci

Pietro Mascagni   1863-1945

Cavalleria Rusticana

These little twins of the hilariously misnamed "verismo" school are traditionally given together on the same evening, and are often recorded the same way. Though there are some excellent separate recordings of each, the beginning collector will probably be as glad to get them in one box.

Out of an unhomogenized pool of recordings, two creamy versions rise to the top. Karajan is the more recent and sonically superior, headlining Cossotto, Carlyle, Bergonzi, Taddei, and Panerai in *Pag,* and Cossotto, Bergonzi, and Guelfi in *Cav.* About half the critics give the edge to Karajan, the others leaning toward Serafin's performance with Callas and DiStefano. Be guided by your predispositions, but be aware that the Serafin recording is not in stereo.

Karajan, La Scala Opera.
(3) DG 2709 020 (LP); 3371 011 (CS)

Serafin, La Scala Opera. (M)
(3) Angel CL-3528 (LP)

Jules Massenet   1842-1912

Manon

This is the flagship opera of the French Late Romantic school, nowadays much in vogue again after years of neglect. It is exquisitely represented by a monophonic budget set featuring the enchanting portrayal of Victoria de los Angeles in the title part, ably partnered by Henri Legay and Michel Dens. Conductor Pierre Monteux is a model of idiomatic elegance. Among stereo versions the excellent set starring Beverly Sills is out of print, and the newest one, conducted by Michel Plasson, is competent but the singing of the principals cannot challenge the old Monteux, whose sound, though not stereo, is "hi-fi" and perfectly acceptable.

Monteux, Paris Opéra-Comique. (M) (B)
(4) Seraphim ID-6057 (LP)

Wolfgang Amadeus Mozart   1756-1791

Don Giovanni

Rule one for this opera: do not buy any budget recording. None of them comes close to challenging any of the four outstanding full-price versions, and *Don Giovanni* is too important (many authorities consider it the *greatest* opera) to accept less than the best. The new digital Haitink recording with Thomas Allen in the title role has so far won only plaudits for good singing, a good sense of drama, intelligent conducting, and glistening sonics. The three older recordings recommended in my earlier book still command consideration. They all point out about equal, with Davis having the best sound, Giulini the best conducting, and Krips the best ensemble.

C. Davis, Royal Opera House.
(4) Philips 6707 022 (LP); 7699 133 (CS)

Giulini, Philharmonia Orchestra.
(3) Angel SCL-3605 (LP, CS); highlights on Angel S-35642 (LP)

Haitink, London Philharmonic.
(3) Angel DSCX-3953 (D-LP, CS); CDCC-47036 (CD)

Krips, Vienna Philharmonic.
(4) London OSA 1401 (LP)

The Magic Flute

Levine's recent digital recording has received much praise for its sense of theater and its singers (except for Cotrubas), though British critics have been cool. Whatever its merits, the inclusion of all the original spoken German dialogue, forcing the set onto four discs instead of the usual three, is unduly intimidating both linguistically and financially to the beginning collector. Haitink has a new digital version too, but the spectrum of reviews for it has been less positive than for Levine, especially on account of the slow tempi.

Of older recordings, Böhm's has aged best. The orchestral playing is beautiful and there is wonderful singing, especially from the men. Among the remaining sets Solti is short on charm but has vivid production; Koopman presents an "authentic" version best suited for specialists; Klemperer has perhaps the greatest overall cast but takes a monumental, Beethovenesque approach and omits all of the dialogue; and Karajan's set is plagued by inconsistencies of cast and pacing. The budget monophonic Fricsay recording is still available, but its sonics are woefully faded and the performance, though far from bad, is not particularly notable either.

All of this is to say that for a first buy of Mozart's most beloved (if not greatest) opera, the Böhm recording is the best compromise for a distinguished introduction that bears repeated hearing. If you have favorite singers on any of the other sets you will probably derive enough pleasure to make your purchase worthwhile.

Böhm, Berlin Philharmonic.
(3) DG 2709 017 (LP); 3371 002 (CS); highlights on DG 136 440 (LP); 922 014 (CS)

The Marriage of Figaro

Solti's new digital recording has received wildly mixed reviews. *Opus* put it on their list of "100 Inspired Recordings"; *Gramophone* proclaimed the singers "the most successful all-round cast of singers assembled for this opera"; *Ovation* found in it "an irrestible feeling of joy"; and *Stereo Review*'s critic exclaimed: "Were I to build a new record library with only one version of this opera in it, I would probably choose this one." Yet *Fanfare* dismissed it; *High Fidelity* found it "bewildering to the point of incomprehensibility"; and the *Gramophone* critic who loved the cast went on to express reservations about the orchestra and the conducting, and finally decided that he preferred the Giulini recording!

Obviously I cannot claim a favorable consensus on this set, but in view of the eminence of all principals (soloists include Te Kanawa, Popp, von Stade, Ramey, Allen, and Moll) and the numerical preponderance of effusive reviews, I feel it must be listed but without guarantees.

Safer choices, perhaps, are the older versions by Giulini and Colin Davis. Giulini gets great ensemble out of his eminent cast (Moffo, Schwarzkopf, Wächter, Taddei, et al), the conducting is magnificent, and Angel manages to fit all the music on three discs instead of the usual four. Davis is more expensive, but has better sound, with plenty of sparkle and dramatic feeling, and an outstanding case including (Jessye) Norman, Freni, Minton, Ganzarolli, and Wixell.

C. Davis, BBC Symphony.
(4) Philips 6707 014 (LP); (2) 7699 132 (CS); highlights on Philips 6500 434 (LP)

Giulini, Philharmonia Orchestra.
(3) Angel SCL-3608 (LP, CS); highlights on Angel S-35640 (LP)

Solti, London Philharmonic.
(4) London LDR 74001 (D-LP, CS); (3) London 410 150-2 (CD)

Modest Mussorgsky   1839-1881

Boris Godunov

Boris Christoff is the singer of recent years most closely identified
with his eponymous hero, Tsar Boris. He made two complete recordings, both in print. The earlier one (though mono) is the better buy. Christoff is in better voice than on the Cluytens set, the
conducting by Issay Dobrowen is more idiomatic, the supporting
cast (including Gedda, Zareska, and Borg) is far superior, and the
price is much lower.

Dobrowen, ORTF. (M) (B)
(4) Seraphim ID-6101 (LP)

Giacomo Puccini   1858-1924

La Bohéme

There have been many recordings of this favorite opera, but none,
including the recent Levine performance starring Scotto, Kraus,
and Milnes, has seriously challenged the first stereo version, that
made by Sir Thomas Beecham in 1956. It is still rated at or near the
top by virtually every critic. "Golden singing from a patrician
quartet" said *Opera News* of de los Angeles, Bjoerling, Amara,
and Merrill. The *Penguin Guide,* conferring its coveted Rosette,
called the whole performance "incandescent."

Beecham, RCA Victor Orchestra. (B)
(2) Seraphim SIB-6099 (LP, CS)

Madama Butterfly

The *Penguin Guide* and the book *Opera on Record* (ed. Alan
Blyth) both push Karajan's recording with Freni and Pavarotti for
first place; but both judgments are made by the same man, Edward Greenfield, who is one of the three editors of the *Penguin*

Guide and author of the article in the book. Aside from him, I have found nearly all other critics preferring Barbirolli's 1966 recording starring Scotto and Bergonzi. Even Greenfield admits Barbirolli "comes closest" to Karajan. Scotto recorded the opera again a decade later and in some ways she was even better, but the sound quality and Maazel's conducting are less attractive than on the earlier set.

Recently a series of interesting opera recordings have come out of Hungary. Perhaps the best is the *Madama Butterfly*, conducted by Giuseppe Patané and starring Veronica Kincses and Peter Dvorsky. The performance conception is refreshingly intimate and the singing of Ms. Kincses is enchantingly lovely and convincing. The recording won the *Grand Prix du Disque* but may be a little difficult to find except in specialty and import shops. Nevertheless I think it should stand here as a tribute to Hungaroton's unexpectedly remarkable opera series. (If you want to order it in Hungarian, simply ask for Puccini's *Pillangóki-sasszony!*)

Barbirolli, Rome Opera.
(3) Angel SCL-3702 (LP, CS); highlights on Angel S-36567 (LP, CS)

Patané, Hungarian State Opera.
(3) Hungaroton 12256-58 (LP)

Tosca

There is near-unanimous accord here as reviewers heap praises on the classic Maria Callas performance conducted by Victor DeSabata and co-starring Giuseppe DiStefano and Tito Gobbi. "Irreplaceable," one critic remarked, "and always will be." The monophonic recording has recently been digitally remastered for sound enhancement. Be sure to look at the prefix to the catalog number before buying: the old mono issue is IB, the new one BLX.

The recent Levine recording with Scotto, Domingo, and Bruson has received mostly rave reviews, with only one major critic disliking it. All agree that Scotto is past her prime in voice, though still an interesting interpreter. Most of the attention has been on Levine's passionate conducting; *High Fidelity* went so far as to proclaim the set Levine's best recording of anything.

Still, I think one's first purchase should be the older set. Callas was incomparably insightful and compelling; DiStefano in his heyday had the most melting Puccini tenor of anyone; and Gobbi could out-act any baritone living or dead despite a somewhat dry voice. DeSabata too was a fiery Italian conductor in the Toscanini mold and could hold his own with Levine. With its refurbished sound the recording easily maintains its premiere status.

DeSabata, La Scala Opera. (M)
(2) Angel BLX-3508 (LP)

Gioacchino Rossini   1792-1868

The Barber of Seville

The 1957 stereo edition with Callas, Gobbi, and Luigi Alva, conducted by Alceo Galliera, retains interest for its excellent ensemble and brilliantly expressive singing. A close rival is the 1962 performance with de los Angeles, Bruscantini, and Alva again, Vittorio Gui conducting; the complete set is out of print but Angel has made available an attractive highlights disc at budget price.

Much interest has focused on the new digital recording by Marriner, with Agnes Baltsa, Francisco Araiza, and Thomas Allen. Marriner has returned to a more authentic version of the score, ridding the opera of some of the vulgar performance traditions which have grown like moss upon it. The singing is excellent, the conducting lively, the sound superb.

Galliera, Philharmonia Orchestra.
(3) Angel SCL-3559 (LP, CS); highlights on Angel S-35936 (LP, CS)

Gui, Royal Philharmonic (excerpts only). (B)
Angel RL-32116 (LP, CS)

Marriner, Academy SMF.
(3) Philips 6769 100 (D-LP); 7654 100 (CS)

Johann Strauss II   1825-1899

Die Fledermaus

Critics universally pick the best modern version as that by Boskovsky, with Rothenberger, Gedda, Fischer-Dieskau, Berry, et al. The

1972 recording includes most of the original dialogue, well done. A genial, warm, but never vulgar performance.

Boskovsky, Vienna Symphony.
(2) Angel SBL-3790 (LP, CS)

Richard Strauss   1864-1949

Der Rosenkavalier

I am indebted to Barry Bender of Rose Records in Chicago for pointing out a factual error in my earlier book. I had stated that the *Penguin Guide* awarded its Rosette for sublime performance to the Solti recording starring Crespin, Donath, Minton, and Jung-wirth. That was an error in my note-taking; the Rosette was actually for the Karajan recording with Schwarzkopf, Stich-Randall, Ludwig, and Edelmann.

Nevertheless, the other information I gave about the Solti recording was true: it was recommended by *Opera News* and famed opera authority George Jellinek as first choice, listed by *High Fidelity* as one of the "Great Recordings of the '60s," and placed by *Stereo Review* among the "Best Recordings of the Past 20 Years." *Opera News,* in fact, proclaimed it "one of the finest opera recordings in the history of the phonograph."

So Solti stands, but I am adding Karajan, not merely because of *PG*'s preference, but because it is the close second choice of many critics, and because it has recently been digitally remastered. The refurbished edition has caused reviewers to take a new look at it, especially since Karajan has come out with a new recording with different singers. In comparison, the old recording looks even more attractive, and many critics are beginning to react against the oft-repeated charge that Schwarzkopf's singing is "mannered." As one critic wrote a few years back, this great singer's portrayal of the Marschallin is "a total characterization, with a classical poise that enchants the mind and haunts the memory."

Karajan, Philharmonia Orchestra.
(4) Angel SDLX-3970 (D-LP, CS); highlights on S-35645 (LP)
Solti, Vienna Philharmonic.
(4) London OSA 1435 (LP, CS); highlights on OS 26200 (LP)

Giuseppe Verdi   1813-1901

Aida

In this case the *Penguin Guide*'s rabid enthusiasm for Karajan's
new recording (with Freni, Baltsa, Carreras, Cappuccilli, and Rai-
mondi) is not shared by a majority of other reviewers; most have
major reservations about one aspect or another and prefer the older
Karajan version with Tebaldi, Simionato, Bergonzi, Corena, and
MacNeil.

Solti's 1962 recording with Price, Gorr, Tozzi, Merrill, and
Vickers is another top choice, intensely dramatic, and chosen by
Opus for their list of "100 Inspired Recordings." Of other full price
analogs, Muti's recording remains a favorite of many despite the
conductor's occasional waywardness; the strong cast features
Caballé, Cossotto, Domingo, Cappuccilli, and Ghiaurov. But
Abbado's more recent digital version with Ricciarelli, Obraztsova,
Domingo, Nucci, and Ghiaurov has replaced Muti's in the affec-
tions of some critics, though many still prefer Solti or Karajan.

Budget hunters are directed to Perlea's beloved mono version
where they will find Caballé's *alter voce* Zinka Milanov, partnered
memorably with Bjoerling, Warren, Barbieri, and Christoff.

Abbado, La Scala Opera.
(3) DG 2741 014 (D-LP); 3382 014 (CS); 410 092-2 (CD);
highlights on DG 2532 092 (D-LP); 3302 092 (CS)

Karajan, Vienna Philharmonic.
(3) London OSA 1313 (LP, CS); highlights on OS 25206 (LP, CS)

Muti, New Philharmonia.
(3) Angel SCLX-3815 (LP, CS); highlights on S-37228 (LP)

Perlea, Rome Opera House. (M) (B)
(3) RCA Victrola VIC-6119 (LP)

Solti, Rome Opera House.
(3) London OSA 1393 (LP, CS)

Otello

This is one of those operas that seem to defeat recording studios,
conductors, and casts. Repeated attempts have resulted in only

one undeniably great recording: Toscanini's, now out of print domestically.

Although *Opera News* flayed it, Levine's version with Scotto, Domingo, and Milnes has garnered rave reviews in most other quarters and would seem to be the "best of the newest."

For somewhat less money you can get a budget version conducted by Tullio Serafin. The best-known recent Otello (Vickers) and the greatest recent Iago (Gobbi) are both here, though in less than top form. Some like Rysanek's Desdemona, some don't. The conducting is too stodgy to be exciting. Yet this is a fair enough view of the opera to be worth the modest price.

Levine, National Philharmonic.
(3) RCA CRL3-2951 (LP, CS)

Serafin, Rome Opera House. (B)
(3) RCA AGL3-1969 (LP)

Requiem

Though technically not an opera, the *Requiem* has been called, with good reason, "Verdi's greatest opera." Certainly it is a basic repertory work and makes more sense here than standing alone in an earlier listing.

Three years ago I reported that "At this writing there are a dozen recordings in print and still almost all critics pick Giulini's mid-'60s version as the most consistently satisfying interpretation." Nothing in the interval has caused this opinion to change. If anything, this version's status has increased: *High Fidelity* and *Gramophone* have reaffirmed its greatness, and *Opus* has included it in their list of "100 Inspired Recordings." The soloists are Schwarzkopf, Ludwig, Gedda, and Ghiaurov.

Giulini, Philharmonia Orchestra.
(2) Angel SB-3649 (LP, CS)

Rigoletto

Giulini, so successful with his REQUIEM (see above), is generally adjudged a flop in his *Rigoletto,* which *High Fidelity* called "in many ways the dullest" version of the last 25 years. Sills fans will not be disappointed with the Rudel version on Angel, but a more solid all-around recommendation is Bonynge's set, sung by Sutherland, Tourangeau, Pavarotti, Milnes, and Talvela.

Budget seekers should be satisfied with Cellini's version starring Berger, Peerce, and Warren. There are some cuts, but for the most part this is a memorably exciting performance, with clear mono sound.

Bonynge, London Symphony.
(3) London OSA 13105 (LP, CS); highlights on OS 26401 (LP, CS)

Cellini, RCA Victor Orchestra. (M) (B)
(2) RCA Victrola AVM2-0698 (LP)

La Traviata

Bonynge's recent digital-and-CD version with Sutherland, Pavarotti, and Manuguerra has won high praise from British critics, brickbats from the Americans. I am listing it since it is currently the only high-tech edition, but repeating George Jellinek's warning that it "will please only the uncritical fans of the two superstars."

Like OTELLO, this opera has mostly fared ill before the microphone. Although almost every critic has found something wrong with almost every aspect of Kleiber's recording with Cotrubas, Domingo, and Milnes, it still turns out on points to be the best analog version.

Honorable mention goes to Previtali's budget set with Moffo, Tucker, and Merrill; and those who would like to own a fair sample of the legendary interpretation of Maria Callas are directed to the mono reissue with Ghione conducting and co-starring Kraus and Sereni in a 1958 Lisbon performance.

Bonynge, National Philharmonic.
(3) London LDR 73002 (D-LP); 410 154-2 (CD);
highlights on LDR 71062 (D-LP, CS)

Ghione, San Carlos Opera House. (M)
(2) Angel ZBX-3910 (LP, CS)

Kleiber, Bavarian State Opera.
(2) DG 2707 103 (LP); 3370 024 (CS); highlights on
DG 2531 170 (LP, CS)

Previtali, Rome Opera House. (B)
(2) RCA AGL2-4144 (LP, CS)

Il Trovatore

Colin Davis's recent recording on Philips has got mostly tepid reviews. In the full-price category the palm remains with Mehta, whose singers (Price, Cossotto, Domingo, Milnes, and Giaiotti) are all in peak form. For the budget-minded, there is some splendid singing on the abridged 1952 mono recording conducted by Cellini and sung superhumanly by Milanov, Barbieri, Bjoerling, and Warren.

Cellini, RCA Victor Orchestra. (B)
(2) RCA Victrola AVM2-0699 (LP)

Mehta, New Philharmonia.
(3) RCA LSC-6194 (LP); highlights on LSC-3203 (LP); RK-1197 (CS)

Richard Wagner   1813-1883

Lohengrin

Karajan's new recording and Tomowa-Sintow, Vejzovic, Kollo, Nimsgern, and Riddersbusch has beautiful orchestral playing, but slow tempos and less than ideal singing. A safer and ultimately more exciting choice is Kempe's set with Grümmer, Ludwig, Thomas, Fischer-Dieskau, Wiener, and Frick.

Kempe, Vienna Philharmonic.
(5) Angel S-3641 E/L (LP); highlights on S-36313 (LP)

Die Meistersinger

No performance emerges unscathed in this competition, but the clear winner on overall points is Jochum's version with Ligendza, Ludwig, Fischer-Dieskau, Hermann, and Lagger. Despite the outright failure of Ligendza, and criticism in some quarters of Fischer-Dieskau, the performance as a whole is more passionate, illuminating, and finely recorded than any other.

Jochum, Deutsche Oper.
(5) DG 2713 011 (LP); 3378 068 (CS)

Tristan und Isolde

Two recent recordings have aroused virulent criticism in some quarters. Kleiber's recording is discussed in detail in the Introduction to this book as an example of wildly divergent opinions. Bernstein has been almost as controversial. I cannot recommend either in good conscience at this time for a first purchase.

Far safer are two older versions. If you must have stereo, Karajan has excellent sound (some think it better than Kleiber's digital sonics) and wonderful singers (Dernesch, Ludwig, Vickers, Berry, and Ridderbusch). But the classic performance is the 1952 mono recording with Flagstad, Thebom, Suthaus, Fischer-Dieskau, and Greindl, conducted by Wilhelm Furtwängler, of which *High Fidelity* says "Age can never dim the magnificence of this achievement." It is now even more desirable at budget price.

Furtwängler, Philharmonia Orchestra. (M) (B)
(5) Seraphim IE-6134 (LP, CS); highlights on 60145 (LP)

Karajan, Berlin Philharmonic.
(5) Angel SCL-3777 (LP, CS)

Die Walküre

Boulez's digital recording from the 1980 Bayreuth Festival must be discounted on the basis of production values and singing. It is a live performance, disfigured by a high level of stage noise; and Gwyneth Jones's vocalizing, to pick just one of the doubtful cast, "lurches between thrilling, incisive accuracy and fearsome yowls" *(Penguin Guide).*

Of the other contenders, Karajan-DG puts up a good fight, but only one reviewer dared score it over Solti's well-cast performance on London, starring Nilsson, Crespin, Ludwig, King, Hotter, and Frick.

Solti, Vienna Philharmonic.
(5) London OSA 1509 (LP, CS)

Der Ring des Nibelungen

Every good opera story (and basic record library book) must have a Grand Finale. Now that we are at The End, you may want to cap off your shopping by blowing your last remaining funds on Solti's landmark recording of the complete *Ring,* of which the preceding DIE WALKURE set is a component. Released between 1959 and 1967, the combination of four interrelated operas still wins plaudits for brilliant sonics, and is universally regarded as "one of the great achievements in the history of art," to quote just one critic.

The casts include the likes of Nilsson, Flagstad, Crespin, Ludwig, Fischer-Dieskau, Hotter, Windgassen and Frick, among many others. The boxed set comes with a bonus of producer John Culshaw's interesting book *Ring Resounding,* and carries a special reduced price. There is a four-disc "highlights" box, and a fascinating three-record "Introduction to the Ring," also at reduced price. At this writing, London has begun to reissue the whole series in remastered digital sound and on CD; so far just the first of the four music dramas, *Das Rheingold,* is thus available.

Solti, Vienna Philharmonic.
(19) London RING-S (LP, CS); highlights on (4) OSA 1440 (LP); "Introduction" on (3) RDN-S-1 (LP)

Das Rheingold only on (3) London 414 101-1 (D-LP); 414 101-2 (CD)

Those who wish to expand their opera collection still further may find this list of twenty-five "next-most-basic" operas valuable:

Britten
Peter Grimes

Debussy
Pelléas et Mélisande

Donizetti
Don Pasquale
L'Elisir d'Amore

Gilbert & Sullivan
The Mikado

Gluck
Orfeo ed Euridice

Humperdinck
Hansel and Gretel

Lehár
The Merry Widow

Menotti
Amahl and the Night Visitors

Monteverdi
L'Incoronazione di Poppea

Mozart
The Abduction from the Seraglio
Così fan tutte

Ponchielli
La Gioconda

Puccini
Turandot

Purcell
Dido and Aeneas

Strauss, R.
Elektra
Salome

Verdi
Un Ballo in Maschera
Don Carlos
Falstaff
La Forza del Destino

Wagner
Der fliegende Holländer
Parsifal
Tannhäuser

Weber
Der Freischütz

Title Index

A

A Midsummer Night's Dream
Mendelssohn, 76, 86
A Night On Bald Mountain
Mussorgsky, 115
Academic Festival Overture
Brahms, 92
Adagio for Strings and Organ
Albinoni, 21
Adagio for Strings
Barber, 196
Aida
Verdi, 216
"Air on the G String"
Bach, 21, 29
Alborada del gracioso
Ravel, 162
Alexander Nevsky
Prokofiev, 183
Also sprach Zarathustra
R. Strauss, 152
Amahl and the Night Visitors
Menotti, 221
"America" Variations
Ives, 202
"American"
Dvořák, 105
An American in Paris
Gershwin, 200
Ancient Airs and Dances
Respighi, 167
Andante Cantabile
Tchaikovsky, 126
Andante favori
Beethoven, 52
Andante Spianato and Grand Polonaise
Chopin, 72

Apollo
Stravinsky, 191, 194
Appalachian Spring
Copland, 197
"Appassionata"
Beethoven, 51
"Archduke"
Beethoven, 53
Ave, verum corpus
Mozart, 61

B

Bacchanale
Saint-Saëns, 103
Bachiana Brasileira No. 5
Villa-Lobos, 194
Bartered Bride: Overture and Dances
Smetana, 124
Belshazzar's Feast
Walton, 174
Billy the Kid
Copland, 198
Blue Danube Waltz
Strauss, 118
Boléro
Ravel, 163
Boris Godunov
Mussorgsky, 212
Brandenburg Concerti (6)
Bach, 22

C

Calm Sea and Prosperous Voyage
Mendelssohn, 76
Candide: Overture
Bernstein, 196

Cantabile
   Franck, 109
Canzoni for brass
   Gabrieli, 17
Capriccio espagnol
   Rimsky-Korsakov, 119
Capriccio italien
   Tchaikovsky, 126
Carmen
   Bizet, 206
Carmina Burana
   Orff, 181
Carnaval
   Schumann, 83
Carnival of the Animals
   Saint-Saëns, 120
Carnival Overture
   Dvořák, 104
Cavalleria Rusticana
   Mascagni, 208
"Choral" Symphony #9 in d
   Beethoven, 47
Chromatic Fantasy and Fugue in d
for Harpsichord
   Bach, 37
Clair de lune
   Debussy, 141, 142
"Classical"
   Prokofiev, 186
Cockaigne Overture
   Elgar, 144
Concerti Grossi
   Handel, 30
Concerto for Orchestra
   Bartók, 176
Concierto de Aranjuez
   Rodrigo, 168
Coppélia Suite
   Delibes, 138
Così fan tutte
   Mozart, 222
Crown Imperial
   Walton, 145

D

"Dance of the Blessed Spirits"
   Gluck, 21, 26
Dance Panels
   Copland, 198
Dance Suite
   Bartók, 176
Danse macabre
   Saint-Saëns, 122
Danses sacrée et profane
   Debussy, 141
Danzon Cubano
   Copland, 198
Daphnis et Chloé
   Ravel, 164
Das Lied von der Erde
   Mahler, 146
Das Rheingold
   Wagner, 221
"Death and the Maiden"
   Schubert, 79
Death and Transfiguration
   Strauss, 153
Der fliegende Holländer
   Wagner, 222
Der Freischütz
   Weber, 222
Der Ring des Nibelungen
   Wagner, 220
Der Rosenkavalier
   R. Strauss, 215
Dido and Aeneas
   Purcell, 222
Die Fledermaus
   Strauss II, 214
Die Meistersinger
   Wagner, 219
Die Walküre
   Wagner, 220
Die Winterreise
   Schubert, 87
"Dissonant"
   Mozart, 67
Divertimento for Strings
   Bartók, 177

Dolly Suite
Fauré, 145
Don Carlos
Verdi, 222
Don Giovanni
Mozart, 209
Don Juan
Strauss, 154
Don Pasquale
Donizetti, 221
Don Quixote
R. Strauss, 154

E

Egmont
Beethoven, 50
Ein Heldenleben
R. Strauss, 155
"Eine kleine Nachtmusik"
Mozart, 63
El amor brujo
Falla, 159
El Salón México
Copland, 198, 201, 202
Elektra
R. Strauss, 222
Elijah
Mendelssohn, 87
"Emperor"
Beethoven, 48
"Emperor"
Haydn, 55
En Saga
Sibelius, 170
Enigma Variations
Elgar, 144
"Eroica"
Beethoven, 42
España
Chabrier, 103
Euryanthe
Weber, 86
Exsultate, Jubilate
Mozart, 61

F

Falstaff
Verdi, 222
Fanfare for the Common Man
Copland, 199
Fantasia on "Greensleeves"
Vaughan Williams, 173
Fantasia on a Theme by Tallis
Vaughan Williams, 173
Fantasia para un gentilhombre
Rodrigo, 168
Fantasie for Flute and Piano
Fauré, 145
Faust Symphony
Liszt, 138
Faust
Gounod, 208
Feste Romane, (Roman Festivals)
Respighi, 167
Fidelio
Beethoven, 50, 205
Finlandia
Sibelius, 170
Firebird: Suite
Stravinsky, 189
Five Movements for String Quartet
Webern, 194
Five Pieces for Orchestra
Schönberg, 194
Fountains of Rome
Respighi, 167
Four Seasons
Vivaldi, 35
Fourth of July
Ives, 196, 201
Francesca da Rimini
Tchaikovsky, 129
From Bohemia's Fields and Meadows
Smetana, 106
"From the New World"
Dvořák, 107
"Funeral March"
Chopin, 74

G

Gaité Parisienne
    Offenbach, 117
Gayne (Excerpts)
    Khachaturian, 161
German Requiem
    Brahms, 95
Gigues
    Debussy, 140
Gloria in D
    Vivaldi, 36
Gloria in G
    Poulenc, 182
Goldberg Variations for Harpsichord
    Bach, 37
Grand Canyon Suite
    Grofé, 200
Grande pièce symphonique
    Franck, 109

H

"Haffner"
    Mozart, 64, 65
"Hammerklavier"
    Beethoven, 52
Hansel and Gretel
    Humperdinck, 87, 221
Harold in Italy
    Berlioz, 70
Háry János: Suite
    Kodály, 180
Havanaise
    Saint-Saëns, 123
Hebrides (Fingal's Cave) Overture
    Mendelssohn, 76
Hungarian Dances, (Orchestral Versions)
    Brahms, 95, 100
Hungarian Rhapsodies
    Liszt, 113
Hungarian Sketches
    Bartók, 177
"Hunt"
    Mozart, 62

I

Ibéria
    Debussy, 140
Il Trovatore
    Verdi, 218
Images pour orchestre
    Debussy, 140
Introduction and Rondo Capriccioso
    Saint-Saëns, 123
Invitation to the Dance
    Weber, 86
Invocación
    Rodrigo, 168
Ionisation
    Varèse, 194
Israel Symphony
    Bloch, 197
Italian Concerto in F
    Bach, 25
"Italian Symphony"
    Mendelssohn, 77

J

"Jagd"
    Mozart, 62
Jesu, Joy of Man's Desiring
    Bach, 26
Jeu de cartes
    Stravinsky, 189
Jeux
    Debussy, 141
"Jupiter"
    Mozart, 65

K

Kanon in D
    Pachelbel, 34
Karelia Suite
    Sibelius, 170, 174
Kinderscenen
    Schumann, 87
"Kreutzer"
    Beethoven, 53

L

L'Apprenti Sorcier
  Dukas, 143
L'Arlésienne Suites: Carmen Suites
  Bizet, 90
L'Elisir d'Amore
  Donizetti, 221
L'Histoire du soldat: Suite
  Stravinsky, 194
L'Incoronazione di Poppea
  Monteverdi, 222
La Bohéme
  Puccini, 212
La Boutique fantasque
  Respighi, 117
La Création du monde
  Milhaud, 180
La Damnation de Faust
  Berlioz, 70
La Forza del Destino
  Verdi, 222
La Gioconda: Dance of the Hours
  Ponchielli, 118, 222
La Mer
  Debussy, 140
"La Notte"
  Vivaldi, 21
La Traviata
  Verdi, 218
La Valse
  Ravel, 166
"Largo"
  Handel, 26
Le Boeuf sur le toit
  Milhaud, 180
Le Coq d'or Suite
  Rimsky-Korsakov, 119
Le Sacre du printemps
  Stravinsky, 191
Lemminkäinen's Return
  Sibelius, 170
Les Preludes, (Symphonic Poem
No. 3)
  Liszt, 113

Lieutenant Kije Suite
  Prokofiev, 183
Lincoln Portrait
  Copland, 198
"Linz"
  Mozart, 65
"Little Music Book for Anna
Magdalena Bach"
  Bach, 26
"Little Night Music"
  Mozart, 63
Leonore No. 3
  Beethoven, 50
Lohengrin
  Wagner, 219
"London"
  Vaughan Williams, 173
Love for Three Oranges: Suite
  Prokofiev, 184
Lucia di Lammermoor
  Donizetti, 207
Luonnotar
  Sibelius, 170
Lyric Suite for String Quartet
  Berg, 193

M

Ma Mere l'Oye
  Ravel, 174
Macbeth
  R. Strauss, 154
Madama Butterfly
  Puccini, 212
Magnificat in D
  Bach, 27
Manfred Overture
  Schumann, 85, 86
Manon
  Massenet, 209
March Militaire
  Schubert, 87
Marche Slave
  Tchaikovsky, 129

Marriage of Figaro
    Mozart, 86, 211
Masquerade Suite
    Khachaturian, 161
Masques et bergamasques
    Fauré, 145
Mass in b
    Bach, 27
Mathis der Maler, (Symphony)
    Hindemith, 178
Mazeppa
    Liszt, 113
Mephisto Waltz
    Liszt, 138
Messiah
    Handel, 31
Metamorphosen
    R. Strauss, 154
Miroirs
    Ravel, 162
Missa Papae Marcelli
    Palestrina, 18
Missa Solemnis in D
    Beethoven, 67
Mississippi Suite
    Grofé, 201
Moments Musicaux
    Schubert, 87
"Moonlight"
    Beethoven, 51
Mother Goose Suite
    Ravel, 120
Moto Perpetuo
    Paganini, 114
Music for Strings, Percussion and Celesta
    Bartók, 177
Mythes
    Szymanowski, 109

N

Night Ride and Sunrise
    Sibelius, 172
Nights in the Gardens of Spain
    Falla, 159
Nocturnes
    Debussy, 141
Norma
    Bellini, 205
Nutcracker
    Tchaikovsky, 130

O

Oberon
    Weber, 86
On Hearing the First Cuckoo in Spring
    Delius, 143
Orb and Sceptre
    Walton, 145
Orfeo ed Euridice
    Gluck, 221
"Organ" Symphony
    Saint-Saëns, 123
Orpheus in the Underworld: Overture
    Offenbach, 118
Otello
    Verdi, 217
Our Town
    Copland, 198
Overture 1812
    Tchaikovsky, 114, 131

P

Pacific 231
    Honegger, 179
Pagliacci
    Leoncavallo, 208
Parsifal
    Wagner, 222

"Pastorale"
    Beethoven, 45
"Pathétique"
    Beethoven, 51
"Pathétique"
    Tchaikovsky, 134
Pavane pour une infante défunte
    Ravel, 165
Pavane
    Fauré, 145
Peer Gynt Suites, Nos. 1, 2
    Grieg, 111
Pelléas et Mélisande
    Sibelius, 111
Pélleas et Mélisande
    Debussy, 221
Pélleas and Mélisande
    Fauré, 145
Peter and the Wolf
    Prokofiev, 184
Peter Grimes
    Britten, 221
Petrouchka
    Stravinsky, 190
Pictures at an Exhibition
    Mussorgsky, 116
Pièce héroïque
    Franck, 108
Pièces de clavecin
    Couperin, 37
Pièces de clavecin
    Rameau, 38
Pines of Rome
    Respighi, 167
Poème for Violin and Orchestra
    Chausson, 104
Pohjola's Daughter
    Sibelius, 170
Pomp and Circumstance March in D
    Elgar, 145
Porgy and Bess
    Gershwin, 207
"Posthorn"
    Mozart, 64

"Prague"
    Mozart, 65
Prèlude à l'apres-midi d'un faune
    Debussy, 142
Prelude to Khovanshchina
    Mussorgsky, 116
Prince Igor: Overture; Polovtsian
Dances
    Borodin, 90
Pulcinella: Suite
    Stravinsky, 191

R

Rapsodie espagnole
    Ravel, 166
"Rasumovksy"
    Beethoven, 67
Requiem
    Fauré, 145
Requiem
    Mozart, 62
Requiem
    Verdi, 217
"Resurrection"
    Mahler, 147
Réverie et caprice
    Berlioz, 112
Rhapsody in Blue
    Gershwin, 200
Rhapsody on a Theme of Paganini
    Rachmaninoff, 150
"Rhenish"
    Schumann, 85
Ride of the Valkyries
    Wagner, 135
Rigoletto
    Verdi, 217
"Ritual Fire Dance"
    Falla, 159
Rodeo
    Copland, 199
Roman Carnival Overture
    Berlioz, 71

"Romantic"
    Bruckner, 101
Romeo and Juliet
    Prokofiev, 185
Romeo and Juliet
    Tchaikovsky, 132
Rondes de printemps
    Debussy, 140
"Rondo alla Turca"
    Mozart, 65
Rosamunde: Incidental Music
    Schubert, 80
Royal Fireworks Music
    Handel, 33
Rumanian Rhapsody #1
    Enesco, 159
Russian and Ludmilla: Overture
    Glinka, 74
Russian Easter Overture
    Rimsky-Korsakov, 119

S

Sabre Dance
    Khachaturian, 115, 161
Salome: Dance of the Seven Veils
    R. Strauss, 154, 156, 222
Saudades do Brasil
    Milhaud, 180
Scheherazade
    Rimsky-Korsakov, 120
Schelomo-Rhapsody for Cello and
Orchestra
    Bloch, 197
Serenade for Tenor, Horn and Strings
    Britten, 174
Sérénade mélancolique
    Tchaikovsky, 128
Serenade
    Haydn, 55
"Serenata Notturna"
    Mozart, 64
Siegfried Idyll
    Wagner, 137

Silent Woods
    Dvořák, 105
Sinfonietta
    Janáček, 179
Slavonic Dances
    Dvořák, 106
Sleeping Beauty
    Tchaikovsky, 132
Songs of a Wayfarer
    Mahler, 156
Songs of the Auvergne
    Canteloube, 193
Spartacus
    Khachaturian, 161
"Spring"
    Beethoven, 53
"Spring"
    Schumann, 85
St. Matthew Passion
    Bach, 29
Stars and Stripes Forever
    Sousa, 115
Suite Bergamasque
    Debussy, 142
Swan Lake
    Tchaikovsky, 133
Swan of Tuonela
    Sibelius, 170
Sylvia: Suite
    Delibes, 138
Symphonic Metamorphosis of
Themes by Weber
    Hindemith, 179
Symphonie espagnole for Violin and
Orchestra
    Lalo, 112
Symphonie fantastique
    Berlioz, 71
"Symphony of a Thousand"
    Mahler, 148
Symphony of Psalms
    Stravinsky, 193
Symphony on a French Mountain Air
    d'Indy, 146

T

Tannhäuser
  Wagner, 222
Tapiola
  Sibelius, 170
Taras Bulba
  Janáček, 179
Te Deum
  Bruckner, 102
Terpsichore
  Praetorius, 18
Thais: Méditation
  Massenet, 114
The Abduction from the Seraglio
  Mozart, 222
The Barber of Seville
  Rossini, 214
The Creation
  Haydn, 54
The Cuckoo and the Nightingale
  Handel, 31
"The Fantastic Toyshop"
  Respighi, 117
"The Great"
  Schubert, 82
The Harmonious Blacksmith
  Handel, 37
The Incredible Flutist
  Piston, 196, 202
"The Jester's Morning Song"
  Ravel, 162
The Lark Ascending
  Vaughan Williams, 173
The Magic Flute
  Mozart, 210
The Merry Widow
  Lehar, 221
The Merry Wives of Windsor
  Nicolai, 86
The Mikado
  Gilbert and Sullivan, 221
The Moldau
  Smetana, 125
The Planets
  Holst, 160

Turandot
  Puccini, 222
Tzigane
  Ravel, 104, 123, 174

U

Un Ballo in Maschera
  Verdi, 222
"Unfinished"
  Schubert, 81
Utrecht Te Deum
  Handel, 27

V

Valse triste
  Sibelius, 172
Variants of "Dives and Lazarus"
  Vaughan Williams, 173
Variations on a Theme by Frank Bridge
  Britten, 158
Variations on a Theme by Haydn
  Brahms, 99
Verklärte Nacht
  Schönberg, 187
Vocalise
  Rachmaninoff, 193

W

"Waldstein"
  Beethoven, 52
Wanderer Fantasie
  Schubert, 87
Washington's Birthday
  Ives, 196
Water Music Suite
  Handel, 33
Wedding March
  Mendelssohn, 76
Welcome to the Queen
  Bliss, 145

The Play of Daniel
    anonymous, 17
The Plow That Broke the Plains
    Thomson, 202
The Rite of Spring
    Stravinsky, 35, 191
The Sorcerer's Apprentice
    Dukas, 143
The Three-Cornered Hat
    Falla, 160
The Unanswered Question
    Ives, 202
The Wasps Overture
    Vaughan Williams, 144
Things to Come Suite
    Bliss, 145
Three Places in New England
    Ives, 201
Till Eulenspiegel's Merry Pranks
    R. Strauss, 155
Toccata and Fugue in d
    Bach, 28, 115
Tombeau de Couperin
    Ravel, 116, 165, 174
Tosca
    Puccini, 213
Totentanz
    Liszt, 113
"Toy Symphony"
    Haydn, 26
Tragic Overture
    Brahms, 99
Transfigured Night
    Schönberg, 187
Tristan und Isolde
    Wagner, 219
Trois Gymnopédies
    Satie, 169
"Trout"
    Schubert, 80
Trumpet Septet
    Saint-Saëns, 121

Well-Tempered Clavier
    Bach, 37
West Side Story
    Bernstein, 202
William Tell Overture
    Rossini, 78
Wozzeck
    Berg, 206

Y

Young Person's Guide to the
Orchestra
    Britten, 158

About the Author

Bill Parker has been a producer and classical music announcer for Minnesota Public Radio since 1975. He has written many articles on music for *Minnesota Monthly* magazine and numerous liner notes for classical recordings. He has managed five retail record stores and has been employed in sales and promotional capacities by both Intersound, Inc. (manufacturers of Pro Arte, Quintessence, and Sinfonia records and tapes) and Delos Records. Currently he is the manager of Grand Music in Saint Paul, Minnesota.